Richard Williams, Philip Yorke

The Royal Tribes of Wales

To Which is Added an Account of the Fifteen Tribes of North Wales

Richard Williams, Philip Yorke

The Royal Tribes of Wales
To Which is Added an Account of the Fifteen Tribes of North Wales

ISBN/EAN: 9783337046804

Printed in Europe, USA, Canada, Australia, Japan

Cover: Foto ©Suzi / pixelio.de

More available books at **www.hansebooks.com**

THE

Royal Tribes of Wales,

BY

PHILIP YORKE, ESQ., OF ERTHIG.

TO WHICH IS ADDED AN ACCOUNT OF

THE FIFTEEN TRIBES OF NORTH WALES.

WITH

NUMEROUS ADDITIONS AND NOTES, PREFACE AND INDEX,

BY THE EDITOR,

RICHARD WILLIAMS,

Fellow of the Royal Historical Society.

.... et nos aliquod nomenque decusque,
Gessimus...................... .... --- ---
VIRG.

Liverpool:
PUBLISHED BY ISAAC FOULKES, 18, BRUNSWICK STREET.
1887.

TO THE

Right Honourable Edward James, Earl of Powis,

LORD LIEUTENANT OF THE COUNTY OF MONTGOMERY,

HIGH STEWARD OF THE UNIVERSITY OF CAMBRIDGE, AND

PRESIDENT OF THE UNIVERSITY COLLEGE OF NORTH WALES,

HIMSELF A REPRESENTATIVE OF MORE THAN ONE OF THE TRIBES WHOSE HISTORY IS

GIVEN IN THE FOLLOWING PAGES,

THIS VOLUME IS BY PERMISSION RESPECTFULLY DEDICATED, BY

THE EDITOR.

CELYNOG, NEWTOWN,
1st August, 1887.

PREFACE TO THE ORIGINAL EDITION.

NATIONS when first possessed of the art of writing, had their events entered on the plain page of domestic history, independent of foreign wars, and distant occurrences. Their most eminent citizens were recorded as founders of their families, and their descendants respected as links of the same chain, however unworthy they may have been of their progenitors. The Patrician families of ancient Rome, had their origin from men famous in their generations. The twelve Tribes of Israel are arranged with great accuracy, and the Phœnicians, their neighbours, were probably not more remiss in this branch of history. They traded to the mines of the Cassiterides, and planted colonies in this island. They might have brought the tracing of pedigrees into Britain; and the Welsh are acknowledged to have assiduously continued the practice, thus supposed to have been primarily introduced. It may be asked what certainty we have of the authenticity of our early genealogies? The same as of every other species of history in other nations; the credit of ancient writers, professed genealogists; men appointed and patronized by the princes of the country, who were prohibited from following any other profession; whose records are still extant, and bear no stamp of fiction, which our poets even would not allow. What credit is to be given to the line of kings, said to have reigned in this island prior to Cæsar's invasion, or from what source Tysilio drew his Brut, is not within the limits of this paper. Our most ancient existing manuscripts are the Triads, and the works of the bards of the sixth century, who celebrate in epic strains the deeds of our heroes, who fought and fell in the cause of their country. The Gododin of Aneurin at that period, is a noble poem, and a curious piece of British antiquity: its plaintive numbers in sad sounds, echo the sense of the sorrowful retreat of the vanquished few from the field of blood, of whom the bard himself was one. During the earlier centuries, the registering of genealogies was the province of the Arwydd-feirdd, and the Ofyddion, during their three years of probation, which preceded their initiation into the higher orders of bardism. It was then optional whether they continued to register the descents of their chiefs, but in general they did; and a bard, and a genealogist became synonymous terms. From the ninth to the twelfth century, the genealogist, sanctioned by royal authority, classed the first families into twenty tribes; five termed royal, and fifteen called common. Other founders of families are recorded, but not included in the tribes, although of greater merit than some who were honoured with that distinction. Why Jestyn ab Gwrgant, a petty Lord of Glamorgan, and a character in everlasting disgrace, should be thus dignified, while he was the founder only of ignominy and loss of dominion to himself, of slaughter and slavery to his country, is difficult to adjust; and that Brochwel Ysgithrog, a prince of Powys in its highest splendor, having Shrewsbury for his capital, and a chief of great power and martial character, should have his name omitted even in the fifteen tribes, is alike inscrutable. Our bards continued their genealogical pursuits to the reign of Elizabeth; from which time bardism, in all its branches, for want of the customary encouragement, suffered an irrecoverable decline. Copies of ancient manuscript pedigree books, falling among persons who had a value for the subject, were carefully preserved, and the descents of families continued to the present century. However numerous these may have been, two pedigree books only have appeared in print; the first by Mr. Davies of Llansilin, in 1716,[1] containing little more than an enumeration of the families descended from each particular tribe. The second by Mr. John Reynolds of Oswestry, in 1739,[2] more copious, but less correct than the former, and both alike con-

[1] "*A Display of Heraldry of most particular Coat Armours, now at use in the six Counties of North Wales, &c.* Collected out of several Authentic Authors. By John Davies of Llansillin Parish in Denbighshire, Antiquary.—Salop. Printed by John Roderick for the Author, in the year 1716."—*Ed.*
[2] "*The Scripture Genealogy beginning at Noah & To which is Added, The Genealogy of the Cæsars. & Also a Display of Heraldry of the particular Coat of Armours now in Use in the Six Counties of North Wales, &c.* By John Reynolds of Oswestry, Antiquarian. Chester. Printed by Roger Adam for the Author, 1739."—John

fused and uninteresting.[1] From the short materials thus before him, the Author hopes allowances will be made for this imperfect attempt. He is sensible to its defects; at the same time he is free to say, that he has spared no assiduities, nor left a corner untried, whence any probable information was likely to arise. He regrets that a nation, possessing so many curious documents of ancient history as the Welsh, should have so long neglected bringing them to the light and public investigation. The Triads, Tysilio, and the rest of our historic manuscripts have yet no other dress than their British garb;[2] and the Latin works of Nennius, Giraldus, Paris, Polydore, Virunnius, Pryce, Llwyd, Powel, and Caius, relative to Wales, remain yet without translations,[3] to the disadvantage of English literature, and general information. Before he concludes, the Author (or historical collector rather) of the following sheets returns his thanks to those gentlemen who have assisted him with their communications: To John Kynaston Powel, Esq. of Hardwick;[4] to the Rev. Samuel Strong of Marchwiel;[5] the Rev. Edward Edwards of Wrexham;[6] the Rev. Edward Davies of Llanarmon Dyffryn Ceiriog;[7] the Rev. John Williams of

Reynolds's mother was John Davies's sister. This work is a very imperfect compilation by Reynolds of MS. materials left by his uncle, and put together with very little knowledge of the subject.—*Ed.*

[1] Since this was written much has been done to remedy the deficiency complained of. In 1846 the Welsh MSS. Society brought out a splendid edition of Lewys Dwnn's *Heraldic Visitations of Wales and Part of the Marches*, in two large imperial quarto volumes under the editorship of Sir Saml. Rush Meyrick, assisted by W. W. E. Wynne, Esq., of Peniarth, and Joseph Morris, Esq., of Shrewsbury. The *Archæologia Cambrensis* from its first publication in 1846 to the present time; the *Cambrian Journal*, 1854—1864; the *Montgomeryshire Collections* of the Powysland Club; various county histories; and *The History of Powys Fadog* in six octavo volumes (1881—1887), by J. Y. W. Lloyd, Esq., and other publications, have added very materially to our information respecting Welsh genealogy.—*Ed.*

[2] Geoffrey of Monmouth's British History must not be considered as a translation of Tysilio.

[3] Ably edited translations of most if not all of these works have since appeared.—*Ed.*

[4] Created a Baronet in 1818, and died in 1822. See p. 86.—*Ed.*

[5] Rector of Marchwiel and Canon of St. Asaph. Died about 1816.—*Ed.*

[6] He was then Curate of Wrexham, and held the Vicarage of Llanarmon yn Iâl from 1782 to 1820, the date of his death. In 1801 he brought out a new edition of Willis's *Survey of St. Asaph*, in two volumes.—*Ed.*

[7] Rector of Llanarmon from 1796 to 1811.—*Ed.*

Llanrwst;[1] and the Rev. Walter Davies of Meifod,[2] an able Welsh antiquary, who will throw more light on this subject. The author hopes that the portrait engravings which have been collected from the best pictures of the several persons that could be obtained, will make some amends for other deficiencies.

[1] Formerly Fellow of Jesus College, Oxford. He held the Head Mastership of Llanrwst Grammar School from 1791 to 1812, and was Rector of Llanbedr y Cenin. He died in 1826.—*Ed.*

[2] He was at that time Curate of Meifod. Shortly afterwards he was nominated to the Perpetual Curacy of Yspytty Ifan. In 1803, he obtained the Rectory of Llanwyddelan, which he resigned in 1807, on being collated to that of Manafon. He resigned the benefice of Manafon in 1837 on his preferment to the Vicarage of Llanrhaiadr yn Mochnant, where he died December 5th, 1849, in his eighty-ninth year. Mr. Davies was one of the best Welsh scholars of his day, an able critic, a good poet, and a voluminous writer. His collected works were published in 1868 in three volumes, under the editorship of the Rev. D. Silvan Evans,·B.D.—*Ed.*

ADVERTISEMENT TO FIRST EDITION.

THE Author of this small work would attempt to enlarge it through the Fifteen Common Tribes, and would hazard another publication (correcting the errors of this) with some additional Engravings, if the Families descended from them were pleased to communicate their Pedigrees, and what biographical matter and anecdote belong to them. This is the more necessary, nay indispensable, as the founders of these Tribes have little, or no notice taken of them in History.

BIOGRAPHICAL INTRODUCTION TO THIS EDITION.

IT is a good proof of the intrinsic value and excellence of *Yorke's Royal Tribes of Wales*, that, after the lapse of nearly ninety years it is still popular, and that a new edition is called for. In the meanwhile, time has brought about great changes, as must ever be the case, more particularly in a busy commercial country like ours. Old families which still flourished in YORKE's time, have decayed or disappeared altogether, while new men have risen to the surface, and have founded new houses on the ruins of the old. It has been my object and my endeavour, while retaining in their integrity the original text and notes, and even with a few exceptions the original spelling, to add by way of notes, such information as I have been able to gather, to indicate these changes, and to bring down to the present date, the story of our old Welsh families, so agreeably told by the genial and accomplished author. The notes and additions for which I am responsible are marked *Ed.* throughout. The fine engraved portraits which illustrated the original edition, have been reproduced by the Typographical Etching system, which the printer has selected, after carefully comparing the numerous processes now in vogue, as being the best adapted for the purpose.

One of the difficulties that a genealogist has to contend with in the present day, is the little attention given now, as compared with former times, to the preservation of Pedigrees and family history. People's minds are so engrossed by the present and the future, that certainly less regard is paid to the past, than used to be the case. Men are too much occupied in the race for riches or honour, to think much about their ancestry. " Let the dead past bury its dead," is the language of the time, and homage is paid to men more and more for what they are than for what their fathers were. Wealth, power, and (which is a more hopeful sign) genius and intellect, will generally command respect for a man, though his father may have been a sweep or a shoeblack.

It has been thought desirable to take this opportunity to publish, in an enlarged form, the brief Account of the *Fifteen Tribes of North Wales*, composed, it is generally understood, by Robert Vaughan, the eminent Welsh antiquary, first published with Notes in the *Cambrian Register* for 1795, and as an Appendix to Pennant's *History of Whiteford and Holywell*, in the following year : also the account of the Tribe of Tudur Trevor, or the Tribe of March, given by Pennant, and by him styled the Sixteenth Tribe.

xii.

The origin of the Tribes is involved in some obscurity, and has given rise to much discussion, for Vaughan's explanation (p. 1, *post*) is by no means satisfactory. That account represents Gruffudd ab Cynan, Rhys ab Tewdwr, and Bleddyn ab Cynfyn, as having " made diligent search after the arms, ensigns, and pedigrees of their ancestors"; while a comparison of dates will shew that it was impossible for those princes to have co-operated in the way referred to, and that they all lived and died before the time when hereditary arms were borne or heraldry existed. With regard to the Fifteen Tribes, Mr. Trevor Parkins, who ably discusses these difficulties in the recent (1883) edition of Pennant's *Tours in Wales*, vol. iii, p. 415, points out that "they belong exclusively to North Wales. They are "principally found in Anglesey and Carnarvonshire, and in those parts of "Denbighshire and Flintshire which did not belong to Powys. Their distribution "is exceedingly irregular, but there seems to be something local in their arrange- "ment. * * * * Many difficulties will be explained, if the Tribes are "believed to have been constituted subsequently to the reign of Owen Gwynedd "[1137-1169], in the last years of national independence, and to have been limited "to the districts which remained un-conquered. The heraldic bearings, some of "which appear to be more modern, may have undergone changes, and been finally "determined upon at a later period. * * * The Tribe of March (or Tudor "Trevor) has no connection with the rest, and its formation is certainly more "recent." Professor Rhys, however *(Ib.*, vol. i., p. 15), is "disposed to put back "the real origin of the tribes into the pre-historic times, when the inhabitants of "Gwynedd were still Goidels, and had a tribal system differing from that of their "neighbours the Ordovices of Powys, who were a Brythonic people, and the "introductors of the Brythonic language into Wales." But whatever may have been the causes which led to the formation of these Tribes, they furnish a highly interesting record of great value to the historian as well as the genealogist, of the history and connections of most of the leading families of North Wales.

PHILIP YORKE, the author of *The Royal Tribes of Wales*, was the son of Simon Yorke, Esq. and Dorothy his wife, and was born at Erthig, near Wrexham, Denbighshire, in the year 1743. His father was a first cousin of Lord Chancellor Hardwicke, and their common ancestry, according to Sir Egerton Brydges, "though of no particular lustre either from its titles or estates was by no means "mean, insignificant in point of property or unrespectable in alliances." His mother was the daughter and heiress of Matthew Hutton, Esq. of Newnham, Herefordshire. Erthig is a fine old mansion, built in 1678, delightfully situated within about a mile of the town of Wrexham. It originally belonged with a considerable estate to an old Welsh family long extinct, of the same name, of the tribe of TUDOR TREVOR. It was purchased in 1715 by John Meller, Esq., a Master in Chancery, who bequeathed it to his nephew (son of his eldest sister), the above named Simon Yorke. Wat's Dyke runs through the property. After a liberal education, Philip Yorke was entered at Benet College, Cambridge, where he proceeded to the degree of M.A. in 1765. He inherited the Erthig estate on the death of his father on the 28th July, 1767, and the following year he was elected F.A.S. On the 2nd July, 1770, he married Elizabeth, younger daughter of the Right Hon. Sir John Cust, Bart., Speaker of the House of Commons, and by her, who died in 1779, had besides a daughter, a son and heir, Simon, born 27th July, 1771, whose son of the same name now resides at Erthig. Mr. Yorke married secondly, Diana, widow of Ridgeway Owen Meyrick, Esq. of Bodorgan, Anglesey, and daughter and heiress of Pierce Wynne, Esq. of Dyffryn Aled, Denbighshire, of the tribe of MARCHUDD (see p. 194, post), by Margaret his wife, daughter of Robert Wynne, Esq. of Garthewin. Of this marriage there was issue, three sons, Pierce Wynne, Philip, and Robert, and a daughter, Lucy. The former died in 1837, leaving by his wife, Elizabeth, daughter of Sir William Bulkeley Hughes of Plas Coch, besides two daughters, a son, the present Pierce Wynne Yorke, Esq. of Dyffryn Aled.

Yorke, for some years represented the boroughs of Helston and Grantham successively in the House of Commons, but constitutional diffidence prevented his speaking there. He was, however, a man of superior endowments and cultivated tastes, which his ample fortune of about £7,000 a year enabled him to gratify. He indeed spent his money lavishly, though not recklessly or foolishly. "Waste not want not" was written up in large letters in his kitchen, but that was all that was known of economy at Erthig, where the owner made great improvements in the house and its surroundings, and added many to its treasures. He was well versed in the classics, especially Virgil, and, as few equalled him as a conversationalist, he was a delightful companion. He loved to gather round his table friends, whose tastes for literary studies and pursuits were similar to his own. Among these was Thomas Pennant, the accomplished author of the *Tours in Wales*, and other well known works. Pennant, who died some years before him, left him a legacy of ten guineas as a token of their friendship.

Yorke made his first appearance as an author in 1795, when he brought out the *Tracts of Powys*, a thin quarto volume, printed by Marsh "at the Druid Press," Wrexham. This formed the groundwork of his later and more important work, *The Royal Tribes of Wales*. It is now very scarce. He dedicated this work to his intimate friend, Pennant, thus :—" To Thomas Pennant of Downing, Esq. "Dear Sir,—I attempted with some pains and to little purpose, the several

"pedigrees of the different descendants of Bleddyn ap Cynfyn, the founder of our
"third Royal Tribe, but communications failing me, the design hath ended for the
"present, at least in this slight Memoir of the Princes and Lords of Powys only.
"Such as it is then permit me to present it you as to one by whom our Antiquities
"have been best understood and best illustrated. I have added the names of all
"the families I can find descended from this as from the nineteen other Tribes;
"from that source alone, the information necessary must be sought; what we
"have abroad is without anecdote, imperfect and uninteresting, and I detach this
"with great submission among them on a service of better intelligence. If with
"success, I would report progress; for I am free to think the race of Cadwalader
"more glorious than the breed of Gimcrack, and a Welsh Card than a Newmarket
"Calendar.—I am, Dear Sir, with great esteem, Your very faithful and obedient
"servant.—Ph. Yorke, Erthig, April 20th, 1795."

Besides the historical sketch of Bleddyn ab Cynfyn, which occupies 37 pages,
the *Tracts of Powys* include "A refutation of Polydore Vergil's remarks about
the ancient Britons" (20 pages); lists of the descendants of the five Royal and
fifteen Noble Tribes of North Wales; "Observations on Crown Manors in Wales,"
afterwards reprinted as an Appendix (No. xvi) to the *Royal Tribes;* the divisions
of Bromfield and Yale; and some letters of Goronwy Owen, Lewis Morris and
others, some of which have been republished in the *Life of Goronwy Owen* and
elsewhere. The sketch of Bleddyn ab Cynfyn ended with the reference to Lord
Herbert of Cherbury (see p. 81 *post*). The author subsequently made great
additions to it and wrote accounts of the other four Royal Tribes framed on the
same model, but not so exhaustive. These he published in 1799 in a handsome
quarto volume of about 200 pages (vii + 192) embellished with twelve fine engraved
portraits under the title, *The Royal Tribes of Wales.* The work was printed by
Mr. John Painter at Wrexham, and upon it rests Yorke's fame as a genial and
accomplished writer on genealogy—a subject which to many is in itself dry and
uninteresting.

In 1802, he published a small volume of thirty four pages quarto, entitled
Crude Ditties, containing about two dozen short poems mostly humorous, but of
little merit. He died on the 19th February, 1804, in the sixty-first year of his
age. The Yorke arms are, *argent* on a saltier *azure* a bezant; crest, a lion's head
erased *proper*, collared *gules* charged with a bezant; motto, "Nec cupias nec
metuas."

ROBERT VAUGHAN, the supposed author of the *Brief History of the Fifteen
Tribes of North Wales* (pp. 172—209 *post*), was the eldest son of Howel
Vaughan, Esq., a descendant of Cadwgan ab BLEDDYN AB CYNFYN, and

Margaret his wife, a granddaughter of Lewis Owen, Vice-Chamberlain of North
Wales and Baron of the Exchequer, an account of whose murder by banditti is
given in p. 114 *post.* He was born in 1592 at Hengwrt near Dolgelley, Merionethshire, to which the family residence had not long before been removed from
Y Wengraig, an old mansion at the foot of Cader Idris, where his ancestors had
resided for many generations. The seat of the original stock was Nannau, from
which in the sixth descent from Cadwgan of Nannau, Howel Fychan or Vaughan
separated and settled at Y Wengraig. Robert Vaughan entered Oxford University as a commoner of Oriel College in 1612, and having passed through the
regular course of studies pursued at that time in Logic and Philosophy, he left
the University without taking a degree and retired to his estate at Hengwrt.
Possessing a good estate, and animated by a patriotic spirit, he devoted himself
with great zeal to the cultivation of those antiquarian and historical studies that
have rendered his name famous and of such authority on all subjects connected
with Welsh history and antiquities. "In genealogy he was so skilled and his
"knowledge on that subject derived from such genuine sources that Hengwrt
"became the herald's college of the Principality, and no pedigree was current till
"it had first obtained his sanction ; a compliment he was justly entitled to if we
"may judge by the immense mass of that sort of learning left behind him which
"evinces an industry almost incredible, and a method and perspicuity rarely to
"be met with in similar collections."—*(Cam. Reg.* iii. p. 279). He was intimate
with most of the eminent literary characters of the age he lived in, and carried on
an extensive correspondence with Archbishop Usher, Sir Simon D'Ewes, Selden,
Sir John Vaughan, and others. The following are only a portion of the fruits of
his diligence and industry :—"*British Antiquities Revived;* or friendly contest
"touching ye sovereignty of the three Princes of Wales in antient times managed
"with certain arguments, whereunto answers are applied. To which is added the
"pedigree of the Right Hon. the Earl of Carbery, Lord President of Wales, with
"a short account of the Five Royal Tribes of Cambria." Oxford 1662 (quarto).
This was the only work published in his lifetime. A second edition was printed
at Bala in 1834, with a memoir prefixed by the Rev. John Jones, of Borthwnog.
He also wrote Notes or Commentaries on the Book of Basingwerk ; on Nennius ;
on the Triads, with an English translation; on Caradoc of Llancarvan's Brut or
Chronicles, with a collation of ten several copies, on vellum ; on Leland's New
Year's Gift ; on Burton's Antoninus ; on Dr. Powell's History of Wales ; on
Usher's Primordia ; Ball's Catalogus Scriptorum ; Annals of Wales from Vortigern
downwards, translated from the original into English with notes ; a short account
of the family of Corsygedol ; a Topography of Merionethshire ; and a Tour to

St. David's, containing short and cursory notices of the places he passed through in going and returning. He also formed at Hengwrt an unrivalled collection of Welsh manuscripts, the greater portion of which are now in the Peniarth library (see p. 115 *post*). The *Cambrian Register*, vol. iii., contains a catalogue of 162 of these, many of which are of very early date,' and several transcripts are in Mr. Vaughan's own handwriting. He also constantly employed a secretary at his house to transcribe valuable manuscripts entrusted to him by others ; and he obtained a large addition to his own collection on the death of Jones of Gelli-lyfdy, another industrious collector, with whom he had made an agreement that the survivor should succeed to the other's library (see p. 115 *post*). Vaughan's notes and copious additions to many of these render them the more valuable, and as materials for illustrating the history and antiquities of Wales, too much importance cannot be attached to them. Transcripts of *Y Seint Greal* and some others have been published under the able editorship of the late Canon Williams of Rhydy-croesau, and the Hengwrt collection has been indeed a vast quarry to which our leading antiquaries have since Vaughan's time resorted, and whence they have obtained most important materials for their works. Robert Vaughan died at Hengwrt in 1666, and was buried in the parish church of Dolgelley.

R. WILLIAMS.

August 1st, 1887.

ERRATA.

PAGE 17, line 12, for *Corysgedol* read *Corsygedol*.
,, ' 28, ,,   4. for *council* read *counsel*.
,, 40, ,, 20, for *langued or* read *langued azure*.
,, 56, ,, 28, for *Dafydd ab* Llwyd read *Dafydd Llwyd*.
,, 61, ,, 12, for *respository* read *repository*.
,, 68, ,, 31, for *English* read *eighth*.
,, 93, ,,   4, after *made* read *by*.
,, 107, ,, 19, for *of Golden Grove* read *at Golden Grove*.
,, 119, ,, 32, for *Conway* read *Conwy*.
,, 129, ,, 14, for *purposes* read *purpose*.
,, 141, ,, 29. for *Dui* read *Dni*.
,, 153, ,, 21, for *of one clothe* read *one of clothe*
,, 173, ,, 14, for *Nicholson* read *Nicholas*.
,, 185, ,, 31, for *gread* read *great*.
,, 192, ,, 14, *dele* the semicolon (;).
,, 197, ,, 14, for *obtained* read *attained*.

ROYAL TRIBES

OF

WALES.

— ⋯⋯ —

GRUFFUDD AB CYNAN ranks first of the five Royal
Tribes.[1] He recovered his crown of North Wales from Trahaern

[1] The five regal Tribes, and the respective representative of each, were considered
as of royal blood. The fifteen common Tribes, all of North Wales, and the
respective representative of each, formed the Nobility; were Lords of distinct
districts, and bore some hereditary office* in the palace. Gruffudd ab Cynan,
Prince of North Wales, Rhys ab Tewdwr, of South Wales, and Bleddyn ab
Cynfyn, of Powys, regulated both these classes, but they did not create them; as
many of the persons, placed at their head, lived before their times, and some,
after. Their precedence, as it stands, is very uncertain and not governed by the
dates; the last of them were created by Dafydd ab Owain Gwynedd, who began
his reign in 1169. We are left ignorant of the form, by which they were called
to this rank. Mr. Vaughan of Hengwrt informs us "that Gruffudd ab Cynan,
"Rhys ab Tewdwr, and Bleddyn ab Cynfyn, made diligent search after the arms,
"ensigns, and pedigrees of their ancestors, the Nobility and Kings of the Britons.
"What they discovered by their pains in any papers and records was afterwards
"by the Bards digested, and put into books, and they ordained five Royal Tribes,
"there being only three before, from whom their posterity to this day, can derive
"themselves, and also fifteen special Tribes, of whom the gentry of North Wales
"are for the most part descended."

* By the laws of Hywel Dda it appears there were twenty-four great officers of the Welsh court.

A

A.D. 1079 ab Caradog, at the battle of Carno,[1] who had been elected by the people, without the merits of descent, on the assassination of our worthy Prince, Bleddyn ab Cynfyn.

In Gruffudd, the succession was restored. He was the son of Cynan, the son of Iago or James, the son of Meurig, the son of Idwal, the son of Anarawd, the eldest son of Roderic the Great; and had not the principality of the north alone, but the supremacy of Wales, vested in him; for it was the condition, in the tripartition of Roderic,[2] and confirmed by his grandson Hywel Dda, that the Princes of South Wales and Powys, should be tributary to the North.

Gruffudd owed his success at Carno to a force of Irish, devoted to his fortunes, from his relation to Auloedd[3] King of Dublin, Man, and the Isles; whose daughter Ranhult, widow of Mathganyn, King of Ulster, by her second marriage, was his Mother. From the same interests, he had been supplied in a former attempt to recover North Wales, when he fixed himself

---

[1] The mountains of Carno, as the mountains of Gilboa, are celebrated for the fall of the mighty. The fiercest battle in our annals, happened in 1079, amidst these hills, when Gruffudd ab Cynan, assisted by Rhys ab Tewdwr, Prince of South Wales, disputed the sovereignty of North Wales, with Trahaern ab Caradog, the reigning usurper. After a bloody contest, victory decided in favour of the first, and Trahaern was slain.—*Pennant.* Carno is in the hundred of Arwystli in Montgomeryshire.—*Ed.*

[2] Roderic ordained that the Princes of South Wales and Powys should each of them pay yearly to the Sovereigns of North Wales, a tribute, called Maelged, of sixty-three pounds.

[3] Auloedd had built a castle on the Menai, near Moel y donn, called Castle Auloedd Frenin, the Castle of King Auloedd.

in Anglesey; but pursuing his success beyond the Menai was defeated by Trahaern at the battle of Bron yr Erw, and driven again, with great loss, within the island.

Gruffudd died in 1136, at the age of eighty-two, and lies buried on the south side of the great altar, in the Cathedral church at Bangor,[1] having reigned fifty-seven years through various fortunes,[2] and with equal interruption from his enemies the English, and his friends the Welsh. His early life was marked by spirit and success, but in his riper years, the desire of peace and his submissions[3] to obtain it, tarnished his former glory.

---

[1] Not a vestige of his shrine is now to be seen.—*Ed.*

[2] Soon after his victory at Carno, he was treacherously surprized at Rûg by one Muriawn Gôch, and, notwithstanding his late eminent success, suffered a long captivity of twelve years* in the castle of Chester. At length he escaped by the bravery of a young man, Kynrig hîr or the tall, of Iâl; who coming to Chester, under pretence of buying necessaries, took an occasion, whilst the keepers were feasting, to carry away his Prince, laden with Irons, on his back, to a place of security.—*Vita Conani.*

[3] Gruffudd had personal rather than political courage (often political villainy). He had fought hand to hand with that hardy Baron Fulke Fitzwarren, who was entrusted by Henry the First with the care of the Marches, and was wounded by him in the shoulder, and fled; but in the end wrested from Fulke, his castle and lordship of Whittington. There was another action in which he was personally engaged; and the circumstances are very extraordinary. Robert of Rhuddlan, nephew to Hugh Lupus, and the possessor of that castle, where he then resided, received in it a visit from Gruffudd, who came to solicit his assistance against his Welsh subjects. This he obtained; but on some quarrel attacked Robert in his castle, took and burnt the baily or yard, and killed such a number of his men,

---

* This could not be: the restless spirit of the Welsh, in this course of time, would have set up another Prince; besides, it contradicts the evidence of Ordericus Vitalis, who says, that Robert of Rhuddlan was slain by Gruffudd on the third of July, 1088, which was only nine years after the battle of Carno.

4

His son Owain Gwynedd more popularly succeeded him;[1] and it may have happened that on this account, the descendants of the tribe, have taken his coat,[2] in preference to his father's bearings, or have borne the father's only in the second quarter. Gruffudd was accomplished: He reformed the Welsh minstrelsy.[3]

that but few escaped into the towers. An extraordinary end attended Robert in a future contest, which ought to become history. On the third of July 1088, Gruffudd had entered the Cynwy, with three ships, and leaving them on the shore at low water, had proceeded to ravage the country, which belonged to Hugh Lupus Earl of Chester, the uncle of Robert. Alarmed at the descent, Robert, while his men were mustering their forces, went down to the sea side, with one soldier only, named Osborne de Orger, where he was slain, and gave up (says Ordericus,) his soul to God, and the virgin, his men coming up too late, to save him; but they recovered his body, which was first interred at St. Werburgh's, Chester, but removed afterwards to Normandy.

[1] Consilio felix Princeps, fortissimus armis ;
Civibus, ille novus Solomon, novus hostibus, Hector.—*Pentarchia.*

Owain Gwynedd reigned thirty-two years. He died in December, 1169, and lies buried at Bangor; whose tomb when Baldwyn, Archbishop of Canterbury coming to preach the Crusade against the Saracens, saw, he charged the Bishop to remove the body out of the Cathedral, when he could find a fit opportunity so to do, in regard that Archbishop Becket had excommunicated him heretofore, because he had married his first cousin, the daughter of Grono ab Edwyn, and that, notwithstanding he had continued to live with her till she died. The Bishop in obedience to the charge, made a passage from the vault through the south wall of the church, under ground, and so secretly shoved the body into the church yard.—*Hengwrt MSS.*

[2] The arms of Gruffudd ab Cynan were, *Gules,* three lioncels passant in pale barry *argent,* armed *azure.* Those of Owain Gwynedd were, *Vert,* three eagles displayed in fess *or.—Ed.*

[3] After Cadwaladr, the Princes who next undertook the reform of our minstrelsy, were Bleddyn ab Cynfyn, and Gruffudd ab Cynan. It was by them enacted, that no person should follow the profession of Bard or Minstrel, but such only as were

and improved the national music : Himself ; his mother and grandmother were born in Ireland, then the land of harps and harmony : whence he brought our best tunes, better performers, and a better order of instruments.   He regulated also the family pedigrees, and heraldic distinctions of our Countrymen,

..................*Sus horridus, atraque Tygris.*

Squamosusque Draco, et fulvâ cervice Leæna,

and established our first game laws.   Of his descendants the house of Gwydir[1] seems most eminent.   Sir John Wynn the historian,[2] was no ordinary character.   He was made a Baronet on the creation of that honour, and his journey to Court, with the particulars[3] kept by himself, is curious.   He was a man of ability, and learned in the histories of his country, which he much embellished, nor did he neglect his common interest, but was shrewd and successful in his dealings.   Hence the people

admitted by the Eisteddfod, which was held once in three years.   They were prohibited from invading each other's province, nor were they permitted to degrade themselves, by following any other occupation.—*Lewis Morris MSS.*

[1] Gwydir, from Gwy, aqua, and Tir, terra ; the lands being much subject to be overflowed by the river Cynwy.

[2] *The History of the Gwydir Family* by Sir John Wynn is of all the works which have been written relating to the general or family history of North Wales the most highly esteemed.   It has been published four times—viz., the first edition edited by the Hon. Daines Barrington in 1770 ; its second appearance in Mr. Barrington's *Miscellanies* in 1781 ; a third edition edited by Miss Angharad Llwyd in 1827 ; and a fourth by Mr. Askew Roberts in 1878, with Notes by that accomplished genealogist and antiquarian the late W. W. E. Wynne, Esq., of Peniarth.   The two last editions contain the portrait of Sir John Wynn from an exceedingly rare engraving by Robert Vaughan, the engraver.—*Ed.*

[3] In the possession of the Antiquarian Society.

were led to think he deceived and oppressed them, and it is the superstition of the place to this day, that the spirit of the old gentleman lies under the great waterfall of Rhaiadr y Wennol, or the swallow,[1] from its swiftness, there to be punished, purged, spouted upon, and purified from the foul deeds done in his days of nature,

> ....*aliis sub gurgite vasto*
> *Infectum eluitur scelus*,..... ....

He made the *amende honorable* of that time, and founded an hospital, and endowed a school at Llanrwst, and gave the rectorial tythes of Eglwysfach, to the support of these charities, and left regulations for their government. In 1615 he had incurred the displeasure[2] of the Court[3] of Marches, since the Lord Chancellor Ellesmere is informed by it, that Sir John

---

[1] But query, Rhaiadr Ewynol=the foaming cataract.—*Ed.*

[2] He was unjustly charged (as he is pleased to say himself) with procuring a petty riot, and for entering into lands, of which he was the King's farmer.

[3] This Court, in the nature of a French Parliament, was first established by Edward the Fourth, who sent his son Edward to reside at Ludlow, where it sate, under the government of his uncle Rivers.* It was confirmed by an Act of Henry the Eighth. The Council, assisting the President, consisted of the Chief Justice of Chester, with the three other then existing Justices of Wales. There were also extraordinary members of Council called in, as the President should think proper. They were allowed six shillings and eight-pence per day, and diet for themselves and their men. "In this Court," says Mr. Lewis, "when it flourished without restraint, as many causes were dispatched in a Term, as in any Court in England, or more, and that he had himself moved in an afternoon above twenty causes, and that the Counsellor for all the motions and pleadings in one cause, in one Term, had but five shillings fee." It was dissolved at the Revolution.

* The Welsh were so turbulent at this time, that it was thought necessary for some person of high distinction to reside on the borders, to strengthen the civil power.—*More.*

SIR THOMAS EGERTON VISCOUNT BRACKLEY.

Lord Chancellor.

Wynn Knight and Baronet, is unfit to be continued a member
thereof, and that his name should not remain in the commission
for Carnarvonshire ; but he made his peace from the sure
means[1] of that moment. The Court of James was corrupt to
an extreme, and beyond the examples of any period.

Sir John died at the age of seventy-three, and lies buried
at Llanrwst. By his wife Sidney,[2] the daughter of Sir William
Gerard, Lord Chancellor of Ireland, he had eleven sons and two
daughters. His eldest son John was a Knight, and died
during his father's life, on his travels at Lucca, at the age of
thirty-one. Domestic disagreements are said to have sent him
so late abroad. He married Margaret[3] daughter of Sir Thomas
Cave of Stanford in Northamptonshire, and left no issue. He
was a man of observation, and some of his foreign letters
remain. The father was succeeded by his son Richard, who was
Groom of the Bed-chamber to Prince Charles, and attended
him and Buckingham, on their matrimonial excursion to Spain,
of which he left a pleasant account.[4] He became Treasurer to

---

[1] See Appendix xii. [By the payment of a bribe of £350.—*Ed.*]

[2] Who died 8th June, 1632.—*Ed.*

[3] "This Lady," says Mr, Pennant, "had four husbands. Her first was Sir
John Wynn the younger ; her second of the Milesian race, for she married Sir
Francis Aungier, Master of the Rolls in Ireland, afterwards created Baron of
Longford. Thirdly, she gave her hand to an Englishman, Sir Thomas Wenman
of Oxfordshire ; and finally she resigned her antiquated charms to my relation,
Major Pennant, a younger son of Downing, who in the year 1656 deposited her
with his ancestors in the church of Whitford."

[4] Preserved by Thomas Hearne.

Sir Richard, in one of his letters to his father from Spain, says "We may

Queen Henrietta. He built the chapel at Llanrwst, from a design of Inigo [Jones ;[1]] the roof was not new, and taken from the neighbouring abbey at Maenan. Parts of that fabric may be traced at Gwydir.

Iuvenius etiam disjecti membra ....

Sir Richard married a Darcy, but died without issue, and was buried at Wimbledon.[2] He was succeeded by his brother Sir Owen, who left a son Sir Richard,[3] who married a daughter of the old cavalier Sir Thomas Middleton of Chirk castle, and had one daughter Mary, the wife of Lord Willoughby, the first Duke of Ancaster. This lady was great grandmother to the present Baroness Willoughby,[4] married to Lord Gwydir, to whom in her right, the place belongs. The Baronetage continued and

think ourselves happy, that have everything in Wales, for both of the kingdoms of Castile and Arragon are not worth one of our worst counties."

[1] Inigo Jones, the great architect, was a native of Llanrwst or of the immediate neighbourhood. The fine old bridge at Llanrwst is considered to be his work.—*Ed.*

[2] See Appendix xiii.

[3] Sir Richard Wynn is stated to have been Chamberlain to Catherine, Queen of Charles the Second, and to have presented to her Majesty a pearl from the river Conway, which is said at one time to have been a conspicuous object in the royal crown.—*Ed.*

[4] This lady, Priscilla Barbara Elizabeth, in whose favour the abeyance of the Barony of Willoughby de Eresby was terminated by the Crown, 18th March, 1780, was the wife of Sir Peter Burrel, Bart., created Baron Gwydyr, May 28, 1796. Upon the death of her grandson, Alberic twentieth Lord Willoughby de Eresby and third Baron Gwydyr on 26th August, 1870, the former title again fell into abeyance between his surviving sisters, in favour of the eldest of whom, Clementina Elizabeth, Dowager Lady Aveland, the present Baroness, the abeyance was terminated in 1871.—*Ed.*

SIR THOMAS MIDDLETON KNIGHT.

ended in Sir John Wynn of Wynnstay, the grandson of Sir John of Gwydir, by his tenth son Henry,[1] and the heiress of Rhiw goch. Sir John of Wynnstay, married Jane the heiress of Watstay.[2] He changed the name as nearer his own, to

[1] Henry Wynn married Catharine, the daughter and heiress of Elizei Lloyd of Rhiw goch, in Merionethshire. Henry was no small pluralist in lay-preferment, and with a kind of law Commendam, he held together the Prothonotaryship of North Wales, was the Judge of the Marshalsea, Steward of the Virge, Solicitor General to the Queen (Henrietta), and Secretary to the Court of the Marches. He sat for the County of Merioneth, in the last Parliament of James the first, and died in 1671. This gentleman, writing to his father, Sir John, the second of April, 1624, and speaking of Parliamentary business, says, "We sit very hard from seven in the morning until one in the afternoon, and after, from two of the clock in the afternoon until seven, in relation to Recusants, state of the Navy, motion against the Lord Treasurer concerning stamps, used by him in stamping his name, which are left with his men. These some held he might lawfully use, but kept safely by him, as the Keeper doth the Great Seal. I cannot chuse but remember what was said by Sir Peter Mutton of Llannerch, in the House, Sir Edward Coke sitting in the chair: "That this time, was not the first that stamps were used, for he had heard before he was born, that stamps were used here, in this kingdom." At which the whole House laughed; which is not to be forgotten in haste. To whom presently Sir Edward Coke called, Sir Peter Stamp.

[2] She was the daughter and heiress of Eyton Evans of Watstay, by Anne the daughter of Dr. Powel, Vicar of Rhiwabon, the Welsh historian. Eyton Evans was the eldest son of Thomas Evans of Rhiwabon, as Wynnstay was then called, which he altered to Watstay, from its situation on Wat's Dyke. Thomas was the son of Richard Evans, the son of old Thomas Evans of Oswestry, Attorney General in the Court of the Marches. Richard married Mary Eyton, daughter and heiress of Edward Eyton of Rhiwabon. This Edward Eyton was the son of William, the younger brother of John Eyton, who suffered death at Holt, for killing William Hanmer, and died without issue; on whom a Welsh Englyn was made,* which signifies that in the year 1534 a great grief befel us in the death of

* It is as follows :—

"Oed Ner mil a banner mal hyn—mawr alaeth,
　Marwolaeth Sion Eutyn,
Pedair ar ddeg teg at hyn
Ar hugain wr rhywiogwyn."—*Ed.*

B

Wynnstay, and in a manner made the place,[1] which had been the residence in times past of Madog ab Gruffudd Maelor, the potent Lord of the Bromfields, and founder of the Abbey

A.D.
1718

of Llanegwest. Sir John died at the age of ninety-one, and

John Eyton, an amiable Man. William, who succeeded his brother John, was the son of John Eyton of Rhiwabon, the son and heir of John ab Ellis Eyton, distinguished for his services at Bosworth, who lies buried at Rhiwabon, and his stone effigy in armour, is ornamented with a collar of S.S.[*] This John ab Ellis Eyton was the son of another Ellis Eyton, who was the eldest son of John hên (or the old) of Eyton and Rhiwabon. The last John was Steward of the Lordship of Bromfield and Iâl, in 1439, and, after the birth of his eldest son Ellis, he was divorced by the church, on the stale ground of consanguinity ; by which ecclesiastical pretence Ellis was made illegitimate, yet he had the Rhiwabon estate given him. The father and mother were again married by licence, and had afterwards issue William Eyton, who in preference to his elder brother, had the Eyton estate, and was ancestor to Edward Eyton Esquire, the present possessor. [The mansion and estate were sold soon after this was written —*Ed.*]

Of the House of Eyton was Madog Eyton of Eyton, Erddlis, and Bersham, who died in 1331, and was buried at Gresford on the feast of St. Matthias. He lies represented in armour in stone, on the south side within the church, in the wall.

[1] In 1678 Sir John inclosed a park for deer, with a stone wall, at Wynnstay, and at the same time, the avenues of oak, elm, and ash, were planted there. [In 1691 he made the fishpond.—*Ed.*]

On the night of the 5th of March, 1858, a disastrous fire took place at Wynnstay, which nearly destroyed the old mansion and the greater part of its contents including the valuable collection of MSS., paintings aud books, with some exceptions. Many of these treasures can never be replaced. The house has since been rebuilt.—*Ed.*

[*] He was an Esquire by creation, which was the fourth class of Esquires, called white spurs. The Ceremony was, that the King put about his neck a silver collar of Esses, and conferred upon him a pair of silver spurs. The five ancient orders of Esquires were, first, those who are elect for the King's body ; second, Knight's eldest sons ; third, younger sons of the eldest sons of Barons and other nobles of higher estate ; fourth, the white spurs by creation ; and fifth, they who are so by office, and by serving the Prince in any worshipful calling. This title of white spur was hereditary, and belonged only to the heir male of the family.—*Prince's Worthies.*

SIR JOHN WYNNE BART.

lies buried at Rhiwabon, under a mass and massacre of marble, ludicrous to look on. He left Wynnstay, and his other estates of great value, to his kinsman Watkin Williams, afterwards Sir Watkin Williams Wynn, the grandfather of my spirited friend of the same name the present possessor.[1] Sir John was a man of pleasure in his youth; late in life he made a visit to the Court, in the early days of Queen Anne, and meeting in the drawing-room after many years absence, his old Westminster school-fellow the Apostolic Beveridge of St. Asaph; "Ah, Sir John! Sir John!" says the good Bishop to him, "when I knew you first, the Devil was very great with you." 'Yes, by Gad, my Lord,' says Sir John, 'and I wish he was half so *great* with me now.'

He was an early improver of Welsh gardening, and introduced a small swan egg pear, that is yet very popular and bears his name.

The house of Llwyn, is of this tribe and family. Maurice Wynn of Gwydir, father of Sir John the historian by his first wife, to his second married Catherine of Beren; by her he had a son, on whom he settled Llwyn; from him is descended

---

[1] This was the fifth Baronet, who died 6th January, 1840. He was succeeded by his son, the late Sir Watkin, who died in May, 1885, leaving one surviving daughter and heiress, Louisa Alexandra, who in 1884 had married the heir to the title, her cousin, Herbert Edward Watkin (the present Baronet), second son of Lieut. Col. Herbert Watkin Williams Wynn, by Anna, daughter of John Lloyd, Esq., of Cefn, a descendant of Cunedda Wledig. Thus, the ancient line of Gwydir and Owain Gwynedd and the Cefn branch of the parent stem of Cunedda Wledig, so long divergent, were once more re-united.—*Ed.*

Owen Wynn Esquire of that place, the existent male heir of the house of Gwydir.[1]

The Wynns of Berthddu, and Bodysgallen, were of this tribe, and a younger branch of Gwydir. Gruffudd Wynn the younger brother of Maurice, and uncle to Sir John the historian, was settled at Berthddu. He married the daughter of Richard Mostyn of Bodysgallen (the second son of Thomas[2] ab Richard ab Hywel ab Jevan Fychan, of Mostyn) and obtained the estate, which hath again reverted to the Mostyn family. The male line ended in Robert Wynn, who died a batchelor, and his estates fell to Margaret, (the daughter of his brother Dr. Hugh Wynn, and, by her mother, the heiress of Plâs hên,

A.D.
1762

---

[1] He died in 1780, having been twice married. By his first wife, Ellenor Seele, of Liverpool, he had three sons and one daughter. His two elder sons dying without issue, the Llwyn estate came to the youngest, the Rev. Maurice Wynn, LL.D., Rector of Bangor Iscoed, the Vicar of Wenlock, who died in 1835 ; the last descendant in this line of the Wynn's of Gwydir. The last descendant in the male line of the house of Gwydir was Dr. Rice Wynn, an eminent surgeon at Shrewsbury, who died unmarried in 1846, aged 69. He was lineally descended from Robert Wynn the fourth son of Maurice Wynn of Gwydir by his first wife, Jane, daughter of Sir Richard Bulkeley (*Hist. of Powys Fadog.* vol. iv., p. 357).—*Ed.*

[2] "Thomas ab Richard ab Hywel first took the name of Mostyn, says Mr. Pennant, on this occasion. Rowland Lee, Bishop of Lichfield and President of the Marches, in the reign of Henry the Eighth, sat on a Welsh cause, and wearied with the quantity of Aps on the jury, directed that the panel should assume their last name, or that of their residence ; and that Thomas ab Richard ab Hywel ab Jeuan Fychan, should be reduced in future to the poor dissyllable Mostyn."

"You may see," says Mr. L. Morris, "in some copies of Gildas Nennius, that the Cambro-British Kings used, on the first coming of the Saxons, the appellation of Mac, instead of Mâb or Fâb, although now entirely disused in Wales, and preserved only in North-Britain and Ireland. It hath of late sunk into the surname there, as Macpherson, Macdonald ; so Ap, properly ab, from Mâb the son, is generally lost in

Corsygedol, and Bodidris,) married to Sir Roger Mostyn of Mostyn. The last Mr. Wynn sat for the boroughs of Carnarvonshire, and will be remembered in the annals of hospitality for his plentiful long table and substantial Christmas dinners. He was not so fond of long sermons, especially in cold weather; and it happened that Bishop Sherlock then of Bangor, his old acquaintance, was on a visit with him at Bodysgallen, on a Sunday, and observing to the Curate at dinner, that he was surprized he had given them no sermon that morning; "Ah, my Lord," says poor Ellis in his broad simple manner, "had I PREACHED when Master Wynn *is* in church, I *shall* have nothing but small beer; but when I do not PREACH when Master is in church, I may have my belly-full of ale and welcome."

The Lloyds of Rhiwaedog were of this Tribe, and of great extraction. The *materna nobilitas* was here also considerable, their ancestor Maredudd ab Jeuan, the Eighth from Owain Gwynedd, having married Margaret, the coheiress of Einion[1] ab

Wales in the surnames Prŷs for Ap Rhŷs, Powell for Ap Howell, Parry for Ap Harry. Ap is the banter of the English, upon our pronunciation of Ab, the true abbreviation from Mâb, a son."

[1] Einion ab Ithel was Esquire to the body of John of Gaunt, who gave him a pension of twenty marks from his manor of Halghton in Cheshire to serve him in Guienne. Ithel, on the death of Walter Lord Manny, succeeded him as Sheriff of Merionethshire for life. Ithel was in great favour with Henry the Fourth, in the beginning of whose reign he died. Jeuan ab Maredudd had matched his son Maredudd ab Jeuan with the daughter of Ithel, who belonged to the House of Lancaster. Jeuan ab Maredudd the father held stedfastly to that house, when Owain Glyndŵr rebelled; so that in the time of that war he and Hwlkyn Llwyd of Glynllifon had the charge of Carnarvon town, and an English captain was in the Castle; in revenge whereof Owain burned his two houses, Cefn y fan or Ystumcegid, and Cesail Gyfarch. In the continuance of this war, Jeuan ab Maredudd died at Carnarvon, and was brought by sea (for the passage by land was shut up by Owain's forces) to Penmorfa, his parish Church, to be buried. Robert

Ithel ab Gwrgeneu Fychan, ab Gwrgeneu ab Madog, ab Ririd Flaidd,[1] Lord of Penllyn, who dwelt at Rhiwaedog. The eldest Son of this match, John Ab Maredudd, was cousin to Owain Tewdwr, and with an hundred gentlemen of North Wales his kinsmen, he went to visit Owain, then in prison at Wysg castle. On his return within two miles of Caerlleon, being beset with enemies, favorers of the House of York, he made an oration to comfort his people, willing them to remember at that time the support of the honor and credit of their ancestors, and concluding

ab Maredudd, the brother of Jeuan ab Maredudd, taking the contrary side, was out with Owain, as may be gathered by a pardon granted him by Henry the Fourth, and Henry his son, then Prince of Wales. From Robert, who did not marry till near eighty, descended the houses of Gwydir, Cesail Gyfarch, and Hafod Lwyfog; and Sir John the historian, his descendant, says, he was the elder brother; from Jeuan ab Maredudd, who was Constable of Cruccaith, the families of Rhiwaedog, Clenenneu, Ystumcegid, Brynkir and Park. It is not material which was the elder brother, the gavelkind and the custom of the country not yeilding to the elder any prerogative or superiority. The father of Jeuan and Robert was Maredudd ab Hywel ab Dafydd ab Gruffudd ab Thomas ab Rodri, Lord of Anglesey, ab Owain Gwynedd, as is evident by the Extent of North Wales, in the twenty-sixth of Edward the Third. During Robert ab Maredudd's time, the inheritance, which descended to him and his brother Jeuan, was not parted after the custom of the country, by gavelkind, but Jeuan being married enjoyed both houses, Cefn y fan and Cesail Gyfarch.

[1] Ririd Flaidd, Lord of Penllyn, took his surname of Blaidd (or the Wolf,) from his maternal ancestor Blaidd Rhudd, or the Bloody Wolf, of Gêst, near Penmorfa, and in his Arms bore a Wolf passant, &c. Some Welsh verses remain concerning him, which may be thus interpreted (the Poet speaks)* " I have a friendly Wolf, that stands by me to crush the insulting foe. It is not the forest Wolf, scattering the harmless flock, but the Wolf of the field of battle : though at other times he is mild and liberal."

From Ririd Flaidd were descended the Lloyds of Rhiwaedog, the Myddletons of Gwaynynog and Chirk Castle, the Vaughans of Glanyllyn, and the Lloyds of Glanhavon.

* " Mae im' flaidd a'm câr o'm caffael—wrtho
  Yn wrtheb archafael ;
  Nid blaidd coed coll ei afael
  Namyn blaidd mies, moesawg hael."—*Cynddelw.*

that it should never be said in time to come, that there an
hundred North Welsh Gentlemen fled, but that the place should
carry the name and memory, that there an hundred North Welsh
gentlemen were slain.   Because some of his kinsmen had brought
with them all their sons, and some others had but one son to
succeed in their name and inheritance, as Hywel ab Llywelyn ab
Hywel and others, he placed all these in the rereward, out of
the fury of the fight, whilst all his own sons were in the
vanward which himself led, where he was sore wounded in the
face, whence he was called 'Squier y Graith, the 'Squire with the
scar, to his dying day : But God gave his enemies the overthrow, he opening the passage with his sword.[1]

Queen Catharine being a Frenchwoman born, the relict of
Henry the Fifth, knew no difference between the English and
Welsh nations, until her second marriage[2] being published, Owain
Tewdwr's kindred and countrymen were objected to, to disgrace
him as most vile and barbarous, which made her desire to see
some of his kinsmen.   Whereupon, Owain brought to her presence
this John ab Maredudd and Hywel ab Llywelyn his near cousins,
and men of goodly stature and personage, but wholly destitute
of bringing up and nurture ; for when the Queen had spoken

---

[1] Gwydir History.

[2] Soon after the death of Henry the Fifth, his widow Catharine became enamoured
by the manly graces of Owain Tewdwr. His introduction was singular : He being a
courtly and active gentleman was commanded once to dance before the Queen, and in a
turn, not being able to recover himself, fell into her lap as she sate on a little stool with
many of her ladies about her.—*Drayton's Epistles.*

to them in different languages, and they were not able to answer her, she said they were the goodliest dumb creatures that ever she saw.

At this time there happened some difference between William Griffith of Penrhyn, Chamberlain of North Wales, and John ab Maredudd, who both bore chief rule in the country ; the one by reason of his authority, that all should reverence and obey him, the other in regard of his descent, kindred, and ability, acknowledging none but the Prince his superior ; hence grew the debate :

> ......*nec Cæsar ferre priorem,*
> *Pompeiusve parem............*

To John ab Maredudd his kindred and friends cleaved steadfastly, like courageous men : so then it began to be a proverb or phrase, to call the family of Owain Gwynedd Tylwyth John ab Maredudd, the race of John ab Maredudd. This variance continued in their posterity long after, till with matches and continuance of time it was worn out.[1]

Our valiant countryman married Gwenhwyfar, daughter of Gronw ab Jeuan of Gwynfryn. By her he had five sons. Morys ab John ab Maredudd, the eldest, had Clenenneu, Rhiwaedog and Park, and married Angharad, the daughter of Ellis ab Gruffudd ab Einion ab Gruffudd ab Cynfrig ab Osbern[2]

---

[1] Gwydir History.

[2] Osbern Fitzgerald was a branch of the Desmond Fitzgeralds, who were settled in Ireland, and descended from Gerald, Constable of Windsor, a military attendant on

Fitzgerald. By her he had three sons; William Llwyd of Rhiwaedog; Ellis who had Clenenneu, and was Sheriff of Merioneth in 1541; and Robert who had Park. The Llwyds were extinct in the male line in William Lloyd, whose sister was the mother of the present William Lloyd Dolben Esquire, of Rhiwaedog.[1]

The Morices[2] of Clenenneu were descended from Ellis, the second son of Morys ab John ab Maredudd. Sir William

William the Conqueror. Osbern is called Gwyddel, or the Irishman. He came into Wales in the time of Llywelyn the Great, and was much favoured by that Prince. From Osbern are descended the Vaughans of Corysgedol, the Wynns of Maes y Neuadd, the Yales of Iâl, the Wynns of Glynn in Ardudwy, whose daughter, and heiress Margaret married Sir Robert Owen of Clenenneu, Llanddyn and Porkington, the grand father to the late Robert Godolphin Owen Esquire.

[The Vaughans of Corysgedol became extinct in the male line upon the death in 1791 of Evan Lloyd Vaughan, Esq., M.P. for Merioneth. William Wynn of Maesyneuadd (Sheriff for Merioneth in 1758) assumed the surname of Nanney. His grandson, John Nanney, the last of this line died in 1868. Sarah Yale the last of the direct line of the family of Yale, of Plas yn Yale, by her Will, proved in 1821, antailed the Plâs yn Yale estate upon William, fourth son of Thomas Parry Jones Parry, Esq., M.P., of Madryn, her mother's grandnephew, who assumed the name of Yale, and was succeeded by his nephew, William Corbet Yale, Esq., the present owner. Robert Godolphin Owen's niece and heiress, Mary Jane Ormsby, in 1815, married William Gore, Esq., who assumed the name of Ormsby before his own of Gore. Their eldest son, John Ralph Ormsby Gore, was, in 1876, created Baron Harlech. The name of Porkington has now been restored to its original form, Brogyntyn.—Ed.]

[1] Rhiwaedog is in the parish of Llanfor, near Bala. The mansion house, and a remnant of the estate, subsequently became vested by descent in two ladies of the name of Iles, by the survivor of whom they were bequeathed to Mrs. Price, of Rhiwlas. The present owner is R. J. Lloyd Price, Esq., of Rhiwlas. The Lloyd's of Plasyndre, and other families in the neighbourhood of Bala, are descended from this ancient stock.—Ed.

[2] Sir William Morice, Secretary of State to Charles the second, and an instrument in his Restoration, was the son of Evan Morice, a younger brother of Clenenneu, settled in Devonshire. Sir William was succeeded in his great office by another of our countrymen, Sir John Trevor, of the house of Trefalyn.

C

Morice of this house married the daughter and heiress of the
Lacons of Llanddyn and Porkington, and the heiress of the three
houses married John Owen (fourth son of Robert Owen, of
Bodsilin,) of the Tribe of Hwfa ab Cynddelw. This gentleman
had been Secretary to Walsingham, and made a fortune of ten
thousand pounds, when his great master left not wherewith to bury
him. The eldest son of this match was the memorable Sir John
Owen of Porkington, Llanddyn and Clenenneu, of whom I shall
speak under his proper Tribe. From Robert, the third son of
Morys ab John ab Maredudd, came the Anwyls of Park. They
ended in an heiress, Catharine, who married Sir Gruffydd
Williams of Marl and Pantglâs, a younger branch of Penrhyn.
Ann, their daughter and heiress, was maid of honor to Queen
Caroline ; was first married to Sir Thomas Prendergast of the
Kingdom of Ireland, and secondly to a gentleman of the same name
and nation. She died without issue, and her estates have passed
away in different alienations. Of a younger branch of Clenenneu,
was Andrew Morice D.D., the twenty-sixth Dean of St. Asaph.
He was instituted to the Deanery on the nomination of Sir
Morice Abbot, Executor to Archbishop Abbot, who had made it an
option. He was ejected from this and his other preferments by the
Parliament, and dying in 1654 was buried in the Cathedral at St.
Asaph. After his death this dignity lay vacant till the Restoration.
He left a son, David Morice, D.D., who held the Vicarages of Bettws[1]

A.D.
1770

A.D.
1634

---

[1] The Vicarage House at Bettws is remarkably small, and was built by the joint efforts
of Sampson Roberts, and Jones, two of its Vicars ;

Stare nequit uno cardine tanta Domus.

19

and Abergele. He is buried in the churchyard of the former A.D.
place, with the arms of Owain Gwynedd engraved on his stone, 1692
exploding as the rest of his Tribe the bearings of the Founder.

The Llwyds of Esclusham and Dulaseu, Baronets, of this
Tribe, descend from Dafydd Gôch of Penmachno. The first
Baronet, Sir Richard Lloyd, was governor of Holt Castle in the
civil wars of the last [17th] century, and defended it vigorously, but
without effect, against General Mytton. The estates passed to
coheiresses ; Mary married to Sir [Harry] Conway of Bodryddan,
Jane, to Lewis Owen of Peniarth, and Anne to Edward
Ravenscroft of Bretton.

Of a younger son of Dulaseu was descended Humphrey Lloyd,
Bishop of Bangor and Vicar of Gresford. He built the good substantial brick house[1] there, which with the church hath been much
improved by my old friend, its worthy incumbent.[2] The Bishop
built his house in the form of a cross, and the windows consisted of three lights in each window. Since the year 1576,
this church has had four Episcopal Vicars ; Bishop Hughes[3] of

[An old rhyme says of the old Vicarage of Bettws yn Rhos :—
"Vicar Jones and Vicar Sampson,
Joined their pence to build this mansion."
An excellent Vicarage house was built in 1861, on a new site, at a cost of about £1,700,
in lieu of the old one above referred to.—*Ed.*]

[1] See Appendix xiv.

[2] The Rev. Henry Newcome, a nephew of Bishop Newcome, for nearly 40 years
Vicar of Gresford. The Vicarage was rebuilt by Archdeacon Wickham, Vicar, in 1850,
at a cost of about £2,500.—*Ed.*

[3] Bishop Hughes was of the house of Cefn Garlleg, of the Tribe of Marchudd ; was
Bishop of St. Asaph in 1573, and died in 1600, and was succeeded by the translator

St. Asaph, Bishop Bellot[1] of Chester, Bishop Parry of St. Asaph,
and Bishop Lloyd of Bangor.[2]   Dr. Lloyd was the third son
of Richard Lloyd D.D. Vicar of Rhiwabon, and was born at
Trawsfynydd.   He was, says Wood, a great tutor at Oriel and
becoming known to his countryman Archbishop Williams, when
the King and Court were settled at Oxford, he was the means
of his preferment.   Bishop Lloyd died in 1688, and was buried
at Bangor.

A.D.
1610

Morgan.   Hughes left lands and revenues for founding a Free-school at St. Asaph.   He
procured a faculty from the Archbishop of Canterbury, to hold the Archdeaconry of
St. Asaph and other benefices, to the value of fifty pounds per annum, in Commendam.
The Archdeaconry has since that time been annexed to the Bishoprick.   Bishop
Hughes (Strype says) held, in consequence of the faculty above mentioned, sixteen
Livings, seven with Cures and nine Sinecures at the same time; that is to say, he had
Llysfaen in 1573, Castell Caer Einion in 1574, Cwmm in 1574, Gresford in 1577,
Llandrinio in 1577, Bettws yn Rhôs in 1577, Meifod in 1578, Llandrillo in Edeyrnion
in 1582, Llanycil in 1582, Abergele in 1582, Llandrillo yn Rôs in 1583, Llangwm in
1585 Whitford in 1587, Mallwyd in 1587, Llanfawr in 1588, and Llanrwst in 1592.
The amount of these livings at this time would be 4000l. per annum.

[1] Bishop Bellot was translated from Bangor, to Chester   He died at Berse Hall, or
Plâs Power, in 1596, and lies buried in the Chancel at Wrexham.   He was employed
by Elizabeth, as one of the English Biblical Translators.   It was some time before the
Clergy had shaken off their monastic austerities, and Bellot would on no account admit
a female into his family.   Orator Herbert [George Herbert the poet], of Cambridge
(brother to the first Lord Herbert of Cherbury) in his Book of Rules to Country
Parsons, lays it down, "'That if he be unmarried and keep house, he hath not a woman
in the house, but finds opportunities of having his meat dressed, and other services done
by men servants at home, and his linen washed abroad."   There was an old Divine not
long since living in Anglesey, of such transparent purity, that he would not suffer his
shirts, either at home or abroad, to be washed in the same tub with the women's shifts.

[2] To these may be added Dr. Narcissus Marsh, Vicar in 1689, who, the following
year, became Bishop of Ferns and Leighlin, and subsequently Archbishop of Cashel,
Dublin and Armagh in succession.—Ed.

The Brynkers of Brynker were of this Tribe. They descended from Rodri, Lord of Anglesey, the second son to Owain Gwynedd, by his second marriage. Their Ancestor Jeuan, the second[1] son of the valiant John ab Maredudd, was settled by his father at Brynker, an estate since alienated to the Wynns of Wern.[2] From this house the good Lord Lyttelton on his Welsh tour, writes to Archibald Bower, and says playfully : "But what Bala is most famous for, is the beauty of it's women, and indeed I saw there one of the prettiest girls[3] I ever beheld ; but such is my virtue that I have kissed none since I came to Wales, except an old maiden lady, a sister of Mr. Brynker, at whose house I now lodge, and who is the ugliest woman of her quality in Great Britain ; but I know a Duchess or two, I should be still more afraid of kissing than her."

A.D.
1755

---

[1] The third son, Robert, was slain in his father's time, in a fray near Ruthyn. Thus says the Gwydir Historian : "The Thelwals* of Ruthin, being ancient gentlemen of that country, who came into it with the Lord Grey, on whom King Edward the First bestowed the country of Dyffryn Clwyd, were in contention with a septe or hundred of that country, called the family of Gruffudd Gôch. These being more in number than the Thelwals, although the Thelwals carried the whole offices of the country under the Lord there, the Lord of Kent, then treasurer of England, drave the Thelwals to take to the castle of Ruthyn for their defence, where they besieged them, until the siege was raised by John ab Maredudd, his sons and kindred, to whom the Thelwals sent for aid. In that exploit, Robert, the third son of John ab Maredudd, was slain by an arrow in a wood, called Coed Marchan, within view of the Castle of Rhuthyn ; in revenge whereof many of the other side were slain, both at that time and afterwards. Owain, the fourth son of John ab Maredudd, was settled at Ystumcegid, and Gruffudd at Isallt.

[2] It was afterwards sold to Sir Joseph Huddart, Kt.—Ed.

[3] This gentlewoman is still living [about 1790].

* Of this house was Thelwal who published his digest of Writs.

The Gethins of Fedw dêg now extinct were of this Tribe. The first that bore the name was Rhŷs Gethin,[1] or the swarthy, ugly, terrible; he was brother to Hywel Coetmor, who anciently possessed Gwydir, sold by his son Dafydd to Maredudd ab Jeuan, Welsh nephew, or first cousin once removed, to the renowned John ab Maredudd, and ancestor to the Wynns of Gwydir. Hywel lies (with his effigy in armour) in Llanrwst church. Rhŷs and Hywel were the sons of Gruffudd,[2] the son of Dafydd Gôch of Penmachno, the natural son of Dafydd, Lord of Denbigh, the brother of our last Prince Llywelyn. Dafydd, who resided at Denbigh, was seized near the place by his own Countrymen, and carried laden with irons to Edward the First, then at Rhuddlan; thence he was taken before the Parliament, sitting at Shrewsbury. At this august assembly, was tried and condemned Dafydd. His perfidy to Edward, and his treasons to his country, rendered him an object of detestation to all. Eleven Earls and an hundred Barons were commissioned to try him, as a subject of England, for he had received from Edward an English Barony,[3] and a pension. He was the first who suffered

---

[1] Rhŷs Gethin lived in the parish of Bettws y Coed near Llanrwst, at a place called to this day Hendre Rhŷs Gethin; it is a little above Pont y Pair. His two sons, Hywel and Jeuan, had their residence on each side the river Lleder near Cromlech Hwfa, above Llanrwst. Jeuan had a house also at Penman maen, in the Parish of Dolwyddelan.

[2] There is a stone figure of this Gruffudd, recumbent in armour, in the church of Bettws y Coed, with this inscription;

Hic jacet Gruffudd ab Davydd Gôch.
Agnus Dei,
miserere mei.

[3] In the Writ for the trial of this Prince, Edward paints his ingratitude pathetically. " Quem susceparamus orphanum, ditaveramus de propriis terris nostris, et sub alarum

the death of a traitor, in the form of the sentence now in use, which he underwent in it's fullest extent ; and his head, with that of his brother Llywelyn, was exposed on the highest pinacle of the Tower of London.[1]

Gruffudd's encomiast, the Friar,[2] thus concludes his history. "Full oft the Earls of Chester met him and were defeated ; full oft the men of Powys attempted his overthrow, but without effect. The friends of Trahaern projected his destruction, but could not prevail. At length he sat on a peaceful throne, surrounded with wealth and prosperity, and conducted the public with success. He lived in friendship with the neighbouriug Kings ; Henry the First King of England, Morchath of Ireland, and the King of Denmark and the Isles. His fame extended to distant as well as adjacent countries. North Wales wore a flourishing aspect. The people were employed in building castles, in raising churches, planting trees, orchards and gardens, and

---

nostrarum chlamyde foveramus; ipsum inter Majores nostri Palatii collocavimus." This last favor was made his destruction. By his acceptance of the Barony (Frodsham in Cheshire) he was held liable to be tried and condemned by the Peers of England. Cromwel pursued the same rule with the Duke of Hamilton, as Earl of Cambridge, and to a similar effect.

[1] Pennant.

[2] Gruffudd ab Cynan his troublesome life and famous acts are compiled in Welsh, says Sir John Wynn, by a most ancient Friar, or Monk of Wales ; and, continues the historian, this was found by the posterity of the said Gruffudd in the house of Gwydir, and at the request of Maurice Wynn Esquire,* who had the same written in a most ancient book, and was lineally descended from him, was translated into Latin by Nicholas Robinson, Bishop of Bangor. [This translation, in his own handwriting, is preserved at Peniarth, and a transcript of the Welsh text, and of the Latin, was made by the late Canon Williams, of Rhydycroesau, and published in *Arch. Cambrensis* for 1866.—*Ed.*]

* Sir John's father.

protecting them with fences and ditches. They repaired ruined fabrics, and adopted the Roman method of husbanding the produce of the soil. Gruffudd founded churches near his principal residences ; his halls and entertainments were distinguished by their grandeur and magnificence. North Wales glittered with churches, as the firmament with stars. Gruffudd governed the people with a steady sceptre, and maintained peace with the neighbouring kingdoms. His sons, who were yet but young, he placed on the frontiers of the State, to guard and defend it against the bordering nations, who should renew hostilities against him. The petty Princes repaired to his Court, when they were reduced to distress by foreign powers, to solicit his advice and protection. He was at length overtaken by old age, which deprived him of his sight. Thinking he had secured by his victories the esteem and admiration of posterity, he devoted himself to works of charity, and once thought of monastic retirement, that he might lead a life of prayer, and manifest his contempt of temporal grandeur. Perceiving his dissolution to approach, he called for his sons, put his affairs in order, and prepared for death after the example of King Hezekias. His goods he divided, and his justice will endure for ever. He left a legacy of twent shillings to Christ-church in Dublin, where he was born and educated and the same sum to all the principal churches in Ireland. He bequeathed twenty shillings to the church of St. David, and to the Monastery at Chester, but more to the Monastery of Bangor ; ten shillings to Holyhead, the same to Penmon, to Celynnog, to Enlli, to Meifod, Llanarmon, Dinerth, and many other principal churches. He did not forget the

Bishop, Archdeacon, and the rest of the Priests of Bangor, and bound them by legacies to defend the Holy Spirit, the searcher and knower of all things. Then David the Bishop, Simeon the Archdeacon, a man of mature age and experience, the Prior of Chester, with many other religious and learned men, came to anoint his body with oil, in conformity to the injunctions of the Apostle James. His sons were among them, and he blessed them and foretold their fortune, and what peculiar character each would support, and as the Patriarch Jacob did on taking his dying leave of his sons in Egypt. And he solemnly enjoined them to combat their enemies with vigor and constancy, after the examples he had set them.

Angharad his Queen was present, to whom he bequeathed one half of his personal estate, with two Rhandir or portions in land and the customs at Abermenai. His daughters and nephews were also present, and he left to each a legacy sufficient to their maintenance.

The Welsh, the Irish, and the men of Denmark, lamented Gruffudd, as the Jews mourned for Joshua the son of Nun. He was eighty-two years old, and was buried on the left side of the great altar at Bangor. And let us pray that his soul may enjoy rest in the bosom of God, with the souls of other pious and good Kings, for ever. *Amen.*

A.D. 1136

Gruffudd in his person, was of moderate stature, having yellow hair, a round face, and a fair and agreeable complexion, eyes rather large, light eyebrows, a comely beard, a round neck, white skin, strong limbs, long fingers, straight legs, and handsome feet.

D

He was moreover skilful in divers languages, courteous and civil to his friends, fierce to his enemies, and resolute in battle; of a passionate temper, and fertile imagination.

He married Angharad, the daughter of Edwyn ab Grono, the founder of the tribe of that name; and by her had three sons and five daughters.[1] Our Friar in his singular and digressive manner, thus describes her: She was an accomplished person; her hair was long and of a flaxen colour, her eyes large and rolling, and her features brilliant and beautiful. She was tall and well proportioned, her leg and foot handsome, her fingers long, and her nails thin and transparent. She was good tempered, cheerful, discreet and witty, gave advice as well as alms to her needy dependants, and never transgressed the laws of duty.

---

[1] His sons were Cadwallon (who was slain in his father's lifetime), Owain Gwynedd, and Cadwaladr; his daughters' names were Gwenllian, Marred, Rannilld, Susanna, and Annes.—*Ed.*

P.S.—Inigo Jones's birthplace—see *ante* p. 8 *note.* It is often stated by biographers of this eminent architect that he was born in London, where his father carried on business as a clothworker; but it has always been a tradition generally accepted in the neighbourhood of Llanrwst, that he was born either at that town, or at Dolwyddelan. Barrington adds that in his time, the tradition was so circumstantial as to suppose that he was christened by the name of *Ynyr,* which after his travels into Italy he exchanged for *Inigo* as sounding better. (See Introduction to *History of the Gwydir Family).—Ed.*

RHYS AB TEWDWR.

THE Founder of our second royal tribe was Rhŷs ab Tewdwr, distinguished by the name of Mawr,[1] or the Great. In him the legal succession of South Wales was restored.[2] He was moreover the choice of the people, on the murder of the usurper Rhŷs ab Owain. With Gruffydd ab Cynan[3] he shared the victory at Carno; and the fortunes of that field, set them both on their hereditary thrones. His first adversities had a slight beginning, which in the end led to his destruction. Einion and Llywelyn, sons of the Lord of Dyfed and 'chiefs of some eminence in South Wales revolted, but were defeated, and fled ; Einion to Iestyn ab Gwrgant[4] Lord of Glamorgan, whom Rhŷs

[1] Major.

[2] Rhŷs was the son of Tewdwr, the son of Einion, the son of Owain, the eldest son of Hywel Dda, the legal Prince of South Wales ; but elected to the North in preference to the sons of Idwal foel, the right heirs. [He resided at Dinefor Castle.—*Ed.*]

[3] Gruffudd ab Cynan had landed from Ireland at Port clŷs,* near St. David's. Rhŷs, defeated by Trahaern, had taken sanctuary at that place; and hearing of Gruffudd's arrival, he went with all the clergy to meet him ; and, falling on his knees, implored his help against his adversaries, promising to do him homage, and to reward him with a moiety of his revenues. Gruffudd, pitying his condition, yielded to his request ; and having together overthrown their common enemy, Rhŷs was put into quiet possession of South Wales.—*Panton Papers.*

[4] In the year 1091, Iestyn, Lord of Glamorgan, rebelling against Rhŷs ab Tewdwr, Prince of South Wales, invited many Barons and Knights out of England to his aid, when, joining his power to them, he led them to Brecknock. Then Bleddyn ab

* Port Clŷs near St. David's meant only some fortified spot in that neighbourhood, quasi pars pro toto. It is a name borrowed from the English Portcullis, and that from the Latin Porta clausa.

28

had raised to a royal tribe. Him Einion[1] associated in rebellion, and together they brought the Normans under Robert Fitzhamon, a Baron of England, and gentleman of the chamber to William Rufus, and with his council and concurrence. The old and gallant Rhŷs met[2] them near Brecknock, was unsuccessful, and

Maenyrch, Lord of Brecknock, whose wife was sister to Rhŷs, sent instantly to him for succour; when making the best levy he could on the sudden, he came forthwith to Brecknock, and joined himself with Bleddyn and his men; and being far less in number than their adversaries, they very unadvisedly fought a most dismal battle to all South Wales; for they both falling by the sword, left it a prey to strangers, and the welfare of their children at the mercy of their enemies. Then Bernard Newmarch, or Newmarket, a Norman, seized upon the Lordship of Brecknock, the possession of which remained in his blood until the time of Henry the Eighth, when, by the attainder of the last Edward Stafford it came to the crown.—*Panton Papers.*

[1] Einion, a discontented Welsh nobleman, persuades Iestyn, Lord of Morganwg (of Glamorgan) to implore aid from England against Rhŷs, Prince of South Wales. Led by Robert Fitzhamon, twelve Knights (namely, de Londres, Grenville, Turburville, St. Quintin, Seward, Umphreville, Berkerolles, Sully, Le Soer, Le Fleming, St. John and Sterling) with their followers, willingly attended the call; defeat Prince Rhŷs, and are nobly rewarded by Iestyn. They were on the point of departing and on shipboard when Einion (whom Esmond had treated ungratefully) persuades them to return, and to revenge his cause, by driving the thankless Welsh Lord from his dominions. This they accomplished, and allotted to Einion the craggy and mountainous districts, and kept possession of the rest, settling their families in the country. This Colony with the Flemings settled by Henry the First in Pembrokeshire, proved fatal to the independence of South Wales.

[2] Queis iter aggressis, occurrit Rhesus in armis;
Undique cóncurrunt acies; pugna aspera surgit,
Ingruit armorum rabies; sternuntur utrinque;
Sternitur Haymonis pubes, sternuntur et Angli,
Proque focis, Cambri, dum vos certatis, et aris:
Acriter et pugnans, medio cadit agmine Rhesus,
Cum quo totus honor cecidit, regnumque Silurum.—*Pentarchia.*

This battle is stated by the best authorities to have taken place in 1089. It was fought at a place called Hirwaen Wrgant. The aged and gallant prince was pursued

fell gloriously in the ninetieth year of his age, and the fourteenth of his reign. By his wife the daughter of Rhiwallon, the brother of Bleddyn ab Cynfyn, he left two sons; Gruffudd, who succeeded him, and Grono, at the time of his father's death a prisoner in England, where he died.

With Rhŷs sunk the sun of South Wales, and all its glories; his successor Gruffudd being stiled Lord only of that | country. He was sent for security to Ireland, where he remained till he was twenty-five years of age. He came then secretly to South Wales, to visit his sister Nêst, the beautiful[1] mistress of Henry the First, and who brought him his eminent son Robert of Gloucester.[2] She was now married to Gerald de Windsor, by the favor of Henry, Constable of Pembroke. Gruffudd remained in South Wales, till he raised the suspicions of Henry, who

and taken in Glyn Rhoddni, now generally called Rhondda, and beheaded at a place called from that circumstance *Pen Rhys*; being then upwards of ninety-two years of age, not as stated in the text, in his ninetieth year. A monastery was subsequently erected at Pen Rhys to commemorate his death. An Eisteddfod was held there in the time, and under the protection of Owen Glyndwr. Rhys ab Tewdwr's arms were: *Gules*, a lion rampant *or* within a bordûre indented.—*Ed.*

[1] Her beauty had excited Owain, the wicked son of Cadwgan ab Bleddyn, to an atrocious act. He burst into the castle of Pembroke by night, and carried off Nêst and her children to Powys, her husband escaping very narrowly; and the castle was left in flames. Whether she yielded to the ravisher from choice or necessity is left in doubt; but Owain sent back to Gerald his children at her request.

[2] Robert Earl of Gloucester was very eminent as a soldier, as a statesman, and scholar. He was the instrument of restoring his nephew, Henry, to the throne of England, altho' that event took place after Gloucester's death. Geoffrey of Monmouth dedicates to him his Latin translation of Tysilio; and Robert was a general friend to learning, and learned men, in that early age of English literature. William of Malmsbury, the Poet and historian, was patronized by him.

engaged Cynan Prince of North Wales, the father in law and great uncle to Gruffudd, to seize and imprison his son and nephew.

Gruffudd fled to the church of Aberdaron, and Cynan attempting to force the sanctuary, was resisted by the Clergy, which gave Gruffudd time to escape and to reach the wilds of Ustrad-Towi. Here he collected his friends, sallied forth, and destroyed the possessions of the English. He extended his ravages to Dyfed, attacked Carmarthen, demolished the town and dismantled the castle ; but attempting Aberystwyth, was surprized, defeated, and driven again within the wilderness of Ustrad-Towi. Henry once more attempted his destruction.[1] I find him next restored to his favor, but on a false accusation was ejected from lands which that Prince had given him.

[1] Henry engaged the wicked Owain ab Cadwgan to assasinate Gruffudd, or to make him prisoner. Robert of Gloucester, the nephew of Gruffudd, by his sister Nêst, was employed in the same service. Owain, at the head of an hundred men, on entering the forest at Ustrad-Towi, perceived the footsteps of men ; he pursued, killed some, and dispersed the rest ; then seizing on their cattle, he returned with his plunder towards the main body. At this time Gerald, the Constable of Pembroke, made his appearance, intending to join the King's forces. Meeting the people who had fled from Owain, they complained of the injury they had just received, and implored his assistance. In an instant the idea of revenge rushed on his mind for the insults his honor had received by the outrage Owain had committed on his wife. He instantly entered the forest in pursuit of that Chief, who, being warned by his followers of the approaching danger, refused to fly, confident that his pursuers intended him no injury, they like himself being vassals of the King of England. As soon as Gerald and his forces drew near, they discharged a volley of arrows. Owain finding his mistake, with much spirit called on his men to support him, telling them, that, though their enemies were seven to one in number, they were only Flemings, who would be affrighted at the name of a Welshman, and distinguished by nothing but drinking deep at carousals. On the first onset,

On the accession of Stephen, hostilities were renewed, and Gruffudd solicited the aid of North Wales to recover his inheritance. Accordingly he went into that country, and in his absence, his wife, Gwenllian, a woman of an high spirit, collected her friends, and with her sons entered Cydweli, the land which the ancestors of Maurice de Londres had ravished from her family. Gruffudd ab Llywelyn, who commanded for Maurice, and was an enemy to Gruffudd, met Gwenllian, and a bloody scene ensued, wherein Gwenllian[1] and her son Morgan, were defeated and slain, and her son Maelgwn made prisoner.

In the succeeding year Gruffudd, in concert with Owain and Cadwaladr[2] the sons of Gruffudd ab Cynan, made a successful irruption ou South Wales, and returned with a large booty;[3] no light object in the warfare of that period.[4]

Owain ab Cadwgan was slain, an arrow having pierced his heart. His death dispirited his followers, and gave them so great distrust of the King's forces, that they dispersed and returned into their own country. In this manner, says Warrington, died suitably to the tenor of his life, this bold and profligate Chieftain.

[1] The place where this battle was fought, is to this day called, Maes Gwenllian, Gwenllian's Field. Warrington (but he speaks doubtfully) thinks Gwenllian was taken and beheaded after the battle. But I hope that was not the case :

...........................*Nullum memorabile nomen*
Fœmineâ in pœnâ est, nec habet victoria laudem.

[2] Cadwaladr's daughter had married Anarawd, the son of Gruffudd ab Rhŷs. A violent dispute having arisen between the father and the son in law (who were in the relation of uncle and nephew also) it was decided by single combat, in which Anarawd fell ;

...........*animosus Anarawd*
A socero cœsus..................Pentarchia.

[3] ....prædæ et spoliorum ardebat amore.

[4] In this expedition they had a conflict with the Flemish, the Normans, and the English, near Cardigan ; in which the latter were defeated, and lost three thousand

A.D.
1137

This year (says Powel) died Gruffudd ab Rhŷs ab Tewdwr, "the light, honor and support of South Wales;" who by his wife Gwenllian, the daughter of Gruffudd ab Cynan, had Rhŷs his son who succeeded.

Our Chroniclers are encomiastic of this character. The Lord Rhŷs ab Gruffudd, say they, "was no less remarkable in courage than in the stature and lineaments of his body, wherein he excelled most men." In 1143 he distinguished himself against the Normans, and Flemish, in Dyfed. His life was a continued warfare, too much engaged against his countrymen and relations; exhausting the national strength in domestic hostilities.[1] On the submission of North Wales to the Second Henry, and in the pacification which ensued, Rhŷs was not included, but alone supported himself against the English, and obtained terms from them. In the absence of Henry in Normandy, Rhŷs renewed the war, encouraged by the Welsh prophecies, that the King would not return. Henry however was soon in South

men. In consequence of this event the Countess of Clare, the sister of the Earl of Chester, a widow lady singularly handsome, was left in a castle attended by many female attendants, distant from every friend, and surrounded by the Welsh, who menaced her with every possible indignity. The poor Countess and her damsels had already felt each horror by anticipation, when they were unexpectedly relieved by the romantic gallantry of Milo Fitzwalter, who encouraged by King Stephen ,and accompanied by a few chosen warriors, rode night and day to the beleagured fortress, and although he found it environed by numbers of Welsh, brought away the Ladies inviolate.—*Gerald Camb.*

Few anecdotes redound more to the honor of that spirit of chivalry, which almost alone illumined the gloom of the early Centuries.—*I. P. A.*

[1] ....ne tanta animis assuescite bella :
Neu patriæ validas in viscera vertite vires.

Wales, and Rhỹs unable to resist, submitted to do him homage, and gave hostages for his obedience. This ceremony was performed at Woodstock, and Rhỹs swore fealty to the English King, and to Henry his son.

The following year he is again in arms, and, invading Cardigan, subdued that country.[2] Encouraged by his success the spirit of contention became general in Wales; the Prince of the North, Owain Gwynedd, and all his sons, his brother Cadwaladr, and the Lord of Powys, joined Rhỹs. Their first attack under Dafydd, the son of Owain Gwynedd, and with success, was on Flintshire.

A.D. 1163[1]

Some forces had been raised in Henry's absence, for the reduction of Rhỹs; with these the King of England marched to Oswestry. I here omit the history of this event, which was disastrous to the English, and very honorable to the Welsh, as it appertains to the next tribe; but it should seem disgraceful to Henry,[3] that in revenge of his disappointment, he put out the eyes of his Welsh hostages, among whom were two sons of Rhỹs,[4] and two of Owain Gwynedd. Rhỹs pursued his success

---

[1] This date should be, I think, 1165.—*Ed.*

[2] In revenge of the death of his nephew, Einion, who was murdered by his servant, Walter ab Llywarch, at the instigation of Clare Earl of Gloucester.

> ....*impiger Einion,*
> *(Pro dolor!) a famulo jugulatus fraude Lomarcho.*—Pentarchia.

[3] "Barbarity," says Mr. Andrews, "to hostages was not esteemed a crime in the early ages."

[4] Ohses ab Henrico crecatus rege secundo.—*Pentarchia.*

E

in South Wales, took the castles of Cardigan and Cilgerran ;
the last, a place of great importance, and in it his cousin
Robert,[1] the son of Nêst his aunt, in her second marriage with
Stephen, Constable of Cardigan.

In 1169[2] Henry was at Pembroke, on his passage to Ireland.
Rhŷs met and presented him with eighty-six horses, of which the
King accepted thirty-six, and returned the remainder. Rhŷs was
restored to his peace, and Henry gave him Cardigan, Ustrad-Towi,
Arustli and Elfel : He also paid him a visit at Tŷ gwyn, and
restored his son Hywel, who had been long an hostage in Henry's
hands. The politic Henry rendered this journey and his return
through South Wales conductive to the interests of his Country ;
for by conversing familiarly with the Welsh Princes, loading them
with presents, and conferring shewy, though unsubstantial dignities
on the most ambitious, he found means to break that union,
which had hitherto rendered all his measures against their
independency abortive. On the return of Henry from Ireland,
Rhŷs attended him at Talycarn, and was made Justice[3] of South
Wales. Hence he was attached to the English interests, and an
instrument in the subjection of his country ; and he brought all
the Lords of South Wales, who had usually opposed Henry to
do homage to that Prince at Gloucester.[4]

---

[1] This Robert, surnamed Fitzstephen, was one of the first invaders of Ireland, with
Strongbow Earl of Pembroke, under Henry the Second.

[2] This must have been in 1171.—*Ed.*

[3] This office, which was hereditary, continued to the twenty-seventh of Henry the
Eighth, and ended in the Lord Ferrers of Chartley.

[4] ....dominumqe potentem
    Imposuit.... ....

In 1176 he made a great feast[1] in his castle of Cardigan, to
which he invited many Normans and English. ' These civilities
were of short continuance, for the same year they treacherously
murdered his son-in-law Einion. To awe them, Rhŷs built the
castle of Rhaiadr, in precipitous, strong ground (near the noted
cataract of that name) above the Wye.

In 1182 the sheriff of Hereford, Ranulph de Poer, murdered
the Lord of Gwent, a Welchman of distinction. In revenge,
his countrymen put Poer to death, with many of his friends.
Henry in wrath marched to Worcester, where Rhŷs met and
appeased him, and promised his sons and nephews as hostages;
but the young men, considering how former pledges had been
treated, refused to appear, and Henry seems satisfied without
them.

In 1186 Rhŷs lost his son Cadwaladr, by a private assassination;
and his kinsman, Llywelyn, the grandson of Gruffudd ab Cynan,
was imprisoned by his brothers, who put out his eyes.[2]

[1] In 1176 the Lord Rhŷs made a great feast at Christmas in his castle of Cardigan,
on finishing that fortress; and he caused it to be proclaimed throughout all Britain a
year and a day beforehand. Thither came many strangers, which were honorably
received, and worthily entertained, so that no man departed discontented. And among
deeds of arms and other shews, Rhŷs caused all the Poets of Wales, which are makers
of songs and recorders of gentlemen's pedigrees and arms, to come thither; and
provided chairs for them to be set in his hall, where they should dispute together, to
try their cunning and gift in their faculties; where great rewards and rich gifts were
appointed for the overcomers. Among them they of North Wales won the prize of
poetry; and among the musicians, Rhŷs's own household-men, and in particular the son
of Eytyn the Crythor, were accounted the best.—*Guttun Owain.* [Rhys in the year
1164 founded the famous Cistercian Abbey of Strata Florida (Ystrad Fflur), where
several princes of the house of Dinevor were interred.—*Ed.*]

[2] Hic quibus invisi fratres...... ....

A.D.
1118   On the death of Henry the Second,[1] Rhŷs renewed hostilities,[2] and took the castles of St. Clare, Abercorran and Llanstephan; and in the last his son, Maelgwyn, then in rebellion against him.

Returning with success,[3] he lost his daughter, Gwenllian, a lady of great beauty and accomplishments, the wife of Ednyfed Fychan[4] (the able General and Minister to Llewelyn the Great), and the great great grandmother to Owain Tewdwr, the grandfather of Henry the Seventh.

During the absence of Richard and his imprisonment in Germany, Rhŷs pursued the war, and subdued South Wales. A cruel feud now arose among his sons, although allied against their father; and Anarawd, having taken his brothers Hywel and Madog prisoners, put out their eyes. Soon after they took and imprisoned the father himself, who recovered his liberty through his blind son Hywel.

---

[1] "Henry," says Carte, "used to tire all his Court with continual standing, and suffered himself so much by this practice, never sitting but when he eat or rode, that it was supposed to be, in conjunction with the kicks he received from horses, the cause of the swelling of his legs, and to have hastened the breaking up of his constitution."

[2] Rhŷs was highly esteemed by Henry the Second, insomuch that whenever he came to his court, the King always in person, with his Nobles, was wont to receive him. But after the death of Henry, the Lord Rhys coming to England, Richard the First did not honour him, as his father was wont to do. Rhŷs was much displeased, and returned home without speaking to the King. This happened at Oxford.—*Passim.*

[3] Hi nostri reditus expectatique triumphi!

[4] Of Ednyfed Fychan and his numerous and illustrious posterity, we shall have occasion to treat hereafter, under MARCHUDD AB CYNAN, the eighth Noble Tribe of North Wales.—*Ed.*

In 1197 the plague raged in Wales, and this restless[1] chieftain perished in it, and was buried[2] at St. David's. By his wife Gwenllian, the daughter of Madog ab Maredudd, Lord of Bromfield, he had four sons and two daughters. He[3] was succeeded by his eldest son, Gruffudd. The first I learn of him is in an English prison, whither he had been sent by his wicked brother, Maelgwyn, and his brother-in-law, Gwenwynwyn. He was released by the English Justiciary, Fitzpeter, who assisted him also in their defeat. Gruffudd died in 1202, on St. James' Day, and was buried at Ustradfflur.[4] He was succeeded by his elder son Rhŷs. Rhŷs died in 1222, being says Powel, "*a lusty gentleman.*" His inheritance was divided between his brother, Owain, and his uncle, Maelgwyn. Owain married Angharad, daughter of Maredudd ab Robert, Lord of Kedewain, and left two sons, Llywelyn and Maredudd : Of the elder I learn nothing, but that he left a son, Thomas. Maredudd, the younger brother

---

[1] Hi motus animorum atque hæc certamina tanta,

[2] *Pulveris exigui jactu,* compressa quiescent. [His monumental effigy still remains in the Cathedral of St. David's, in a good state of preservation.—*Ed.*]

[3] Rhŷs was the eldest of six towardly sons, that his father, Gruffudd, had by Gwenllian the fair daughter of Gruffudd ab Cynan, Prince of North Wales; and he surviving them all, obtained the dominion of South Wales, which he well and worthily ruled.[4]—*Panton Papers.* [The Lord Rhys's brothers were Anarawd, Meredydd (lord of Ceredigion), Cadell, who had a portion of Dyfed, Rhys Vychan and Owen—*five* in all ; his sisters were Gwladys and Nest.—*Dwnn's Vis.* ii., p. 99, note.—*Ed.*]

[4] This prince is celebrated in the Welsh Chronicles for his martial prowess and nobility of mind.—Williams' *Em. Welshmen.*

[*] Spes Patriæ, columen pacis, lux urbis et orbis ;
Gentis honos, decus armorum, fulmenque duelli ;
Quo neque pace prior, neque fortior alter in armis.—*Pentarchia.*

A.D. of Llywelyn, was better known, and, says Powel, "this year
1268 died Maredudd ab Owain, the defender of South Wales."
Thomas married the daughter and heiress of Philip, Lord of
Iscoed, and by her had a daughter, Elen, who married Gruffudd
Fychan, Lord of Glyndyfrdwy, and by him was mother to our
great Glyndŵr[1].

I find but five descendent families from this Tribe; Wynn of
Dôl-Bachog,[2] Owen of Cefn-Hafod, Lloyd of Plâs-uwch Clawdd,
Evans of Tre-Castell, and Jones of Haim.

---

[1] She was also the mother of Tudor ab Gruffudd Fychan (slain in the battle of
Mynydd-y-Pwll-Melyn in 1405), from whom descended the Vaughan's of Corsygedol,
the Hughes's of Gwerclas, Barons of Kymmer in Edeirnion, and other good families.—Ed.

[2] Of the Dôl-Bachog family I can trace nothing. Of Cefn-Hafod I am equally
ignorant, as of the Lloyds of Plâs-uwch Clawdd near Rhiwabon, and Jones of Haim.
But there is a place called Haim wood, near the junction of the Severn and Vernew.
Mr. Evans of Towyn is one of the Tre-Castell family, [Dol-bachog is now an ordinary
farm house in Trefeglwys, Montgomeryshire; and so are Tre-castell in Llanwnog;
Cefn-hafod, or rather Cefn-hafodau, in Llangurig; and Haim or Hem, in Forden,—all
in the same county. The Owen's of Cefn-hafodau are now represented by Arthur
Charles Humphreys Owen, Esq., of Glansevern, and by Mr. Baxter Owen, of Glandulas,
in that county. The late William Owen, Esq,, K.C., of Glansevern (who died in 1837),
traced his descent by uninterrupted male succession from Rhodri Mawr, King of all
Wales, through Cadifor ab Dinawal, whose wife was a daughter of the Lord Rhŷs.
The present owner of the Glansevern estate, Mr Humphreys Owen, is his
great grand nephew. The other families above named became extinct long ago. One
of the most illustrious of Rhŷs ab Tewdwr's descendants was Giraldus Cambrensis (or
De Barri) one of the brightest luminaries of the twelfth century, who was the fourth
son of William De Barri, by Angharad, daughter of Nest, the daughter of Rhŷs ab
Tewdwr. Among numerous other families now extinct descended from Rhŷs ab Tewdwr,
were the Wynns of Coed Llai, or Leeswood, near Mold, who became extinct apparently
in 1793, upon the death of Margaret, daughter of Sir George Wynn, Bart., and wife of
Richard Hill Waring, Esq.—(Hist. of Powis Fadog, v., p. 230)—the Griffiths of
Cefnamwlch in Lleyn (Camb. Journal, 1854, p. 53)—the Jones's of Berendeth,
Pembrokeshire (Lewys Dwnn's Vis., i., p. 196)—the Lloyd's of Nantmel (Ib. p. 259),
the Owen's of Presteign (Ib. p. 261), and the Wynrs of Graianog (Ib. ii., p. 280).
Perhaps the only family still existing which can trace its descent in a direct line
paternally from Rhŷs ab Tewdwr, is that of Lewis of Harpton Court, Radnorshire, of
which the late Sir George Cornewall Lewis, Bart., M.P., was a distinguished representative (Lewys Dwnn's Vis., i., p. 253). The Powells of Brandlesome Hall, Lancashire,
also claim similar descent (Burke's Landed Gentry.) —Ed.]

BLEDDYN AB CYNFYN.

BLEDDYN AB CYNFYN ranks the third Royal Tribe. He had a title to Powys in female succession from his great grandmother, Angharad;[1] but his crown of North Wales, was usurpation, in common at first with his brother, Rhiwallon, who fell in the battle of Mechain; and the whole was then his own.[2] From his father, Cynfyn ab Gwerystan, he had no claims; by his mother, the daughter and heiress of Maredudd ab Owain, Prince of South Wales, he was half brother to Gruffudd ab Llywelyn ab Seisyllt, the preceding Prince of North Wales,[3] who was himself an usurper also; moreover on the death of Owain ab Edwyn, Bleddyn accumulated the sovereignty of South Wales, again uniting the whole dominion of his maternal ancestor

---

[1] Angharad was the grandaughter and heiress of Merfyn, the third son of Roderic the Great, in whose favour his father gavelled off the Principality of Powys, which comprehended Montgomeryshire, parts of Shropshire, and parts of the present Counties of Brecknock, Denbigh, and Radnor.

[2] " Bleddyn ab Cynfyn bob cwys,
　　Ei hun bioedd hen Bowys."—*Rhys Cain.*

[3] This warlike Prince was put to death by his own subjects, and his head sent to Harold, who commanded the armies of the Confessor Edward with success against our countrymen. Harold brought Gruffudd's widow out of Wales, and married her; she was sister to the powerful Saxon Earls, Edwyn and Morcar, the sons of Algar, and grandsons of Leofric, Earl of Mercia; which latter led an army against Swane, King of Denmark, in 1003, and died in 1057, being the husband of the famous Godiva, who freed Coventry from an heavy tax, and gave rise to the well-known story of Peeping Tom.

Roderic; and like him gavelling his lawful inheritance, he divided Powys between his sons Maredudd and Cadwgan.[1]

It remained not long separate, but was reunited in Maredudd on the murder of his brother Cadwgan,[2] (a superior person of that time, whom Camden calls "the renowned Briton,") by their nephew Madog, the son of Ririd, the fifth son of Bleddyn ab Cynfyn; and the extinction of his nephews the sons of Cadwgan, by Maredudd himself.

The story of our country under its native Princes is a wretched calendar of crimes; of usurpations, and family assassinations; and in this dismal detail we should believe ourselves rather on the shores of the Bosphorus (things oddly coincident[3]), than the banks of the Dee.

[1] In 1073 Bleddyn was slain in battle, as some say, but according to others treacherously murdered in Powys Castle by Rees ap Owen ap Edwin and the Gentlemen of Ystrad Tywi, having worthily governed Wales thirteen years. Bleddyn according to Powel was "verie liberall and mercifull, and loved iustice and equitie in all his reigne."—He is said to have built Dolforwyn Castle, between the years 1065 and 1073. He had other sons besides Maredudd and Cadwgan, namely, Llywarch, Madog, Rhirid, and Iorwerth. His arms were, *Or* a lion rampant *gules*, armed and langued *or.—Ed.*

[2] Cadwgan was killed in an ambush by Powys Castle, which he was then erecting. Powel of Ednop in his *Pentarchia*, a wild, incorrect Latin MS. poem, in James the First's time, thus describes his Coat of Arms, [*Or* a lion rampant *azure* armed and langued *gules*] :—

Aurea magnanimi Cadugani parma leonem,
Cœruleum, rapidumque, cruentis faucibus effert.—*Tracts of Powys*, p. 2 *note.*

[3] The Celts or Gauls were descended from Gomer, the eldest son of Japhet, who was the eldest son of Noah, and from the Provinces of the Upper Asia they migrated to the countries on the Lake Meotis, on the North side of the Euxine Sea; and, as they were called Cimmerians in Asia, so they communicated their name to that famous Strait,

Our Law of distribution, the custom of gavelkind,[1] had the the same ill effect, applied to the succession as the freedom of the State ; it balanced the power and raised the competition of the younger branches against the elder ; a Theban war of Welsh brethren ending in family blood, and national destruction. Nor was the elder more delicate, accumulating again by every means his broken patrimony. It might apply to the colonization of new countries, and was in this, the only manner of portioning our

which has been since called Cimbrian or Cimmerian Bosphorus. Here they had not continued long, when the increase of their progeny made it necessary to penetrate farther into the country, and, as it is supposed they fell down the Danube, along whose banks they encamped, as their manner of life was, for the convenience of their cattle ; and so shaping their course Westward, entered Germany, from whence they advanced into France ; for the Inhabitants of France, as Josephus tells us, were anciently called Gomerites, as being descended from Gomer ; and from France they came at length into the Southern parts of this Island. And therefore we find that the Welsh, the ancient proprietors of Britain, called themselves Gomeri or Cymry, and their language Cymmraeg ; which words bear so great analogy to the original appellation, from whence they are derived, that we may reasonably conclude the true ancient Britons, or Welsh, to be the genuine descendants of Gomer, the eldest son of Japhet. But this will be farther evinced from the affinity between the Celts or Gauls, and the ancient Britons, with respect to religion, language, laws, and customs.—*Owen's History.*

[1] " What aggravated this mischief," says Lord Lyttelton, " was another ancient custom which prevailed among the Chieftains and Kings of Wales, of sending out their infant sons to be nursed and bred up in different families of their principal Nobles or Gentlemen ; from whence it ensued, that each of these foster fathers, attaching himself with a strong paternal affection to the child he had reared, and being incited by his own interest to desire his advancement above his brothers, endeavoured to procure it by all the means in his power. Thus, as most of their Kings cohabited with several women who generally brought them many children, several parties were formed among their Nobility, which breaking out at their deaths, involved their kingdoms in blood and confusion. Minors were never allowed to reign ; but it often happened that when a Prince, excluded in his infancy, attained to manhood, he then aspired to the throne he had lost on account of his nonage, and found a party to assist him in those pretensions."

F

children. It is yet distinguishable in Welsh lands; and still intermixing them, may sometimes interfere with a compact demesne, and the pleasures and space of modern gardening and home improvements, but the liberal spirit of our gentry hath much lessened, by reasonable exchanges, these last inconveniences of this ancient distribution. The term *gafel,* in the Welsh, implies an holding, because each son held a share in his father's land, and the youngest had a claim to the paternal residence.

Maredudd ab Bleddyn, to quote our dry monk, and historical[1] collector, Caradog of Llancarfan, "under severe contrition for his hellish practices against his brothers and nephews," died in 1132. He was, notwithstanding a man of spirit and abilities, but his ambition to unite Powys, led to great cruelties and oppression. His conduct and courage, when attacked by Henry the First of

[1] Our most ancient British History is called Brut y Brenhinoedd, or the Chronicle of the British Kings, because it concludes with Cadwaladr the last King ; and to distinguish it from the continuation by Caradog, which is called Brut y Tywysogion, or the Chronicle of the Princes. It begins with the Trojan colony, and ends with the reign of Cadwaladr, the abdicated King of the Britons. It hath gone among us under the name of Tyssilio, a bishop, the supporter of the British Church against the usurpations of Austin the monk, and the son of Brochwel Ysgithrog ;* but he seems to have been only the continuer of it,† from the Roman conquest to his own time, about the year 660.

A.D. 606 * Brochwel commanded the Britons at their memorable defeat near Chester, which led to the massacre of the Monks of Bangor Monachorum. His son Tyssilio, besides his Welsh work, wrote an Ecclesiastical History of Britain, which Archbishop Usher said he had seen. There is also a short dialogue in Welsh verse between two Monks extant, which is ascribed to Tyssilio. From Ysgithrog are many descendants, chiefly in Montgomeryshire, and I have given in the Appendix with truth the character of one of them, whom I had the pleasure of knowing well.—*Appendix* xv, *Blayney.*

† This is the history so miserably mangled by Geoffrey of Monmouth in his Latin translation. "If Geoffrey," says Mr. Morris, "had worded the exploits of Corineus and Arthur, as the original history in the British tongue required, there would not have been that air of fable in his translation." Most of the objections of Camden, Milton, Burton, Nicholson, &c., took their rise from their falling foul of a bad translation, instead of an Original, which they had never seen.

England and deserted by Gruffudd ab Cynan, the reigning Prince of North Wales, does him credit. He defended the passes into Powys with judgment and success; and Henry, endangered in these defiles, was struck by an arrow, that his armour resisted, which he said came not from a Welsh, but an English bow; and offering terms to Maredudd withdrew his army on the receipt of a small sum of money and a thousand cattle. A.D. 1118

Maredudd died fourteen years after, in entire subjection to the English Prince. He had married two wives; by his first, Hunydd, the daughter of Eunydd[1] ab Gwernwy, the founder of the Tribe of Dyffryn Clwyd and Allington, and one of the A.D. 1132

It was afterwards continued to the death of Cadwaladr, by some other hand. Caradog, of the Abbey of Llancarfan, collected and continued this history to the year 1156. The Monks of Conway, and Ustrad-fflur pursued it to 1270, just before the death of the last Prince. Humphrey Llwyd translated this book from Welsh into English, adding some things from Matthew Paris and Nicholas Trivet, but died before he published it; and it was left in the hands of Sir Henry Sidney, President of Wales, who recommended to Dr. Powel to augment and print it, which he did, and dedicated it to Sir Philip Sidney, the son of Sir Henry, in 1584. The Monks of Ustrad-fflur and Conway seem purposely to have discontinued their history, unwilling to relate the final conquest of their country, and the death of Llywelyn. This part was completed by Humphrey Llwyd himself, assisted by the collections of Guttyn Owain.

[1] Eunydd was the son of Gwenllïan,* the daughter of Rhŷs ab Marchan. This is the lady that is commonly styled the heiress of Dyffryn Clwyd. She had great possessions in it, having the property of seven townships, in the neighbourhood of Ruthin. Bleddyn ab Cynfyn married her to his cousin Gwernwy, and, to make him a suitable match for her, and in reward of his military services to himself, bestowed upon him seven townships; Almor, Trefalun, Gresford, Allington, Lleprog fawr, Lleprog fechan and Trefnant. Ithel, the son of Eunydd, had six sons, who jointly gave the

* Gwenllïan, id est, White Linen. Linen was so rare in the reign of Charles the Seventh of France, who lived about the time of our Henry the Sixth, that the Queen of France could boast of two shifts only, of that commodity.

Fifteen [Tribes] of North Wales, he had several children; by
the second, Eva, the daughter of Blettrws ab Ednowain, and
granddaughter to Ednowain bendew, one of the Fifteen [Tribes], in
him first erected also, he had a son, Iorwerth gôch, or the red
Edward, who married Maude daughter to Roger de Manley, by
whom he was father to Sir Gruffudd Fychan,[1] Lord of Crigion
and Bergedwyn [Burgedin,] ancestor to the several houses of the
Kynastons. He was called the wild Knight of Caer Hywel,
from his romantic life, and the seat of his residence of this name
in Montgomeryshire.[2]

To return to Maredudd. That sole possession, which unhappily
to himself was obtained in Powys, did he again mutilate and

land whereon the parish church of Gresford is built; "this is a fact well known," says
Lewis Dwnn. The sepulchres of the grandchildren of the said Ithel ab Eunydd are in
the church of Gresford. Should not the gentlemen of this Tribe carry their
ancestress's Arms, *azure* a fess *or* between three nags' heads, erased *argent;* at least
quartered with their own, since she was so considerable an heiress. [Of Eunydd (or
Efnydd) ab Gwernwy and his descendants we shall treat more fully under EFNYDD, the
fourteenth Noble Tribe of North Wales.—*Ed.*]

[1] Sir Gruffudd was a Knight of Jerusalem, originally the Order of the Holy
Sepulchre there; whence removing, they were incorporated with the Knights
Hospitallers or Templars, then resident at Rhodes; and until this direful French
visitation, which has plundered their estates, and ruined their commanderies in that
country, were continued in respect as Knights of Malta.

[2] Caer Hywel is a mansion still known by that name on the banks of the Severn, at
Edgerley, in the County of *Salop,* and not far from the ford on the Vyrnwy, designated
in the Mabinogi of the *Dream of Rhonabwy* as "Rhyd y Wilure." Among the
Kynastons we find another "wild Knight," Humphrey Kynaston the Wild, who during
his outlawry in the reign of Henry the Seventh, inhabited a cave in the bold sandstone
rock at Ness Cliff, called after him Kynaston's Cave, and concerning whose feats many
tales are still current in that neighbourhood. Iorwerth Goch had also a younger son,
Iorwerth Fychan, the lineal ancestor of the Powys's, Lords Lilford *(Burke's
Peerage.)—Ed.*

divide (but it was our custom so to do) between his eldest son Madog, and his grandson Owain Cyfeiliog, the son of his younger son Gruffudd, who died before him. And here it may be necessary and at some length, to mark the partitions since made, as the source of families from this Tribe. To the share of Madog was the division of Powys given, from him named Powys Fadog; a mutability in initial consonants, to harmonize and vary the diction, frequent in our own and not uncommon in other languages; to Owain the upper moiety, which, from his son Gwenwynwyn, was called Powys Wenwynwyn.[1]

Madog ab Maredudd, who succeeded as Lord of Bromfield,[2] a title taken on the partition by this line of the Powysian Princes, was a leading man of those times; having to his own power in Powys united that of his nephew and ward Owain. He was the constant confederate of Rondel the Third, and of his son Hugh Cyfeiliog, the fourth Earl of Chester.

Madog was the ally also of Henry the Second in his Welsh wars, and commanded his navy in an unsuccessful attempt on Anglesey: nor was he more fortunate against his countrymen at the battle of Consylt,[3] on the English part. He had been offended with Owain Gwynedd, the reigning Prince of North

[1] Pars ea Powysiæ de quo cognomine adepta est.—*Pentarchia.*

[2] With respect to this fine Lordship, and in some short observations relative to North Wales, may I be allowed to quote myself in a paper I wrote a few years since on the subject. See Appendix, xvi.

[3] In this action near Flint, Henry de Essex, hereditary standard-bearer of England, threw away the flag, and fled crying aloud, "THE KING IS SLAIN." The English however rallied, and made an handsome retreat.

Wales, who claimed his allegiance; yet was this in conformity with the rules of Roderic, by which the Princes of South Wales and Powys were under sovereignty to the North.[1]

Be this excused to him, his character was good beyond the examples of that time; for he was "one that feared God, and relieved the poor."[2] He resided frequently in England, died at Winchester, and was buried at Meifod, a church he rebuilt near Mathrafael, the seat of these Princes, on the reduction of Shrewsbury,[3] their ancient capital, by Offa in the eighth century.[4] He married [first] Susannah, the daughter of Gruffudd ab Cynan, Prince of North Wales, and founder of our first Royal Tribe. By her he had three sons, and a daughter, Marred, the wife of Iorwerth Drwyn-dwnn,[5] and the mother of our great Llywelyn.[6]

A.D.
1160

[1] The Princes of South Wales were to pay four tons of honey, and the Princes of Powys four tons of flour, to the Sovereigns of North Wales.

[2] Powel.

[3] Many of the fields and places near Shrewsbury (then called Pengwern) still retain their Welsh Names. It was once again in the hands of the Welsh, and taken by our great Llywelyn in 1215.

[4] Early in the following century, the able Egbert, who had united the Saxons under one kingdom, gained from us the city of Chester, with large maritime dependencies; and would have probably subdued North Wales, but was recalled by a Danish invasion. Egbert, during the reign of our Prince, Merfyn frych, had carried his arms into all parts of North Wales.

[5] Iorwerth Drwyn-dwnn, or Edward with the broken nose, the eldest son of Owain Gwynedd, was set aside the succession on account of this deformity. [He resided at Dolwyddelan castle, but was eventually compelled to flee for refuge from the cruelty of his brother Dafydd, to Pennant Melangell, a celebrated sanctuary in Montgomeryshire, near which, at a place called Bwlch Croes Iorwerth, he is said to have been killed.—Ed.]

[6] Madog married secondly a Norman lady, Maude, daughter of Roese de Verdun,— his union with whom proved most unhappy, and ended in his ruin. In consequence of disagreements, this lady left him and went to Henry the Second, King of England,

Madog built the Castles of Oswestry, Caer Einion, and Overton, where he resided, and which received from him the additional name of Madog.

In the customs of his country, he continued to gavel his broken patrimony, and divided his moiety of Powys between his sons Gruffudd Maelor, Owain, Eliza [Elissau], [Owain] Brogyntyn, Cynfrig [efell] and Einion efell. The three last were illegitimate, but it was not unusual to put such, when eminent, in an equal succession ; and it is observable, that four of the tribes of Israel were of Jacob's natural issue, but appointed to the same distinction with the rest.

Gruffudd Maelor succeeded as Lord of Bromfield,[1] "a man wise and liberal ;"[2] nor was he less brave, or less a friend to his country. He was valiantly engaged at the head of the men

who summoned the prince to Winchester to state his case, at the same time requesting him not to bring more than four and twenty horse with him, the lady Maude not to bring any more with her. On the appointed day Madog came with his four and twenty horsemen. Maude came also with twenty four horses, but two men on each horse, whereupon Madog was overpowered and cast into prison at Winchester, where he died. While in prison he was compelled to settle the lordship of Oswestry upon his wife, and the heirs of her body by whomsoever begotten. After Madog's death, Maude married John Fitz Alan, Earl of Arundel, by whom she had a son, John Fitz Alan, Earl of Arundel, and Baron of Oswestry and Clun. Thus the English obtained the lordship of Oswestry. (Cae Cyriog MS., quoted in Hist. of Powys Fadog, vol. i., pp. 119-120.) Madog's arms were, argent a lion rampant sable, armed and langued gules.—Ed.

[1] In Welsh Maelor, so called from Maelor ab Gwran ab Cunedda Wledig, to whose share this district fell, on the general division of North Wales among the sons and grandsons of Cunedda in the sixth century.

[2] Powel.

of Bromfield in the battle of Crogen[1] or Chirk, whence the second Henry, with considerable loss, made a difficult retreat, and was in imminent danger from an arrow, that had been critically aimed, but intercepted by Hubert de Clare, the Constable of Colchester, who stepped before him, and, at the price of his own life,[2] preserved that of his friend and master. Gruffudd died in 1191, and was buried at Meifod. By his wife Angharad,[3] the

[1] It has been erroneously said, that the term Crogens was used in contempt and derision of the Welsh ; but that was not the truth : the English meant to express by it animosity, and the desire of revenge. It alluded to this action, where Henry was worsted, and in great personal danger. Many of the English were slain, and buried in Offa's Dyke, below Chirk Castle ; and the part so filled up is to be seen, and forms a passage over it, called to this day, Adwy'r Beddau, or the Pass of the Graves.

[2] Lord Lyttelton places this event at the siege of Bridgnorth ; our histories state the fact as I have done.

[3] On account of consanguinity, she being his first cousin, Madog was divorced from her, on the persuasion of Archbishop Baldwyn, when he visited North Wales. "At this time," says Giraldus, " Dafydd ab Owain Gwynedd, the reigning Prince of North Wales, had no other part of the principality, save Rhuddlan Castle, and the adjacent territory, which he held with a garrison of English, and where Archbishop Baldwyn lodged one night to visit the King's[*] sister Emma, the wife of Dafydd." A spirit of enmity generally existed between the people, as well as the Princes of South and North Wales. When Dafydd ab Owain Gwynedd, Prince of the North, had honorably received some fugitives from the South, his courtiers insisted that it was too much condescension in him to favor the subjects of a rival Prince, who would not shew the least respect to any of his. Dafydd upon hearing this swore a great oath, that he would not rest until he would be satisfied, whether the Lord Rhŷs of South Wales, would not honorably receive some messenger, sent by him to his Court. He was some time before he could meet with a person who would undertake the trial. At length Gwgan of Caer Einion in Powys land set off on the embassy ; and arriving at Lord Rhŷs's Court found him in a furious temper, beating his servants and hanging his dogs. Gwgan knowing it was not a proper time to appear, delayed his message until the following day ; and then in a long speech, still extant in MS. he let the noble descendant of Rhŷs

A.D. 1187

[*] Henry the Second.

daughter of our great Prince, Owain Gwynedd, he had one son, Madog,[1] who inherited his estates entire. Him I find serving under John in two Welsh expeditions. From the first the King of England retreated with loss and disgrace; in the second he was successful, and reduced Llywelyn of North Wales, his son-in-law, to hard conditions; who submitted to pay the charges of the war, to do homage for his dominions, and, in favor of his revolted feudatory Madog, to renounce for ever the paramountship of Powys.

The year following Llywelyn and Madog were reconciled, and uniting their force they took all the English garrisons in North Wales, excepting Rhuddlan and Deganwy, and these fell after; and corrupting the third Innocent, a venal Pope, he dispensed with their oaths of allegiance taken to John, then under an

A.D.
1212

---

ab Tewdwr mawr know that he came from Dafydd ab Owain of North Wales, of the stock of royal Cynan, to pay his friendly respects to him ; and if he was well received, he had commission from his Prince to thank the Lord Rhŷs ; if not, he had commission to act on the reverse. The Lord Rhŷs asked Gwgan, in what could his honorable reception exist. Gwgan answered, in giving me a horse better than my own to carry me home ; in giving me five pounds in money, and a suit of clothes ; in giving my servant who leads my horse by the bridle, a suit of clothes and one pound. Come in said the Lord Rhŷs, I will give thee the noblest steed in my stud, for the sake of thy royal master ; and above thy demand, I will double the sums, and treble the suits of apparel. Which promise was performed, and Gwgan returned to the mutual satisfaction of both Princes.

[1] Gruffydd Maelor had *four* sons and three daughters. The sons were Madog, his successor, Maredudd, Roderick, and Owain ; and the daughters, Christina, Catherine, and Gwenllian Fechan. His arms were *argent*, four pales *gules*, a lion salient *sable*, armed and langued *azure.—Ed.*

G

interdict,[1] and a Nuncio was sent into Wales for this purpose. "They were moreover put under the pains of cursing, if they failed to annoy and trouble him to the utmost of their power."[2] John returned with an army to Powys, and had gained some ground, and demolished the Castle of Mathrafael, which was not restored, when he was recalled by the revolt of his English Barons.

A.D. 1215

A.D. 1200

A.D. 1236

The last service, in which I find Madog, was in South Wales, in concert with our great Llywelyn, when they reduced and ruined many of the English Castles; and returned home with a large booty, no light object in the warfare of those times. He built the Cistertian Abbey of Llanegwest, of the Cross, or de Valle Crucis, one of the last founded, and first dissolved; and was buried in the church of his own Monastery [there]. By his wife Gwladys,[3] the daughter of Ithel ab Rhŷs ab Morgan of Ewias, ab Morgan hir, ab Iestyn ab Gwrgant, the fourth Royal Tribe, he had one son Gruffudd, who had the fortune to inherit his estates entire[4]

The great interests, with the good abilities of this Lord rendered him considerable, and he took an active share in these turbulent times. He was strictly attached to Henry the Third,

[1] This assumption of the Court of Rome was first practised in England against Stephen.

[2] Powel.

[3] Or, as some say, Ysota.—*Ed.*

[4] Madog had *four* sons :—Gruffydd, his successor ; Maredudd, Lord of Rhiwabon (killed in 1240 by Prince David ab Llywelyn) ; Hywel, who left no male issue ; and Madog Fychan who also died without issue.—*Ed.*

whom he pressed into North Wales, and joined there, to effect the release[1] of Gruffudd ab Llywelyn, who was kept in close prison by his brother Dafydd, the reigning Prince.

In the succeeding reign of Llywelyn, the son of Gruffudd, he engaged himself with equal attachment to the Prince of England, Edward, who possessed the Earldom of Chester, with large maritime Welsh dependencies. He assisted him (but without effect) in his first attempts on our country, for Edward was driven back[2] by Llywelyn, co-operating with the rebel force of Montford;[3] of both he took ample revenge[4] afterwards.[5]

[1] This was accomplished ; but the unfortunate Gruffudd, being delivered to Henry, did but change his confinement from the Castle of Cruccaith, to the Tower of London ; whence attempting his escape he perished by a fall from the ramparts [and his head first meeting the pavement, being a very bulky man, was driven into his body, between the shoulders and collar bones.—*Matt. Paris.*] On this event, Henry the Third declared his son Edward, Prince of Wales, in preference to his nephew Dafydd, the reigning monarch. And it is observable, that Edward never departed from this claim, since after his conquest in 1282, he annexed to himself, by the statute of Rhuddlan, only "Terram de Snowdon," holding the rest of the country, as his own, and declares Llywelyn not an enemy but a traitor.

[2] Of one of these Welsh expeditions,* in his father Henry's time, there is a letter preserved by Matthew Paris, from a soldier of fashion, describing the distresses of the English army in very spirited terms. "We lie here," says he, "watching, praying, fasting, and freezing ; we watch for fear of the Welsh, who beat up our quarters every night ; we pray for a safe passage homeward ; we fast, for hardly have we any food, the halfpenny loaf being raised to five pence ; and we freeze for want of warm clothing, and having only a linen tent to keep out the cold." *A.D. 1246*

[3] Llywelyn had a conference at Hawarden Castle, with Montford, where they established peace between Cheshire and Wales, in order to promote their several and respective designs ; and on June the twenty-second in the year following, Montford obliged his captive, the English monarch, to make an absolute cession to the Welsh *A.D. 1264*

* Apud Gannoe, i. e. Diganwy.

Bromfield was laid waste to punish Gruffudd, and Powys fell to the victor; who on his submission restored him to his estates. He died in his Castle of Dinas Brân,[1] and was buried with his father in the neighbouring Abbey of Llanegwest.[2] By his wife Emma, the sister[3] of James, Lord Audley, an English captain, terrible to the Welsh, with his German cavalry, which they destroyed afterwards, he had four sons; to Madog the elder, he

A.D.
1270

Prince, not only of his fortress, but of the sovereignty of Wales, and the homage of its Barons, heretofore paid to Henry; and in the treaty of Montgomery, it was agreed between Henry and Llywelyn, that the Dee should be the boundary from Wirrall in Cheshire, to Holt in Denbighshire, and thence in a direct line to Pengwern, or Shrewsbury.

[4] At Evesham and Buellt.

[5] "On the occasion of the conquest, and the death of Llywelyn, two ecclesiastical poets," says Knighton, "one a Welshman, and the other an Englishman, wrote as follows."

WALLENSIS,
" *Hic jacet Anglorum tortor, tutor Venedorum,*
Princeps Wallorum Leolinus, regula morum,
Gemma coævorum, flos regum præteritorum,
Forma futurorum; dux, laus, lex, lux populorum."

ANGLICUS SIC,
" *Hic jacet errorum princeps, et prædo virorum,*
Proditor Anglorum, fax lucida, secta reorum,
Numen Wallorum, trux dux, homicida piorum,
Fæx Trojanorum, stirps mendax, causa malorum."

[1] Regibus Anglorum fuit hic Griffinus amicus,
Aversatus herum Leolinum, cujus ob iram
Se bene munitum Castello semper in illo
Continuit latitans, nomen locus indidit inde;
Orbati teneris nati linquuntur in annis.—*Pentarchia.*

[2] This is the last event related in the British copy of our History; what remains to the conquest of Wales, by Edward the First, was added by Humphrey Llwyd.

[3] Or, as Powel and others say, *daughter.*—*Ed.*

53

gave the Lordships of Bromfield and Iâl, with the reversion of
Moldsdale, Hopesdale, and Maelor Saesneg,[1] his mother's jointure,
and so called from her nation ; to Llywelyn the Second, the
Lordships of Chirk and Nantheudwy ; the Third son Gruffudd,
had Glyndyfrdwy, but from the interests and remorse of Earl
Warren only, who obtained for him from Edward this lot of his
inheritance, and the grant which conveys it is dated from Rhuddlan,
the tenth of his reign.   He held this Lordship under the King
of England in chiefty, and was called by the Welsh, y Barwn
gwynn, the white Baron.   He was father to Madog grupl, or
the cripple, the great great grandfather to Owain Glyndŵr, who
succeeded lineally to these estates.   The fourth son Owain was
intended for the church, but died a natural death in his youth,
and his portion Cynllaeth, from him called Cynllaeth Owain,
came to his brother Gruffudd who survived him, and so in
descent to Glyndŵr, and was forfeited to Henry the Fourth.

From this disposition of Powys Fadog, will be missed the
Cwmmwd's[2] of Dinmael, Edeyrnion, Merffordd, Croes Oswallt,
Mochnant is Rhaiadr, and the Lordship of Whittington.   To
two of his legitimate children, Owain and Elisa, Madog ab
Maredudd had given Mechain is Coed, in the upper Powys, and
lands in the neighbourhood of Chirk Castle.   Dinmael and
Edeyrnion had been parcelled off by him[3] to his natural son

[1] Maelor Saesneg, i. e. Saxon or English Maelor, the detached part of Flintshire.

[2] Commot or Cwmmwd, was the third of a Cantref, which contained fifty townships.
From Cwmmwd we derive Cymmydog, a neighbour.

[3] Our histories do not notice another son of Madog ab Maredudd, Llywelyn. He
probably died before his father, and before the division of his estates among his

Owain Brogyntyn. He had portioned upon Powys Fadog, two other of his natural sons, Cynrig and Einion efell;[1] the first was stiled Lord of Eglwys Egle, held lands in Moldsdale and the township of Treuddyn; Einion was Lord of Cynllaeth, had Croes Oswallt or Oswestry, where his father had built a Castle, and the Lordship of Whittington. The Cwmmwd of Merffordd had been given by Bleddyn ab Cynfyn, in reward of military services, to his cousin Gwernwy, the father of Eunydd the [founder of one of the Fifteen] Tribes.[2]

The relations and friends of the family contended with Emma for the direction of the children; sensible, should they be brought up by their mother, their affections must be lost to their country. She had the custody of the two elder, but keeping with difficulty the possession of them, and of the lands of her Welsh jointure, threw both to the care of Edward, alleging that their ancestors had sworn allegiance to the Kings of England, and they were feudally in his wardship. The King accordingly took the children, and committed the charge of them and their estates, Madog the elder to John Earl Warren, and Llywelyn to Roger Mortimer, who strengthened their trusts with

surviving sons; he is however celebrated by Cynddelw, our British Homer, in several Poems: in one he thanks him for a stag which his hounds had killed by Cynddelw's door; in another he enumerates the several battles fought by Madog ab Maredudd, his father; at last the Bard deplores the fall of Llywelyn, saying his house on the banks of the Dee was left desolate. [Llywelyn ab Madog, "the hope of all Powys," was slain just after his father's death in 1160.—*Ed.*]

[1] Efell signifies twins, from the Latin Gemelli, the Latin M being always expressed in Welsh by the letter F.

[2] See under EFNYDD the Fourteenth Noble Tribe of North Wales, *post.*—*Ed.*

two strong Castles; Chirk, built by Mortimer, and Holt,[1] by
Warren; and as might happen, the wards were missed and no
more found.[2]

> ....*Tali curantes arte pūpillos*,[3]
> *Rursus ut ad patrios nunquam rediere penates.*

Tradition says they were drowned in the night, in the Dee, at
Holt. They perished no doubt by some secret and violent death,
at the hands of their Guardians, who by the grants of Edward
succeeded generally to their estates. But it is observable, the
King took a part in the spoil, but he might not share in their
destruction; for in his grant to Warren, the Castle[4] and Demesnes
of Hope are reserved to himself; and he had given Emma a

---

[1] This Roger was more than once justice of North Wales; was the second son of
Roger, Lord Mortimer of Wigmore, and uncle to Roger the Minister, Earl of Marche.
He was summoned to parliament, as Lord Mortimer of Chirk, by Edward the Second,
and was one of the Lords who gave sentence of banishment against the two Spencers;
for which his nephew and himself were imprisoned in the Tower; and where it is said
this Roger died.

[2] The author has here copied a mistake previously made by Powel and other
historians. The four sons of Gruffydd ab Madog ab Gruffydd Maelor were witnesses to
the Settlement made by him on his wife Emma, and after his death in 1270, the four
joined in a renewal and confirmation of it, which proves that they had arrived at the
state of manhood. These settlements were among the *Sebright MSS.*, and are quoted
by Pennant *(Tours in Wales*, 1883 ed., vol. i., p. 266). The children who were
murdered were Llywelyn and Gruffydd, *sons* of the Madog named in the text, and
grandsons of the lady Emma. The foul deed was perpetrated in 1281.—*Ed.*

[3] Ednop, like the French writers of Latin verses of that time (James the First) has
no regard to quantity. The Frenchmen professed it; Nos Gallici non curamus
quantitatem syllabarum.

[4] In this Castle of Hope, commonly called Caergwrle, Edward the First and his
Queen Eleanor, lodged on their journey to Carnarvon, and whilst they were there the
Castle was by some accident set on fire, and burnt. The little village of Hope (in
Welsh Estyn) is called Queen Hope, from Eleanor's visit.

56

temporary composition in land for her jointure of· Maelor Saesneg, which on her death should have reverted to her family, but which Edward kept and annexed to Flintshire,[1] under pretence that the heirs were rebels. And here seems set in violence, ingratitude, and a cruel breach of trust, a wretched instance and example, dreadfully copied afterward in the persons of two of his descendants, Richard of York, and the Fifth Edward, both as to their lives and fortune.[2]

Thus ended the Madocian line of the Powysian Princes : that rag of Powys, which descended to Glyndŵr, was in point of power manerial matters only. Glyndyfrdwy is at present [1799] the possession of Edward Williames Vaughan Salesbury Esquire, second son of the late Sir Robert Howel Vaughan, of Nannau, and had been forfeited in Glyndŵr's rebellion, and sold by Henry the Fourth to a second son of the Salesburys of Bachymbyd, a younger branch of Llyweni. Through the Salesburys, the Pughes of Mathafarn,[3] and the Prices of Gogerddan, it rests in Mr. Salesbury.[4]

---

[1] The four ancient North Welsh counties were Anglesey, Carnarvon, Merioneth and Flint. In South Wales Glamorgan and Pembroke were made Shires so early as Henry the First, on his importation of Flemish, and the common Law of England planted in them.

[2] Nescia mens hominum fati sortisque futuræ,
Et servare modum, rebus sublata secundis !
Turno tempus erit, magno cum optaverit emptum
Intactum Pallanta ; et cum spolia ista diemque
Orderit ....

[3] Dafydd ab Llwyd ab Llywelyn ab Gruffudd, Lord of Mathafarn, wrote in verse the Legend of Tydecho, one of our most capital Saints. This illustrious Bard had a great

I come next to Powys Wenwynwyn, the other division. Bleddyn had gavelled Powys between his sons, Maredudd, and Cadwgan. It reunited in Maredudd, who accumulated the whole by the family slaughter of that period. He divided it again between his son Madog, whence the Fadog division, and his grandson Owain Cyfeiliog,[1] whose son Gwenwynwyn gave name to this moiety. Gruffudd the second son of Maredudd died before his father. He had submitted with him to Henry the First, and was called by this Prince to his baronial Parliaments. I find nothing more interesting respecting him, but he took his share in the family feuds and fightings of that season. He married Gwerfyl, daughter to Gwrgenau ab Hywel ab Jeuaf ab Cadwgan

hand also in bringing in Henry the Seventh, by feeding his countrymen with prophecies, that one of them was to deliver Wales from the English yoke ; by which many thousands were induced to rise under Sir Rhŷs ab Thomas, and join Henry at Milford.

[4] Mr. Salesbury was a colonel in the Guards. He died in 1807, and left the estate to his brother. Eventually it descended to his nephew Sir Robert Williames Vaughan, the third Baronet, of Nannau, who died without issue in 1859, and by whose Will, the Rhûg estates (comprising Glyndyfrdwy) came into the possession of the Hon. Charles Henry Wynn, second surviving son of Lord Newborough, the present owner, who claims descent from the Salesburys, or Salusburys, of Lleweni, through Robert Salesbury, Esq., of Plas issa, Llanrwst. This is supposed to have influenced Sir Robert Vaughan in devising the estate to him. The Salesbury family produced many distinguished men, one of the most eminent being William Salesbury, the translator of the New Testament into Welsh, who was second son of Foulk Salesbury of Plas issa, where he was born early in the sixteenth century.—*Ed.*

[1] His surname, Cyfeiliog, he took from a district so called in Montgomeryshire, containing five parishes. The ruins of his Castle are still seen at Tafolwern in Cyfeiliog. [There are now no ruins to be seen, but the site may be easily distinguished. Tafolwern is in the parish of Llanbrynmair, Montgomeryshire.—*Ed.*]

H

ab Elystan Glodrudd,[1] the founder of our fifth Royal Tribe, and died in 1128. His son Cyfeiliog, who enjoyed his estates entire, was a man of more eminence, and a busier actor in the constant contentions of that restless time. He bore an honorable share in the battle of Crogen, from which the second Henry retreated with considerable loss and personal danger. In 1176 he attended the summons of Henry, to meet him at Oxford, and to confer with him on Welsh affairs.

I next find him in a business of family pillage, in which he plundered Iorwerth gôch, his father's half-brother, of his estates in Powys. This drew upon him the justice of Owain Gwynedd, Prince of North Wales, and of Rhŷs ab Gruffudd, of the South ; and together they drove him from his country, which with the assistance of the English he recovered in part; but was reduced by Rhŷs after the death of Owain, and again restored on proper concessions. He married Gwenllian, the daughter of Owain Gwynedd ; by her he had one son, Gwenwynwyn, who inherited his estates entire, excepting the Cwmmwds of Llannerch hudol and Broniarth, which his father had parcelled off in favor of his natural son, Caswallon. Cyfeiliog founded the Cistertian Abbey of Ystrad Marchell,[2] and died a very aged man in 1197. He

---

[1] Elystan or Athelstane Glodrudd was godson to the Saxon King, Athelstane. —*Tracts of Powys*, p. 16 note.

[2] Virginis et nitidum Marcellæ struxit Asylum.—*Pentarchia*. This once famous abbey (Strata Marcella) stood on the banks of the Severn, about two miles below Welshpool, but not a vestige of it now remains. It was founded according to Bishop Tanner in the year 1170. Owen Cyfeiliog died and was buried there, having previously taken upon himself the habit of religion. His arms were *Or* a lion rampant *Gules* armed *azure ;* or, as some say *Gules*, a lion rampant *or.*—*Ed.*

was a distinguished Bard[1] also, as what he left[2] may testify; and in our Augustan[3] age of Welsh poetry. The Saxons, at

[1] Mr. Andrews has well observed, that the tale of Edward the First's cruelty to the Bards, in the next century, has no foundation, but an obscure tradition, and a hint in the Gwydir history. Edward hath been also accused of having destroyed all the ancient records and writings in Scotland. This is ably refuted by Sir David Dalrymple. But an order at that time subsisted to silence the Welsh Bards. Our countrymen were more severely treated by the Fourth Henry, when the Welsh were rendered by an act of Parliament incapable of purchasing lands, or of performing any office in any town, or of having any Castle or house of defence. English Judges and Juries were to decide disputes between English and Welsh: Englishmen that married Welshwomen* were disfranchised, and no Welshman might bind his child to any trade, nor breed him up to literature. The absurdities of these ordinances counteracted their virulence; and the moderation of the Fifth Henry having laid them to sleep; if not repealed, they were at least forgotten.

[2] His poem, called HIRLAS OWAIN (finely translated into English verse by the Reverend Mr. Williams of Fron), affords a specimen of his martial spirit, as well as of his poetic talents.

[3] Poetry and good language was in greater perfection in Wales, a little before and a little after the Norman Conquest, than it hath been since; and the historical part of our Poems is a great light to Historians, both English and Welsh, Irish and Scotch. Goronwy Owain on this subject says, "I find the old metres were, what all compositions of that nature should be, that is, Lyric verses adapted to the tunes and music then in use. Of this sort were the several kinds of Englynion, Cywyddau, Odlau, Gwawdodyn, Toddaid, Trybedd y Myneich and Clogyrnach, which appear to have in their composition the authentic stamp of genuine Lyric poetry, and of true primitive antiquity. As to the rest, I mean Gorchest y Beirdd, Huppynt hir and byr, being the newest, they were falsely thought the most ingenious and accurate kind of metres. But I look upon them to be rather depravations than improvements in our poetry. What a grovelling, low thing that Gorchest y Beirdd is? And I would have an impartial answer, whether the old, despised, exterminated Englyn Milwr hath not something of antique majesty in its composition. Now, when I have a mind to write good sense in such a metre as Gorchest y Beirdd, and so begin, and the language itself does not afford words that will come in to finish with sense and Cynghanedd too, what must I do?

* Henry no doubt was jealous of the charms of our countrywomen, and fearful of their influence on his English subjects.

least for some time, were no poets; they landed here, without an alphabet. The Normans had their Jongleurs,[1] Troubadours, and Provencial songs, the Monks jingled their Latin doggrel; but until the days of Gower, Chaucer and Lydgate, native English numbers were in a manner unknown;[2] the scholar since hath excelled his master;

> *Nosque ubi primus equis Oriens afflavit anhelis,*
> *Illinc sera rubens accendit lumina Vesper,*

Why, to keep Cynghanedd (i. e. the alliteration) I must write nonsense to the end of the metre, and cramp and fetter good sense; whilst the dictionary is overturned and tormented to find out words of a like ending, sense or nonsense; and besides, suppose our language was more comprehensive and significant than it is (which we have no reason or room to wish) what abundance of mysterious sense is such an horrid, jingling metre of such a length able to contain! In short as I understand that it and its fellows were introduced by the authority of an Eisteddfod, I wish we had an Eisteddfod again, to give them their dimittimus to some peaceable acrostick land, to sport and converse with the spirits of deceased Puns, Quibbles, and Conundrums of pious memory; then would I gladly see the true primitive metres reinstated in their ancient dignity, and sense regarded more than a hideous jingle of words, which hardly ever bear it."

The Welsh poetry had a great compass and variety. Dr. John David Rhŷs the physician and grammarian, who took his degree in Italy, introduces a comparison between the Welsh and Italian poetry, and inserts a whole Italian poem, marked in the manner he has done the Welsh. In Metastasio is a poem similar to a very favorite measure in Welsh poetry; viz.

> *Sopra il santissimo. Natale Ode,* Vol. 9.

In this, the end of the first line rhimes to the middle of the second, and the end of the second to the middle of the third.

[1] This species of Minstrels ended in the conjuring art; hence our Jugglers.

[2] We must not wonder, if the English verse in those early centuries appear uncouth. The bard had to do with a harsh, though nervous language, frowned on by the Court, neglected by the Gentry, and disguised by a most unintelligible mode of spelling.—*J. P. A.*

The son of Owain Gwynedd, Hywel (who fell in the contention for his father's throne) brother to Madog the navigator, hath written his own battles in verse, and some

The Britons had taught the Saxons to read, and given them the first of all things in Christianity itself, which they spread and adorned with ten Cathedrals.[1]

Gwenwynwyn began early the career of his family; and in the life of his father, with his base brother Caswallon, he made

love verses in a most elegant manner, of which we have several copies in Wales. Our Princes and chieftains continued this custom of writing their own actions, as late as Henry the Second's time, the age of Hywel. Poetry was so sacred with these people, that they never suffered invented fables, the chief ingredient in heroic poetry, to have a footing in it, which is the reason that neither the Gauls, Britons, Irish, Picts, Cornish or Armoricans, ever had to this day a poem in the nature of the Iliad or Eneid. "Poetry," says Mr. Morris, hath been with us the sacred respository of the actions of great men; and it hath been so, from the most ancient times, in other nations; as the song of Moses, among the Jews, of the defeat of the Egyptians. Taliesin's historical poem of the Tombs of the Warriors of Britain is a noble piece of antiquity, and strikes great light on the events of those times, when compared with the Triades, the Brut y Brenhinoedd, and the succeeding writers. The book of Triades, in British Trioedd Ynys Prydain, or the Threes of the Island of Britain, seems to have been written about the year 650, and some parts of it collected out of the most ancient monuments of the kingdom, but not from the same fountain as Brut y Brenhinoedd; as there are facts and matters in the Triades not to be found in the Brut, and also several things which the author of the Brut never would have omitted, if he had met with them. The Triades hath always been quoted by our British poets from age to age, though Geoffrey of Monmouth, the Latin translator of Tyssilio, never saw it, or else he would have embellished his translation with its contents, instead of the ridiculous things which he hath added to it from Myrddin Emrys, and oral tradition." It is called by some writers, and by the translator of Camden, the Book of Triplicities. The Britons, as well as other nations of old, had a particular veneration for odd numbers, and especially for that of Three. Their most ancient poetry consists of Three lined stanzas, called Englyn Milwr, the Warrior's Verse. Their most remote history is divided into sections, being combinations of some Three similar events. All men of note, whether famous or infamous, were classed together by Threes; Virtues and Vices were tripled together in the same manner; and the Druids conveyed their instructions in moral and natural philosophy to their people, in sentences of Three parts.

[1] Canterbury, Rochester, London, York, Hereford, Lincoln, Lichfield, Norwich, Worcester and Durham.—*Tracts of Powys*, p. 18, *note*.

a predatory excursion by night, and took and plundered the
Castle of Carreg Hwfa,[1] and put to death their Welsh uncle,
their father's first cousin, Owain ab Madog, then an old man,
whom they found in it.

His next exploit had a better aspect. He recovered his Castle
of Powys,[2] on the terms he had lost it, from Archbishop Hubert
of Canterbury, who commanded the armies of Richard the First
against the Welsh, and held the administration in England,
whilst that Prince was absent in Palestine.[3] He next assisted
the wicked[4] Maelgwn to surprize and imprison his brother
Gruffudd, Lord of South Wales; and his person being delivered
to Gwenwynwyn, he gave him up to the English. Two years
after he conceived a great design; the liberty and extension of
his country to its ancient limits. With views so popular he
raised a large army, and besieged William de Breos in his
Castle of Payn in Radnor. He lay three weeks without effect
before it, whilst Breos had time to collect assistance, and was

A.D.
1198

---

[1] The Castle of Carreg Hwfa was taken and despoiled by the two cousin-germans,
Owain Cyfeiliog and Owain ab Madog, in the year 1162 ; which latter kept possession
of it twenty-five years, when he was besieged in it, and slain in the night by Gwenwynwyn and Caswallon, sons of Owain Cyfeiliog, his former colleague in plunder and
devastation. [This castle stood near the banks of the Vyrnwy, in the parish of Llan-
ymynech, Montgomeryshire. There are no ruins or even traces of it now to be seen.—*Ed.*]

[2] ....Gwenwynwyn sanguinis hæres,
Ante obitum patris, totam subjecit Arustli ;
Inde Polæ Castrum, quod vi possederat Anglus,
Conditione pari, quâ perdidit ante, recepit.—*Pentarchia.*

[3] Richard was but eight months in England, during a reign of ten years.

[4] Powel gives him another character ; but I look to his actions, as I find them
related.

reinforced by the Justiciary of England, Jeffrey Fitzpeter,[1] who had released the Lord of South Wales, his prisoner, and put him at the head of his countrymen, who joined him in great numbers. Gwenwynwyn engaged the whole, and in the open plain near the Castle, and was defeated.

Yet unsubdued, he refused allegiance to his sovereign Llywelyn, but was again reconciled, and took the same oaths of fidelity to him, as he had before done to the King of England; from the last, he had been discharged by a dispensation from Rome. And here it should seem he had some hardship; he was detained a prisoner at Shrewsbury, whither he went to consult the English Council; and however an offence this to his own Prince, who seized his country, it was an ungrateful return from England. He was restored to his liberty by John, three years after; by whose assistance he recovered his possessions; and he attended him in an unsuccessful expedition into Wales the year following.

A.D.
1202

A.D.
1207

The next year [1211] he is in arms on the part of Llywelyn, and with other great men of Wales, they drove John with disgrace from the country. He kept his faith but five years; deserted once more to John, was pursued by Llywelyn, his country taken, and himself driven within the walls of Chester. Reviewing his character, little good is to be found in it; but he was a man of spirit in the field. He had moreover, in a

[1] Fitzpeter was an eminent character. He was dreaded by John, who yet dared not to remove him from his great office. When John heard of his death, he exultingly cried, "And is he gone then? Well, let him go to hell, and join Archbishop Hubert. By God's foot I am now for the first time King of England."—*Matthew Paris.*

religious sense, improved his father's foundation of Ystrad Marchell.
By his wife Margaret, daughter of Lord Rhŷs of South Wales,
he left one son Gruffudd.[1]

Him I find, with other leading men of Wales, soliciting the
third Henry to release Gruffudd, the brother of Dafydd, the
reigning Prince; an event already related. Two years after he
was restored to his estates (forfeited to Dafydd) by Henry, who
exercised this power as Sovereign of Wales, and to whom
Dafydd had made his entire submission. He steadily for a
time adhered to the English, and was alone among his countrymen in that particular, refusing to join Dafydd; again he returned
to his allegiance, during the life of that Prince.

I find him next in exile, and his estates confiscated by the
succeeding Prince, Llywelyn; but again he temporized, and

[1] Before I part with Gwenwynwyn, let me relate from Giraldus an incident which
passed between his father Cyfeiliog and our Henry the Second. "We had excommunicated," says the historian, " Owain Cyfeiliog, because he was the only one of the
Princes, that hȧd not paid proper respect in person to us. This Owain was the most
eloquent of all the Welsh, and governed his part of the country with great prudence.
He had contracted an intimate friendship with Henry, and sided with him generally
against his countrymen. In consequence of this, some time after, sitting at table with the
King at Shrewsbury, Henry handed him a piece of his bread, as a mark of his Royal favor.
Owain immediately cut it into pieces, as it were eleemosynary bread, or that which is
given among different people ; and then removing it at some distance from him, and
again bringing it nearer to him, he ate each piece separately. Upon the King desiring
to know the reason of this, Owain with a feigned smile replied, " I show my master by
this manner of breaking the bread, how he ought to conduct himself in ecclesiastical
matters ;" alluding to the King's keeping in his own hands the vacant preferments
longer than he ought to have done, and not distributing them among the persons proper
to take the care of them. [Gwenwynwyn's arms were, Or a lion's gamb dexterways
erased *gules*, armed *azure*. Eyton *(Antiquities of Shropshire*, vol. vii., p. 15) says that
Gwenwynwyn's wife, Margaret, was the daughter of Robert Corbet, lord of Caus, not
of the Lord Rhŷs as above stated.—*Ed.*]

again joined his Welsh Sovereign; and as the test of his sincerity, he took and demolished the Castle of Mold,[1] a frontier English garrison. He must have still changed, for it is matter of complaint,[2] on the part of Llywelyn, that Edward the First had received and protected his rebel subject Gruffudd ab Gwenwynwyn. He [Gruffudd] married Margaret[3] the daughter of Hywel y Pedolau,[4] and had six sons, among whom his lands

---

[1] Mold in Welsh is called Wyddgrug,=conspicuous. [Gwenwynwyn was living in 1246, as appears from a deed, dated 22 April, 30 Hen. III. *(Dwnn's Vis.* ii., 124 *note.)* —*Ed.*]

[2] Many causes of animosity subsisted between Edward, Llywelyn, and the Welsh, previous to the final rupture. In the year 1277, the Barons of Snowdon, with other Noblemen of Wales, had attended Llywelyn to London, when he came thither at Christmas to do homage to Edward, for the four Cantreds of Rhòs, Rhyfoniog, Tegengl, and Dyffryn Clwyd; and bringing, according to their usual custom, large retinues with them, were quartered at Islington, and the neighbouring villages. These places did not afford milk for such numerous trains; they liked neither the wine nor the ale of London; and, though plentifully entertained, were much displeased at the new manner of living, which did not suit with their taste: they slighted the English bread, and their pride too was disgusted by the perpetual staring of the Londoners, who followed them in crowds to gaze at their uncommon garb. " No," cried the indignant Britons, "we never again will visit Islington, except as conquerors;" and from that instant they resolved to take up arms.—*Carte from a MS. in the Mostyn collection.*

[3] Or, according to *(Dwnn's Vis.* ii., p. 242), Gwenllian. In the *Hist. of Powys Fadog* (vol. v., p. 43), Gruffudd is stated to have married Hawys, daughter of Sir John L'Estrange of Ness Strange and Cheswardine, Knight. He died in 1289, and was buried in the church of the Franciscans, or Grey Friars, Shrewsbury. He bore *Or,* a lion rampant *Gules.*—*Ed.*

[4] Sir Hywel y Pedolau was son of Gruffudd ab Iorwerth ab Maredudd ab Methusalem ab Hwfa ab Cynddelw, one of the Fifteen Tribes contemporary with Owain Gwynedd. Sir Hywel was so strong a man, that he could, it is said, straighten horse shoes with his hands; whence his name y Pedolau, i. e. of the horseshoes. His mother was King Edward the Second's nurse; and he being a foster-brother to the King was in great favor, and was knighted by him. And here I am led to doubt the policy of Edward

I

were divided. To Owain[1] the eldest were given the Cwmmwds of Arustli, Cyfeiliog, Llannerch hudol, and the half of Caer Einion; Llywarch[2] the second, had Mochnant uchaf, and Mechain uwch coed; John the fourth part of Caer Einion; William or Wilcock, as the Welsh call him, Mowddwy; Gruffudd Fychan had Deuddwr, Ystrad Marchell, and the Tairtref,[3] or three towns on the borders, which came to the family by the marriage of their great great grandfather, Gruffudd ab Maredudd, with the heiress of the house of Elystan Glodrudd; Dafydd the Sixth and youngest had the remaining fourth of Caer Einion. Owain married Hawys, the daughter of Philip Corbet, Baron of Caus, and by her had an only daughter, Hawys gadarn, or the hardy.

the First in making his second son Edward a Welshman, and bringing his Queen for that purpose to lie in at Carnarvon, his elder son Alphonsus being then alive; and since the union of England and Wales was a great object, and for which eventually we are much obliged to him,* it seemed to be made more difficult by this measure, as the Welsh might not have easily resigned their countryman and adopted King. [For a fuller account of Sir Hywel y Pedolau and his descendants, see under HWFA AB CYNDDELW, the first Noble Tribe of North Wales, post.—Ed.]

[1] Owain ab Gruffudd ab Gwenwynwyn was summoned to a parliament at Shrewsbury, where he acknowledged his lands to be held under the Crown of England in capite, under the tenure of free Baronage, and resigned to the King and his heirs the sovereignty of Powys. Rhŷs of South Wales had done the same at an earlier period. The Sovereigns of North Wales preserved their title of Princes till 1282, on the death of the last Llywelyn. The kingly title ended with Gruffudd ab Cynan.

[2] Or, Llywelyn according to Powel.—Ed.

[3] Tair Trêf lies in the Parish of Myfod, adjoining Mathrafael, the seat of these Princes of Powys. (Tracts of Powys, p. 23, note.)—Ed.

* "I confess," says Vaughan of Hengwrt, "we have reason to bless God for his mercy to us in our happy establishment under one Monarch. We may well say we were conquered to our gain, and undone to our advantage."—Periissemus nisi periissemus.

Her uncles (Wilcock excepted, whence was saved to his descendants this lot of his inheritance, and the lordship of Mowddwy
is to this day, through the De Burghs, in his heirs general,
the Myttons of Halston)[1] contended by the gafael, that she
could not as a female inherit her father's land; forgetful that
from such Powys was first derived to their family; and her
uncle John raised a force to support his claims, and besieged
his niece and her husband in the Castle of Pool [Powis Castle].
They were relieved by Roger [Mortimer] the Minister Earl of
Marche,[2] and for this service Mortimer had grants from them in

[1] Since this was written, the lordship of Mawddwy, and most of the other possessions of
the Myttons of Halston, have passed into other hands, chiefly through the reckless
improvidence of the celebrated "Jack" Mytton who spent the whole of his fine property
that was not out of his reach by entail, including £60,000 cash. Of timber alone, it
is said, that he sold £80,000 worth. He died in the King's Bench Prison, in March,
1834, in his thirty-eighth year, and was succeeded by his son, John Fox Mytton, who
died in February, 1875. After John Mytton's death, Halston was sold to the late
Edmund Wright, Esq. Sir Edmund Buckley, Bart., is the present lord of the Manor
of Mawddwy.—*Ed.*

[2] There were twenty Lord Marchers. of whom this powerful Peer, with the title of
Earl of Marche, was one. They sat among the English Lords, and had the titles of
those places they had won from the Welsh. They had originally regal jurisdiction in
their several Baronies, where the King's writs did not run. This was intended as a
strength against the neighbouring enemy; but Edward the First, in his statute of
Rhuddlan, withdrew this power, for he was able of himself to rule our countrymen.
None were erected after that period: they held of the King immediately, that is, in
capite, and were accordingly bound to him in personal suit and service, and to find him
a certain number of soldiers. In the third of Edward the Second, for the Scotch war I
find the Barony of Powys had to send four hundred; Rhòs and Rhyfoniog, that is,
Denbigh, two hundred; Ruthin two hundred; Dyffryn Clwyd one hundred; Nantheudwy and Glyndyfrdwy, two hundred; Bromfield and Iâl, two hundred; numbers
exceeding the present Militia proportions.* Henry the Eighth finally reduced their

* I believe there is little doubt, from these comparative proportions, that North Wales had considerably
more inhabitants than it hath at present, many, as in these times, being necessarily drawn off by trade, and
other engagements.

Powys. The cause was then taken before Edward the Second, the feudal Judge of the controversy, and whilst yet before him, he seized and imprisoned the uncles in the Castle of Harlech. They had lost their Court patron, Thomas Earl of Lancaster,[1] then without favor and soon without his head, at Pomfret [Pontefract]. The King decided that her issue, whether male or female, should inherit her estates, and if her uncles who litigated left no male issue, their lands should accumulate to her also; and this was afterwards the case. Moreover he had given her an husband in Sir John Charleton, a gentleman of his chamber,[2] who was summoned by writ[3] to Parliament in the seventh year of this King, as Lord Powys; whence a Barony in fee was created, descendable to his heirs general. And here I get within the land of dates; land seldom to be found in the *latitudes* of

broken power. Many of these Baronies had fallen to the Crown from purchase, inheritance, or forfeiture. He resumed all or most of the jurisdictions that were left, and deprived the Marchers of the same, leaving them in effect but as Lords of Manors in England. He then ordained Justices† of Assize himself, and Justices of the Peace, Sheriffs, and other Officers; and divided the country more correctly into counties; and erected Great Sessions and other Courts for its government, by Officers of his own, and according to the Laws of England, and left little or no authority to the Lords Marchers. The former policy, and presents of the Kings of England to their Nobles, had continued from the Norman Conquest until Edward the First; insomuch that at that time Wales was almost come into the possession of divers English Lords, who held the same of the Kings of England, and not of the Princes of Wales.

[1] Lancaster possessed the Lordship of Denbigh in virtue of his marriage with the heiress of the Lacys.

[2] Valectus Regis. Hence Valet.

[3] There was no representation in the Commons-house from Cheshire or Wales till the Welsh incorporating acts of Henry the Eighth.

† Henry the English gave us but four Judges to the whole Principality; the Puisnes were added by Elizabeth. Only eight Justices of the Peace were allowed to each Shire by Henry, who formed the new Counties of Monmouth, Denbigh, Montgomery, Brecknock and Radnor.

Welsh genealogy, where such things were usually forgotten. This first Lord of an English house (Appley, in Shropshire,) the son of Sir Alan Charleton, was a man of civil and military talents, had attended his Sovereign, moreover, as his Chamberlain, in his frequent and unfortunate northern expeditions. He followed for a time then the reforming factions of Lancaster, the refuge and receptacle of all that were distressed and discontented; was defeated, and taken with them at Boroughbridge, but escaped the proscriptions which ensued; came again into favor, and suffered in the insurrection against the King, when his house was pillaged by the London mob. I find him next in early employments and in great consideration with Edward the Third, who sent him on his service to Brabant, and afterwards to Ireland, as Justice or Chief Governor; and he took with him thither his brother Thomas, Bishop of Hereford, as Chancellor of that kingdom. Our old books speak of him in high esteem for his fidelity, prudence, and valour; nor amidst his greater employments had he neglected the interests and accommodation of his countrymen; and he obtained from Edward the Second two weekly markets at Pool and Machynlleth, and two fairs in the year at each place.[1] He died at the age of eighty-five; his wife, the Powys heiress, some time before him; and as I learn from Dugdale and John Salisbury of Erbistock, she lies buried in the dissolved house of the grey Friars of her own foundation at Shrewsbury. John their son, who succeeded,[2] was

A.D.
1353

---

[1] ....Clarum et venerabile nomen
Gentibus, et nostræ multum quod profuit urbi.—*Lucan.*

[2] This, the second John de Charleton, married Maud, daughter of Roger Mortimer, first Earl of March (see *Mont. Coll.*, i. 259). He died Aug. 30, 1360.—*Ed.*

summoned to Parliament, from the twenty-eighth to the forty-seventh of Edward the Third; was Chamberlain of the household to this King, as his father had been to his predecessor; attended him in that useless and expensive expedition to France in 1339, as did his son [John de Charleton, the third of that name], the Black Prince, in the same kingdom, and to the same effect, in 1370. [The last named John de Charleton] died [July 13, 1374,] leaving by his wife Joan, daughter of Ralph, Earl of Stafford,[1] John his son, then under age, and a younger son

---

[1] Ralph Bagot, Lord Stafford, a great soldier and one of the founders of the Garter, was created Earl of Stafford in the twenty-fifth of Edward the Third, and died in the forty-sixth of that reign. He was the son of Edmund, Lord Stafford, who died in the second of Edward the Second, the son of Nicholas, who was killed by the fall of Droselan Castle, which he had undermined, and was besieging in Wales, in the tenth of Edward the First. He was the younger brother of Henry, who died without issue, the two sons of Henry Lord Stafford, who first relinquished his paternal name of Bagot, and assumed his mother's name of Stafford. His father, Harvey Bagot, was a collateral ancestor and a younger brother of Lord Bagot's house; and marrying Millicent, the daughter and heiress of the Staffords, possessed in her right the title and estate of that great family. To return to Ralph, the first Earl. He left issue, Hugh, his son and heir, who died in the ninth of Richard the Second, leaving issue, Thomas. Thomas died without issue, the sixteenth of that reign, having married Anne, daughter and heiress of Thomas of Woodstock, Duke of Gloucester, murdered at Calais; but on account of their tender age, they never lived together. He was succeeded by his brother William, who dying unmarried four years after, was succeeded by his brother Edmund, who married this Anne, the widow, if so she might be called, of his elder brother Thomas; and fell, on the part of Henry the Fourth, in the battle of Shrewsbury, leaving by her Humphrey his son and heir, then very young. In him were concentred the great Earldoms of Buckingham, Hereford, Stafford, Northampton and Perche. He was also Lord of Brecknock, Caus and Holderness, and in the twenty-third of Henry the Sixth was advanced to the Dukedom of Buckingham. [His portrait is here given.] He fell in the battle of Northampton, on the part of that King, in 1460; as his eldest son, the Earl of Stafford, had fallen on the same side, in the first battle of St. Alban's. His grandson, the Earl of Stafford's son Henry, was restored and succeeded

HUMPHREY STAFFORD OR **BAGOT.**

Duke of Buckingham.

Edward. John was Justice of North Wales, had summons to Parliament from the sixth of Richard the Second to the third of Henry the Fourth, when he died[1] leaving no issue. He was succeeded by his brother Edward. This Lord was a sufferer in Glyndwr's[2] rebellion, and obtained pardon for his tenants in Powys, who submitted, and had been engaged in it. He was warmly attached to Henry the Fourth, who gave him the Garter. In the succeeding reign, he took an active part with the Clergy against the sectaries of that season, persecuted the Lollards, discovered and seized Sir John Oldcastle in Powys where he had been concealed, and who was sacrificed[3] by our fifth Henry

his grandfather,but afterwards lost his head at Salisbury, on the orders of Richard the Third. He was succeeded by his son Edward, restored again by Henry the Seventh, and executed by his cruel son Henry the Eighth. He was succeeded by his son Henry, restored to the barony of Stafford ; Henry by his son Edward ; Edward again by his son Henry. Henry died unmarried in 1637, and was succeeded in this fee barony by the heir general, his sole sister Mary, created afterwards Countess of Stafford. She married Sir William Howard, Knight of the Bath, the second son of Thomas Earl of Arundel, the virtu Lord. Sir William was created Viscount Stafford, and lost his head very unjustly amidst the cruel parties of Charles the Second's time. His family was again restored, and the male line became extinct in the last reign [George the Second] only. What claims remain in heirs general to the barony, I am not competent to say ; but Earl Gower left the title open, being created Marquis of Staffordshire, and not of Stafford. [Sir George William Jerningham, Bart., in 1824, obtained the reversal of the attainder of Viscount Stafford, and claimed for himself the ancient barony of Stafford as lineal heir of his great grandmother, Mary Howard, wife of Francis Plowden, Esq., grand-daughter of Viscount Stafford. In this he was successful, the House of Lords resolving 6th July, 1825, that he had made out his claim. He died 4th October, 1851. The present peer is his grandson. (Burke's Peerage.)—Ed.]

[1] This Lord had met the Duke of Lancaster at Leominster, when on his march from Bristol to Chester, after his landing at Ravenspurg.

[2] Owain had burnt the suburbs of the town of Pool.—Carte.

[3] Lord Cobham," says Lord Orford, "was the first author, as well as first martyr, among our Nobility ; a man, whose virtues made him a reformer, whose valor a

his old friend and wild companion,) to an ecclesiastical bribe[1]

martyr, whose martyrdom an enthusiast." He was suspended by a chain fastened round his waist over a slow fire. This torturing death he bore with constancy; and with his last breath he conjured Sir Thomas Erpingham, that if he should see him rise from the grave in three days, he would then intercede with the King in favor of his brethren, the Lollards. The Lordship of Broniarth was granted to the family of Tanad of Aber Tanad, the fifth of Henry the Fifth, for the assistance they gave in the apprehension of Oldcastle ; in it is a field, called to this day Lord Cobham's garden. Sir Gruffudd Fychan, Lord of Byrgedwyn, Treflydan, Garth and Caer fawr, in the opening of the fifteenth century, with his elder brother Jeuan, are parties to a deed in the possession of Mr. Mytton of Garth ; whereby Edward Charleton, Lord of Powys, grants them several privileges for assisting in taking Sir John Oldcastle, in the third of Henry the Fifth, when the King himself was absent in France. From Dafydd Lloyd, eldest son of Sir Gruffudd, are descended the Lloyds of Llai, of Marrington, and Welsh Pool ; from Cadwaladr, the second son, the Lloyds of Maes mawr, of Rhandir, and Humphrey ab Roger of Treflydan. Reinallt, his third son, under his claim as the youngest, had the family house at Garth. His grandson, John ab Gruffudd ab Reinallt, was the first who took the name of Wynn, pure or white ; whether from the flaxen colour of his hair, the paleness or delicacy of his complexion, or from some amiable qualities of his mind. " Humphrey Wynn, son of John Wynn of this House, was living in the year 1560." The sixth in descent from Humphrey married Dorothy, daughter of John Powel Esquire of Worthen, and had issue an only daughter Dorothy, married to Richard Mytton Esquire of Pont Is Cowryd, who had issue Devereux Mytton Esquire, the present. [1799] worthy possessor of Garth and Pont Is Cowryd. [Mr. Mytton died in 1809, and (his eldest son Richard having died in his lifetime) was succeeded by his grandson, the Rev. Richard Mytton, LL.B., whose son Richard Herbert Mytton Esquire succeeded him. The last named gentleman died in May, 1869, and his eldest son, Devereux Herbert Mytton Esquire, is the present owner of the estates. The above statements with reference to the grant of the lordship of Broniarth are not quite correct, the author having committed the error of ascribing to the family of Tanad the original grant, instead of to their *predecessors*. From documents at Brogyntyn, it appears that the lordship was granted to Ieuan and Sir Griffith Vaughan, the two sons of Griffith ap Ieuan ap Madog ap Wenwys, by Sir Edward Charleton, on 10th March, 8*th* Henry the Fifth (1420), being about three years after the capture of Lord Cobham. Ieuan Llwyd ap David, of Abertanad, by his marriage with Maud, granddaughter of the above-named Ieuan, acquired *half* of Broniarth, and his grandson Thomas Tannatt, in the reign of Elizabeth, purchased the *other* moiety of Humphrey Lloyd, a descendant of Sir Gruffudd Vaughan. *(Mont Coll.* iv., p. 366.)—*Ed.*]

[1] Archbishop Chicheley had earnestly forwarded this French war, which that country

for his French war. Charleton sent his son-in-law, Sir John Grey, to bring him a prisoner to London; and for this service Lord Powys had the thanks of Parliament. He was summoned as a Peer, from the third of Henry the Fourth to the eighth 'of Henry the Fifth, and died in 1421, leaving issue by his wife Eleanor, the widow of Roger Mortimer Earl of Marche,[1] two

---

itself then deprecated ; and it gives Mr. Andrews very good room to doubt the tennis-balls story, said to have been sent by the Dauphin to Henry at that time. Chicheley dreaded lest Henry should lend an ear to his Parliament, who still harped on the vast advantages which might be gained by seizing the possessions of the Church, and wished to amuse him with war ; and, by way of composition, the Abbey lands, which depended on foreign Monasteries, and which had been given to the English Clergy, were yielded to the King by the Priesthood, and he complimented them again, by persecuting the Lollards.

[1] By Mortimer she was mother of Anne, Countess of Cambridge, the heiress of England and Wales, and to whom our gracious Sovereign, in every rule of right, the Catholic line necessarily excluded, is lawful heir and lineal successor.

[Victoria, daughter and only child of Edward, Duke of Kent, fourth son of] George the Third, the eldest son, by Augusta of Saxegotha, of Frederick, Prince of Wales, the son of George the Second, the son of George the First, the son of Ernest Augustus, Elector of Hanover, by Sophia, the daughter of Frederick Elector Palatine, and Elizabeth, the daughter of James the First, the son of Lord Darnley and Mary, Queen of Scotland, the daughter of James the Fifth, the son of James the Fourth by Margaret, the eldest daughter of Henry the Seventh by Elizabeth, the eldest daughter of Edward the Fourth, the eldest son of Richard Duke of York, the son of Richard of Conisburg Earl of Cambridge, by Anne daughter and heiress of Roger Earl of Marche, the son of Edmund, Earl of Marche, by Philippa daughter and sole heiress of Lionel Duke of Clarence, the third son of Edward the Third. This Edmund was the son of Edmund Mortimer, the son of Roger, the first Earl of Marche of this family, the son of Edmund, the son of Roger, the son of Ralph by Gwladys Ddu, or the Black, the heiress of her brother Dafydd ab Llywelyn, the son of Llywelyn ab Iorwerth, or Leolinus Magnus, Prince of North Wales, the eldest son of Iorwerth Drwyn-dwnn, the eldest son of Owain Gwynedd, the son of Gruffudd ab Cynan, the son of Cynan, the son of Iago or James, the son of Idwal, the son of Meurig, the son of Idwal foel, the son of Anarawd, the eldest son of Rhodri fawr, or Roderick the Great, the son of

K

daughters, Joan and Joyce. Joan married Sir John Grey of
Heton,[1] who had the moiety of her estate, of which the Castle
and Lordship of Powys were a part. He was, in the language
of our Chroniclers, a man of great action, of great descent also,
the son of Sir Thomas Grey of Berwick by Jane, daughter of
John Lord Mowbray. He distinguished himself in the Fifth
Henry's French war; had large grants from this Prince in that
kingdom, with the Earldom and Castle of Tankerville; but it
does not appear he held English privileges, from his foreign
honor; and his grandson seems to have discontinued the title.
He remained in service in France, and Henry gave him the

Merfyn frŷch, and Esyllt, the daughter and heiress of the last Prince Cynan Tindaethwy,
the son of Rhodri Molwynog, the son of Idwal iwrch (or the roe) the son of Cadwaladr,
the last King of the Britons, who abdicated, and died at Rome in 688. Her present
gracious Majesty is right heir, in lineal succession, to the British, Cambro-British, Anglo-
Saxon, Anglo-Norman, English and Scottish Kings.

I would just observe here that the last Prince of Wales, Llywelyn, and his brother
David, Lord of Denbigh (be their father legitimate or not), left but each a daughter ;
and Edward the First compelled both to become Nuns to prevent their having issue,
to create him or his successors any disturbance ; so that in no case do this family stand
in the way of our present gracious [Queen]'s regular succession to Wales.—*Tracts
of Powys*, p. 30, *note.*

[1] Of the house of Heton, in Northumberland, was Sir Thomas Grey, who fell in that
strange unintelligible plot at Southampton with the Earl of Cambridge, in the second
year of Henry the Fifth. Shakespeare has told this story pathetically, but I conceive
unjustly to the sufferers. They were put to death, and their crimes rather declared
afterwards to the people, than proved to public satisfaction before their execution.
Cambridge had married the heiress of the Crowns of England and Wales. Shakespeare
has heightened another scene, and marries Anne, the daughter and coheiress of Warwick
(the widow, as he states her, of Edward Prince of Wales) to Richard Duke of Gloucester,
who murdered her husband ; whereas Anne was never married to Edward, but
betrothed to him only.

Garter, till with the Duke of Clarence,[1] and other distinguished soldiers,

Qui multum fleti ad superos, belloque caduci,

he fell in the unfortunate action at Baugé in 1421. By his wife Joan he left a son, Henry de Powys, who is styled Earl of Tankerville. He was a child at his father's death, and in the sixth of Henry the Sixth was knighted with his young Sovereign at Leicester by the regent Duke of Bedford. He married Antigony, the illegitimate daughter of Humphrey, the regent Duke of Gloucester, and died in the twenty-eighth of Henry the Sixth, leaving issue Richard and Humphrey, and a daughter Elizabeth married to Sir Roger Kynaston of Hordley; whence a claim in that family to this fee Barony.[2]

[1] Clarence had been deceived by false intelligence. He thought the van of the Scots had been separated from the main body, and attacked them with his cavalry alone. Finding his error, he fought desperately to redeem it ; but numbers overpowered him. A Knight, named Swinton, wounded him in the face, and the mace of Lord Buchan deprived him of life. In the battle, besides Clarence, the Lords Roos and Tankerville were slain ; the Earls of Dorset, Somerset, and Huntingdon, were taken prisoners. Buchan, who had been made Constable of France for this service, lost both life and victory, four years after, in the battle of Vernuoil against Bedford, the younger brother of Clarence. Petrarch attributes the defeat suffered by the French, about this time, to their drunkenness. Their success under Dumourier of late is said to have arisen from it.

[2] The barony of Powys which fell into abeyance on the death of Edward Grey, in 1551-2, has been the subject of some litigation. It was claimed in 1584, by Henry Vernon, Esq. of Stokesay, in the County of Salop, in right of his grandmother, Anne, cousin and coheir of Edward the last Lord Powys, but the claim was not prosecuted. In 1731, it was again formally claimed by John Kynaston, Esq., of Hordley, in the County of Salop, whose claim was opposed on behalf of the Vernon family, by Sir Nathaniel Curzon, Bart. (ancestor of the present Lord Scarsdale). The petitions and documents in support thereof on both sides were referred to the [Lords'] Committee of

To return to Richard. He shared in that contentious time, and was attainted in the Parliament at Coventry in the short interval of Henry's, or rather his Queen's, success, in 1460. I find him next restored, and at the siege of Alnwick with the Earl of Warwick, in the second of Edward the Fourth; and in the sixth of that king he died, leaving by his wife Margaret, the daughter of James Lord Audley, a son John, then six years old. He was a soldier also, as most men in that time, of his station, seem to have been. He served under the Earl of Oxford at the siege and sack of Ardres. He ·had summons to Parliament from the twenty-second of Edward the Fourth, by the style of Grey de Powys, to his death. At the former

A.D.
1494

Privileges, but Mr. Kynaston dying in 1733, no decision was given. In 1800, Mr. Kynaston's grandson, John Kynaston Powell, Esq., of Hardwick, in the County of Salop, again claimed the barony. Counter petitions were presented to the House of Lords, and referred to their Committee of Privileges, by Lords Scarsdale, Lilford, and Powis. The Committee having been informed that there were then living coheirs of John, Earl of Worcester (who died in 1470), the son of John Lord Tiptoft, by Joyce de Charleton, coheiress with Joan de Charleton, wife of Sir John Grey (Earl of Tankerville), and lineal ancestor of the said Edward Grey, directed notice of the claim to be given to them as possible coheirs of the barony, whereupon Mr. Kynaston Powell ceased to prosecute his claim.—(See account of Proceedings in *Mont. Coll.*, i., pp. 362-423.)—*Ed.*

In or about the year 1447, Henry Grey, at the instigation it is said of the Queen (Margaret of Anjou) under some pretence, summoned Sir Gruffudd Fychan, of Guilsfield (who as we have seen, *ante* p. 72 *note*, had taken an active part in the arrest of Sir John Oldcastle), to appear before him at the castle of Pool. He at first demurred, but receiving what he considered "a safe conduct," he resolved to comply with the summons. No sooner, however, had he arrived at the court-yard of the castle, than he was apprehended, and, in the presence of Henry Grey, beheaded on the spot. Several Welsh poets wrote pathetic elegies upon his death. Sir Gruffudd had been knighted, it is said, on the field of Agincourt for his distinguished exploits in that battle.—*(Mont. Coll.*, i., p. 335, and ii., p. 139.)—*Ed.*

period he was just come of age; but the Barony was his own
since the attainder and execution of Tiptoft, the learned but
temporizing Earl of Worcester,[1] during the short restoration of
Henry the Sixth, when the abeyance ceased. John married
Anne, the daughter of William Herbert Earl of Pembroke, the
first of that name, and left a son John. He died at the age
of nineteen, leaving by his wife Margaret, daughter of Edmund
Lord Dudley, a son Edward, aged one year. Edward married
Anne, one of the daughters[2] of Charles Brandon, Duke of
Suffolk. By her he had no issue; but by Jane Orwel, daughter[3]
of Sir Lewis Orwel, he left four illegitimate children, Edward
Grey, and three daughters. The last Lord served in France,
and attended his father-in-law, Suffolk, in the campaign of 1524,
when some French towns were taken, but nothing very memorable done, or perhaps in the way of conquest should be
attempted.[4] He died in 1551. He suffered a recovery of his

[1] The first Earl of Worcester of the name of Tiptoft was son to Joyce, the younger
sister and coheiress of the Charletons. "When he fell," says Caxton, "the axe did
then at one blow cut off more learning than was left in the heads of the surviviug
nobility."

[2] By his second wife Anne. Suffolk's third wife was Mary, sister to Henry the
Eighth, and widow of Lewis the Twelfth of France.

[3] "Nothing is more frequent in the Knightly ages," says Mr. Andrews, "than to
find the daughters of Barons, living unmarried with Kings and Noblemen. So
Humphrey Duke of Gloucester married Eleanor, daughter of Reginald Lord Cobham,
whom he had long kept as his mistress. In like manner the Cardinal Beaufort had left
an illegitimate daughter by Alice, daughter of Fitzalan, Earl of Arundel."

[4] The Parliament of 1421 presented an address to Henry the Fifth, in which they
observed that the conquest of France would be the ruin of England; and the reasons
are obvious. In 1420 they had presented two petitions to the same effect.

estates, and by feoffment, will and codicil, settled the same in default of lawful issue on Jane Orwel for her life, remainder to Edward Grey, his natural son by her, in tail. In 1568[1] this Edward Grey conveys the manor of Plâs dinas to Edward Kynaston of Hordley, still in the family, in consideration of his relinquishing his claim to the other estates, as heir at law to the last Lord. In the twenty-ninth of Elizabeth the same Edward Grey conveys the Lordship and Castle of Powys to Sir Edward Herbert, the second son of that able statesman, fine scholar, and eminent soldier, William Herbert, Earl of Pembroke,[2] the second of his name and title, who flourished

---

[1] This date was wrongly given in the text as 1560 ; it should be 1568, being the tenth Elizabeth.—See *Tracts of Powys* and *Mont. Coll.*, i., p. 378.—*Ed.*

[2] Sir John Price in an Epistle Dedicatory to this Lord, with his Latin defence of the British History against Polydore Vergil, the last collector of the Peterpence in England, compliments Pembroke as a scholar and critic. Sir John did not live to publish this book, which was printed by his son, Richard Price, in 1573, about twenty years after the father's death. Sir John first published the Lord's Prayer, Creed, and the Ten Commandments in the Welsh tongue [in 1546], and gave us the topography of Wales, which was augmented by Humphrey Llwyd, and stands at the head of our earlier Welsh histories. He had also assisted his friend Leland in his Assertio Arthurii. Sir John Price was of Brecknockshire, a Doctor of both Laws, and one of the King's Council in the Court of the Marches ; and, says Mr. Morris, "was a man of good abilities, and had opportunities of understanding the history of the Ancient Britons, being one of the Commissioners employed by Henry the Eighth to survey the Monasteries, that were to be dissolved. By his defence he does not appear to have carefully perused the British copy of Tyssilio, interrupted perhaps by the hurry of business ; for he hath not urged all that he might have said to the matter in dispute, provided he had carefully compared the original with the translation, and if he had also had a thorough knowledge of our Ancient British Bards, who best knew the use of words, and whose works were indeed the root and foundation of the Ancient British History ; the histories of the origin of most nations being on the same footing."

under four Princes,[1] of different aspects, and in difficult times. Sir Edward died in 1594, having restored the Castle; and had sepulture at [Welsh] Pool. He married an heiress of the Stanleys of Hertfordshire, the daughter of Thomas Stanley of Standon, Master of the Mint, and was succeeded by his son, William, made Knight of the Bath, at the coronation of James the First, and by his son, Charles, created Lord Powys.[2] He married Eleanor, the daughter of Henry Percy, the eighth Earl of Northumberland, and had one son, Percy, who succeeded him. Percy had been made Knight and Baronet, his father then living, by James the First, in his rage of Knighthood[3] and Baronetism. He died in 1666, and was buried at [Welsh] Pool, leaving issue by his wife, Elizabeth, sister of the first Earl of

---

[1] Henry the Eighth, Edward, Mary and Elizabeth.

[2] In his time, Powis Castle was besieged and taken by the Parliament army, under Sir Thomas Myddelton, on the 2nd October, 1644, and Lord Powis was taken prisoner, and sent to London upon his parol, where he remained at his lodging in the Strand ; his estates being sequestrated, and £4 per week being allowed him for his maintenance by the Committee of Sequestrators. Besides his son Percy, he had two daughters, Katherine, wife of Sir James Palmer ; and Lucy, wife of William Abingdon, Esq.—*Ed.*

[3] This ceremony, and so often repeated, must have been disagreeable to James. Sir Kenelm Digby tells us, " he hated a drawn sword, since the fright his mother was in, during her pregnancy, at the sight of the swords, with which David Rizzio, her Secretary, was assassinated in her presence ; and hence it came," says Sir Kenelm, "that her son had such an aversion all his life to a drawn sword.* I remember," proceeds he, " when he dubbed me Knight, in the ceremony of putting a naked sword on my shoulder, he could not endure to look upon it, but turned his face another way ; insomuch that, in lieu of touching my shoulder, he had almost thrust the point into my eyes, had not the Duke of Buckingham guided his hand aright." I remember to have

* James is said to have been painted abroad with a scabbard without a sword, and with a sword, which nobody could draw, though several were pulling at it.—*Passim.*

Craven, one son, William,[1] who was created Earl by Charles the Second, and by his brother James Marquis, and finally after his abdication Duke of Powys. He married Elizabeth, daughter of the Marquis of Worcester, and died in the Court of St. Germain's in 1696. He was succeeded by his son, William, who was restored to the Earldom and Marquisate. He married a co-heiress of the Prestons of Furness in Lancashire, and by her had two sons, William and Edward, and many daughters. Lady Mary, the eldest,[2] fell under the lash of Pope. The last Marquis, William, died without issue, and left his estates to Henry Arthur Herbert of Oakley Park, created Earl Powys by George the Second, who afterwards married Barbara, niece to the Marquis, and daughter of his brother, Lord Edward. The

heard, that when he knighted old Sir William Morice of Clenennev in Carnarvonshire, and turning upon him, after he quitted his sword, " By Christ," says the King, " I fear I have knighted an old woman," and Sir William's picture justifies the notion. James was personally not unknown to the Welsh. He had progressed to Chester in 1617, and was attended by great numbers of our countrymen, who came out of curiosity to see him. The weather was very dry, the roads dusty, and the King almost suffocated. He did not know well how to get civilly rid of them, when one of his attendants, putting his head out of the coach, said, " It was his Majesty's pleasure, that those, who were the best Gentlemen, should ride forwards." Away scampered the Welsh ; and one solitary man was left behind. " And so, Sir," says the King to him, " and you are not a Gentleman then ? " " Oh yes, and please hur Majesty, hur is as good a Shentle-man, as the rest ; but hur Ceffyl, God help hur, is not so good."

[1] He had also a daughter Mary who married George, Lord Talbot.—*Ed.*

[2] But nobler scenes Maria's dreams unfold,
Hereditary realms, and worlds of gold.
She went to France with a large sum of money, got in the Mississippi bubble, with a view of marrying the Pretender, and she had a notion also of going as an adventurer to the South American Gold Mines.

present Earl[1] is the son of this alliance, and is descended from
Sir Richard Herbert, who, on their defeat at Banbury,[2] was
taken and beheaded with his brother, the Earl of Pembroke,[3]
by the rebel army, and in retaliation of similar cruelties, particularly in North Wales, committed by their own. Richard,
the second son of Sir Richard, who died at Banbury, was great
grandfather to the historical, the philosophical, that right whimsical
Peer, Edward Herbert, first Baron of Cherbury; the man at once
and together, the negociator, the scholar, statesman, soldier; the
genius and absurdity of his time and nation.[4]

[1] This was George Edward Henry Arthur Herbert, who died unmarried, in 1801, when
the title became extinct. The estates passed to his only surviving sister, Lady Henrietta
Antonia, wife of Edward, second Lord Clive, who in May, 1804, was created Earl of Powis
—the first of the present line. He died May 16th, 1839, and was succeeded by his son,
Edward, second Earl of Powis, who died January 17th, 1848. Upon his death,
Edward James, the present Earl, inherited the title and estates.—*Ed.*

[2] At the above mentioned battle, Sir Richard mowed his way through the whole
army of Northern men, with his poleaxe, twice and back again; a deed of strength
and valour hardly credible! When ordered for execution, Pembroke asked not for
his own life, but wished his brother, Sir Richard, might be spared, as he was a soldier,
he said, fit to serve any Prince in Christendom. Sir Richard was higher by the head
than any one in the army.—*Life of Lord Herbert.*

[3] Pembroke beheaded Thomas ab Robin of Cochwillan, of the Tribe of Marchudd,
near the castle of Conway, for that he was a follower of the House of Lancaster; and
his wife, it is said, carried away his head in her apron; and, adds Sir John [Wynn] of
Gwydir, "Earl Herbert's desolation consumed the whole borough of Llanrwst, and all
the Vale of Conway, to cold coals,* whereof the print is yet extant, the very stones of
the ruins of many habitations carrying yet the colour of the fire."

[4] This first Lord of Cherbury, in his early youth, had spent some short time in the vale
of Clwyd. Thus he speaks in respect to that matter. "After I had attained the age of
nine, during all which time I lived in my grandmother's house at Eyton, my parents
thought fit to send me to some place, where I might learn the Welsh tongue, as

* Cinders.

L

To proceed with the descendants: The Kynastons, of whom
were various branches, seated at Stocks, Morton, Walford, Shotton,

believing it necessary for me to treat with my friends and tenants, who understood no
other language. Whereupon I was recommended to Mr. Edward Thelwal, of Plâs y
ward in Denbighshire. This gentleman I must remember with honor, as having of
himself acquired the exact knowledge of Greek, Latin, French, Italian and Spanish,
and all other learning, having for that purpose neither gone beyond seas, nor so much
as had the benefit of any Universities. Besides, he was of that rare temper in
governing his choler, that I never saw him angry during the time of my stay there,
and have heard so much of him many years before ; when occasion of offence was given
him, I have seen him redden in the face, and after remain for a time silent ; but when
he spake, his words were so calm and gentle, that I found he had digested his choler ;
yet I confess I could never obtain that perfection, as being subject to choler and passion
more than I ought, and generally to speak my mind freely, and indeed rather to imitate
those, who having fire within doors chuse rather to give it vent, than suffer it to burn
the house. I commend much more the manner of Mr. Thelwal ; and certainly he,
that can forbear speaking for some while, will remit much of his passion ; but as I
could not learn much of him in this way, so I did as little profit in learning the Welsh,
or any other of those languages that worthy gentleman understood, having a tertian
ague for the most part of the time, being nine months, I staid in his house." From
comparing dates it must have happened, that, whilst young Herbert was at Plâs y
ward, the lady of the house, Catherine of Beren, was living. She had married Edward
Thelwal to her fourth husband. She was a singular character ; and I wonder Herbert
should not have noticed her. By Thelwal she had no children ; by her first husband,
Salisbury, the heir of Lleweni, she had Thomas Salisbury, who was executed in
Babington's Plot the twenty-first of September, 1587. Her second son, Sir John
Salisbury the Strong, succeeded at Lleweni. Her estate at Beren had followed the
heiress of the Lleweni house into the Combermere family, and was sold by the present
[1799] Sir Robert Cotton to the late Honourable Thomas Fitzmaurice. Catherine's
second husband was Sir Richard Clough ; by him she had two daughters ; one married
to Wynn of Melai ; the other to Salisbury of Bachegraig, whence is descended our
ingenious country-woman, Mrs. Piozzi.* Her third husband was Maurice Wynn of
Gwydir ; her daughter by Maurice married Simon Thelwal, the eldest son of her last
husband by a former marriage. Simon's son, Edward Thelwal, married Sidney, the
daughter of William Wynn of Garthgynan, the fourth son of Sir John [Wynn] of

* Hester Lynch Salisbury, Dr. Johnson's friend, better known as Mrs. Thrale (her first husband's
surname). She died at an advanced age in 1821.—*Ed.*

CATHARINE of BEREN.

Bradenheath, Otley,[1] Hordley, Hardwick, Bryngwyn,[2] Trewylan,[3] Lee, Kinersley, Knockin, Ryton, Llwyn y Mapsis, and Pant y

Gwydir, the historian; and their daughter and heiress married Sir William Williams of Llanforda, the eldest son of the Speaker. Hence the connection with Sir John Wynn of Wynnstay, who was first cousin to Sidney, and who left his great property to Mr. Williams, her grandson, afterwards Sir Watkin Williams Wynn, the grandfather of the present [1799] Sir Watkin Williams Wynn. Catherine died in the life of Thelwal, and was buried at Llanufudd without a monument, notwithstanding her numerous descendants; from which she was called Mam Cymru, the mother of Wales. [It is related that after the funeral of her first husband, Catherine left the church in company with Maurice Wynn who proposed to her, but he was too late, Sir Richard Clough having done so and been accepted on the way *to* the graveyard. She promised him, however, that in case there should be another opportunity, he should be her third husband, and he was. The portrait here given is of her when a young and blooming woman. At the Wrexham Exhibition, in 1876, the Rev. R. H. Howard exhibited one taken of her in old age.—*Ed.*]

[1] Of the House of Otley was Sir Francis Kynaston, of whom and his wife an alabaster monument remains in the church of Ellesmere. He died in 1590. There was another and later Sir Francis of the same House, an Esquire of the body to Charles the First, who translated the loves of Troilus and Cressida from Chaucer into Latin. Otley came to the Kynastons by the marriage of Kynaston of Stocks to Elizabeth, daughter and heiress to William Otley of Otley. [The Kynastons of Otley or Oteley, became extinct in the male line, on the death in 1781, without issue, of Edward Kynaston, when the estate passed to his nephew, the Rev. Charles Mainwaring, whose descendant, S. K. Mainwaring, Esq., is the present owner. *(Burke's Landed Gentry.)—Ed.*]

[2] Bryngwyn is in the parish of Llanfechain, County of Montgomery. Mary Kynaston, heiress of Bryngwyn, conveyed the estate on her marriage to William Mostyn, Esq., of the ancient Flintshire family of Mostyn. Their son, William, assumed the additional name of Owen on succeeding to the estate of Woodhouse, County of Salop, and represented the County of Montgomery in four Parliaments, namely, from 1774 to 1795, the date of his death. The heavy costs of contested elections, amounting it is said to £70,000, necessitated the sale of Bryngwyn, and it now belongs to the coheiresses of the late Martin Williams, Esq. *(Mont. Coll.*, v., p. 255*).—Ed.*

[3] Trewylan is in the parish of Llansantffraid, County of Montgomery. Edward Kynaston, Esq., the last male heir of this branch, died without issue in 1778, having by his Will entailed this estate upon the male issue of his cousin, Catherine, the wife

byrsle,[1] descend from a common ancestor, Sir Gruffudd Fychan of Caer Hywel, the son of Iorwerth, the son of Maredudd, the son of Bleddyn, the founder of the Tribe. The family of Hordley and Hardwick is still extant.[2] It descends from Sir Roger Kynaston of Hordley, fourth son of Gruffudd Kynaston of Stocks. Sir Roger was an eminent soldier and partizan of the House of York, and distinguished in the battles of Blore, Banbury, and Barnet. On occasion of the first were given him the Arms of Audley, the enemy's general, who fell in the fight, and, as the family papers inform me, by Sir Roger himself.[3] I conjecture his crest, an armed hand, in the act to strike, issuing from a sun in full glory, is derived from Barnet battle, and allusory to the accident which gave Edward the victory.[4] Sir Roger was

of . . . Moody, Esq., upon condition that they took the surname of Kynaston. Her great grandson, Edward Kynaston Kynaston, Esq., is the present owner of the estate. *(Mont. Coll.*, iv., p. 154.)—*Ed.*

[1] John Salisbury, in 1660, records an Arthur Kynaston of Pant y byrsle, then living as a famous and faithful genealogist. His correspondence with Mr. Robert Vaughan of Hengwrt is still extant in manuscript. [The Kynaston family of Pant y byrsle ended in an heiress, Catherine, who married Richard Jones of St. Martin's. *(Hist. Powys Fadog*, iv., p. 94.)—*Ed.*]

[2] Sir John Roger Kynaston, Bart., who died unmarried, 7th March, 1866, was the last lineal male representative of this stock. Upon the death of his sister Amy, widow of the Rev. Evelyn Sutton, on 19th October, 1867, the Hardwick estates passed by devise to her grandnephew, the Rev. Walter Charles Edward Owen, who has taken the name of Kynaston.—*Ed.*

[3] The descendants of Sir Roger bear the Audley Arms in their first quarter.

[4] The devise on the Arms and Ensigns of the Earl of Oxford, a Lancastrian, was a star shooting forth rays, and Edward's was a sun. Warwick's men, seeing the star advancing through a fog, mistook it for Edward's standard, and fell upon their friends

Constable of Harlech Castle, thrice Sheriff of Shropshire, and
once of Merioneth; an office then of trust and emolument.
He married, first, Elizabeth, the daughter of Lord Cobham, and
widow of Lord Strange; by her he had one son, Sir Thomas
Kynaston, who died without issue. Sir Roger died the eleventh
of Henry the Seventh. His second wife was Elizabeth, daughter
of Henry Grey, Earl of Tankerville, by Antigony, daughter of
Humphrey Duke of Gloucester. By her he had Humphrey,
called the Wild; a gentleman remembered by many strange
pranks; still the talk of the neighbouring peasantry. The cave
in the rock at Ness cliff, called Kynaston's cave, was the retreat
of himself and mad companions. He was outlawed the sixth
of Henry the Seventh, pardoned the next year, and died in
1534.[1]

To return to the common ancestor, Sir Gruffudd Fychan. He
was father to another Gruffudd Fychan, the father of Gruffudd
Fychan of Stocks, the father of Philip, the father of Madog who
first took the name of Kynaston, the father of John, Steward
of Ellesmere in the thirteenth of Richard the Second, the father
of Madog Kynaston of Stocks, killed in the battle of Shrewsbury, who married Isolda, daughter of the Earl of Northumberland, and was father of John Kynaston, who had his pardon
from Henry the Fourth, the father of Gruffudd Kynaston of

with such fury, that they were broken and dispersed, before the Earl of Oxford could
rectify the error. These last, believing themselves betrayed, fled towards the enemy
with great precipitation.

[1] See note, p. 44, *ante*

Stocks, Steward of Ellesmere in the ninth of Henry the Sixth, father of Sir Roger of Hordley his fourth son the soldier, who was the father of Humphrey the Wild, the father of Edward Kynaston, who died the thirty-fourth of Elizabeth, the father of Roger Kynaston, the father of Edward Kynaston, the father of Roger Kynaston, the father of Edward Kynaston, member for Shrewsbury, the father of John Kynaston, who sat for Shropshire in many Parliaments, the grandfather by his son Roger of my worthy friend, John Kynaston Powel Esquire, the present [1799] member, to whom I am particularly indebted for his liberal communications.[1]

From Cynrig efell, Lord of Eglwysegle,[2] the twin son of Madog ab Maredudd, and great grandson of the founder of the tribe, are descended the Davieses of Llannerch or Lleweni fechan, and Gwasanau; the last, it is said, is a corruption of Hosannah, and allusory to the Alleluiatic[3] victory gained over the Saxons and Picts beneath it. This old mansion was

---

[1] In 1818, in consideration of his descent from the ancient and noble family of Grey, Lords of Powys, a baronetcy was conferred on Mr. Kynaston Powell, with remainder to his brother, the Rev. Edward Kynaston, who succeeded him on his death in 1822. The Rev. Sir Edward Kynaston died in April, 1839, leaving besides a daughter, one son Sir John Roger Kynaston, of Hardwick, the third Baronet, who died unmarried in March, 1866, when the title became extinct.—*Ed.*

[2] Eglwysegle is a division of the Lordship of Bromfield, and contains the townships of Trebibisham, Broughton, Stanstye villa, Acton, Morton Wallicorum, and Erddig.

[3] "The Victoria Alleluiatica, fought in 420 between the Britons, headed by the French Bishops, Germanus* and Lupus, and a crowd of Pagan Picts and Saxons, who were carrying desolation through the country. This event happened in Easter week, when

> * Quid taceam, Germane, tuam sine sanguine palmam,
> Victaque Cambriacis Saxona tela sonis?—*Passim.*

garrisoned in the civil wars, and taken from the royalists by
the Parliament General, Sir William Brereton. Llannerch came
to the family on the marriage of Robert Davies,[1] of Gwasanau,
with Anne, the eldest daughter and heiress of Sir Peter Mutton,
Chief Justice of North Wales. The last of the male line at
Llannerch was John Davies, who died a bachelor in 1785, and
was succeeded by his sisters, coheiresses; the elder, Letitia of
Llannerch, married to Daniel Leo, Esquire;[2] the younger, Mary

the Christian army, wet with their recent baptism in the river Alun, were led by their
holy commanders against the Pagan host. Germanus instructed them to attend to the
word he gave, and repeat it. Accordingly he pronounced that of Alleluia. His soldiers
caught the sacred sound, and repeated it with such extatic force, that the hills
resounding with the cry struck terror into the enemy, who fled on all sides; numbers
perished by the sword, and numbers in the adjacent river."†—*Pennant.*

[1] This Gentleman was grandfather by his son Mutton Davies to Robert Davies of
Llannerch, an able naturalist and Welsh antiquary; and several of his letters to men
eminent in the same studies remain. He collected the valuable library of MSS. that were
at Llannerch.* His grandson, Robert, the father of the last gentleman, was of a very
hospitable turn; almost daily he had a led horse taken with him to St. Asaph, ready
saddled, to bring home to Llannerch any friend that might not be so immediately ready
to start with him. The old gardens at Llannerch are within my memory; they were
made by Mutton Davies in the foreign taste, with images and water tricks. Among
the rest you were led to a sun-dial, which as you approached, spouted in your face; on
it was written:

> *Alas! my friend, time soon will overtake you;*
> *And if you do not cry, by G—d I'll make you.*

[2] Llannerch is now the property of the Dod family, the late Whitehall Dod, Esq.,
having succeeded to the estate on the decease in 1841 of his grandmother, Mrs. Leo's
cousin, Anne Elizabeth, daughter and heiress of Peter Davies, Esq., of Llannerch, and
wife of the Rev. George Allanson, the last representative of the Davies family.—*Ed.*

† The river at present would not drown a puppy. It might happen in a great flood.

* Five volumes of these are now at Owston in Yorkshire, and the same number have been presented to
the library of Jesus College, Oxford. Davies died May 22nd, 1728, aged 44; and a superb monument has
been erected to his memory in Mold church.—*Ed.*

of Gwasanau, to Philip Puleston,[1] of Hafod y Wern,[2] Esquire.

The Eytons of Coed Llai, or Leeswood, have the same source from Cynrig. They are represented in the Reverend Hope Wynn Eyton, Vicar of Mold.[3] His ancestor, Gruffudd ab Nicholas ab Deicus, married Margaret, the daughter of the old Bosworth soldier, John ab Ellis Eyton, who lies buried at Rhiwabon; and although her husband was descended from Bleddyn ab Cynfyn, and her father from Tudor Trevor, she called all her children after his name of Eyton, and all her sons John, in affection to him also.

From Cynrig descended the Wynnes of Tower. The line ended in Roger Wynne, the younger and surviving brother of that facetious old Gentleman, Dr. William Wynne. Roger died without issue, and left the Tower estate to his widow, who gave it to her niece, the lady of the Reverend Hope Wynne Eyton, the present [1799] worthy possessor.[4] An odd circumstance happened in this house. During the wars of York and Lancaster,

---

[1] The only issue of this marriage was a daughter Frances, who married Bryan Cooke, Esq., whose grandson Philip Bryan Davies Cooke, Esq., of Owston and Gwysanau, is the present owner.—*Ed.*

[2] Ieuan ab Hywel ab Maredudd, the fourth in descent from Rhodri, Lord of Anglesey (the brother of our Prince, Dafydd ab Owain Gwynedd) had a third daughter and coparcener, that married Hywel ab Gronw ab Hywel of Maelor, and by him had two daughters, viz., Gwerfyl, married to Tudor ab Hob y dili ; and Alice, married to John Puleston, a younger son of Emral : She brought Hafod y Wern into that family.—*Gwydir History.*

[3] He died in 1822, having been thirty years Vicar of Mold, and was succeeded in the estate by his eldest son, the late John Wynne Eyton, Esq., who died without issue about 1857.—*Ed.*

[4] See note *supra.*

the place belonged to Reinallt[1]. ab Gruffudd ab Bleddyn, one of the six gallant Welsh captains,[2] who defended Harlech Castle against the fourth Edward. He and his people had continual frays with the citizens of Chester. In 1465 a considerable number of the latter came to Mold fair; a fight ensued and much slaughter on both sides, but Reinallt had the advantage ; took prisoner Robert Byrne, linen-draper, Mayor of Chester, led him to his Tower, and hung him with his own halter in the hall, where the iron staple, to which he was suspended, still remains.[3]

[1] In Reinallt's time the people of Chester so cordially hated the Welsh, that they would not permit any of that nation to inhabit among them unmolested. Lewys Glyn Cothi, a noted bard of that age, and a sharer in the wars and fortune of Jasper Earl of Pembroke (uncle to Henry the Seventh) intended to settle in Chester, and to that end married a widow there; but the next day the citizens, under some pretence or other, took from him all his household furniture, and insisted on his quitting the city. This treatment so much enraged him, that he immediately wrote a poem, which is still extant, and sent it to Reinallt of the Tower, petitioning his assistance to revenge the injury done him by the men of Chester. Reinallt, being ripe for the enterprize, collected his people, went to Chester, and put the citizens, as many as fell into his hands, to the sword ; and if we can credit another poem sent to Reinallt from a Bard of Meirionydd, called Tudur Penllyn, to thank him for that day's work, he had driven several of them, like a flock of sheep, to be drowned in the river Dee.

[2] Another of these valiant Welshmen was Dafydd ab Ieuan ab Einion, who baffled for a long time all the endeavours of Pembroke to take the Castle. "I held a tower in France," said he, "till all the old women in Wales heard of it, and now the old women of France shall hear how I defended this Welsh Castle."—*Gwydir History.*

[3] Another story is told of Reinallt. Four cousins having met at an inn, began to boast of their various exploits. The first was David ab Siancyn ab David Crach of Nant Conwy who began, "This is the dagger with which I slew the Red Judge on the bench at Denbigh." The second, David ab Ieuan ab Einion (referred to *supra*), said "This is the sword and this the ashen spear with which I slew the Sheriff at Llandrillo." The third, Reinallt ab Gruffudd, said "This is the sword with which I slew the Mayor

M

The Parrys of Plâs newydd in Denbighshire, and of Warfield in Berkshire, are of the ancient stock of Cynrig efell. They are very respectably represented in Richard Parry Esquire. His ancestor, Richard Parry, Bishop of St. Asaph,[1] succeeded Morgan[2]

in the See. Morgan, encouraged by Archbishop Whitgift, had

---

of Chester when he came to burn my house." Then they inquired of the fourth, Gruffudd Fychan ab Ieuan ab Einion, a quiet and peaceable man, "What daring deed he had ever performed?" when he replied, "This is the sword with which, had I drawn it in dishonour, I should have accomplished as much as the best of you did."

In two Pedigrees at Nannau, it is recorded that Reinallt died at the age of twenty-eight, at Llandderfel near Bala, in 1466—two years *before* the surrender of Harlech Castle—*(Hist. Powys Fadog*, v., p. 233-5) ; but this can hardly be correct, as his name appears in the printed Rolls of Parliament as one of the defenders of the Castle.—*Ed.*

[1] Bishop Parry was the son of John Parry, Esq., of Pwll Halawg, Dyffryn Clwyd, and Elen his wife. He was born in 1560, and died in 1623. His father was tenth in descent from Cynrig Efell, and so to Bleddyn ab Cynfyn ; his mother was ninth in descent from Iorwerth Foel, lord of Chirk of the house of Tudor Trevor ; while his wife, Gwen, the daughter of John ab Rhys Wynn, of Llwyn Yn, was a descendant of Edwyn ab Goronwy, founder of the twelfth Noble Tribe of North Wales. On the 27th September, 1624, the Bishop's widow married Thomas Mostyn, Esq., of Rhyd, and on the same day her eldest son and heir, Richard Parry, of Pwll Halawg, married Mr. Mostyn's daughter Mary ; and Mr. Mostyn's son and heir, Thomas Mostyn, married Bishop Parry's youngest daughter Ann. The last Richard Parry, of Llwyn Yn and of Warfield, who died in 1834, was lineally descended from the Bishop Parry. He devised this ancient patrimony to his nephew, Col. Francis Haygarth, the present owner. *(Dwnn's Vis.,* ii., p. 320, *note,* and *Hist. Powys Fadog,* v., p. 223.)—*Ed.*

[2] Morgan was of the Tribe of Nefydd hardd or the handsome ; was of St. John's, Cambridge ; Vicar of Welsh-Pool, and afterwards had Llanrhaiadr mochnant. He was made Bishop of Llandaff in 1595, and translated in 1601 to St. Asaph, where he died in 1604. Morgan in his great work, the Welsh Bible, acknowledges therein his obligations to Dr. Powel, the historian, Bishop Vaughan[*] of London, Archdeacon Prŷs,

[*] Dr. Richard Vaughan was a native of Carnarvonshire, of St. John's College, Cambridge, Chaplain to Elizabeth, and successively Bishop of Bangor, Chester, and London. His merit was universally allowed to be equal to his dignity in the Church, but none of his writings were ever printed. Fuller tells us, in his usual style, that he was a very corpulent man, but spiritually minded ; and Owen, his countryman, has addressed to him one of his best complimentary epigrams.—*Granger.*

published the Welsh version of the old and new Testament;
the latter he had corrected only from the former translation of

and to Dr. Gabriel Goodman, Dean of Westminster. Goodman was a pious, profitable,
and learned man; a native of Ruthin, where he founded the school, and an hospital. He
supported Camden in his peregrinations, who through his interest was made Under-
master of Westminster school. Dr. Goodman translated into English, as we now have
it, the first Epistle to the Corinthians. He was forty years Dean of Westminster, and
died in 1601. His nephew, Godfrey Goodman, Bishop of Gloucester, was a man of
learning also, but in many respects a strange character. He died a Roman Catholic, as
he professes himself in his extraordinary will.† He wrote a panegyric on Cromwell,
who ejected him of his preferments. "He was," says Echard, "the only Apostate
Bishop since the Reformation, and was the only Bishop, that left children to beg their
bread;" whereas he was never married, or had any. He died in 1655, and was buried
by his directions near the font in St. Margaret's, Westminster. To revert to Camden.
The accounts of Wales in his Britannia have but little information. We have a
tradition, that he came no further into North Wales than Corwen, was taken there for
an English spy, and insulted by the people. This put an end to his Welsh travels.
Mr. Morris complains of this great man bitterly, in his correspondence with Mr. Richard.
"Have you heard," says he, "what success my reveries had, in converting the Doctor
(Philips) and his friend Pegge from the Camdenian faction? I am now, at my leisure
hours, drawing out some heads on the same subject for the Cymrodorion, who talk of
publishing memoirs, in the nature of those of the royal Academy of Sciences at Paris.
All that I am afraid of is, that we shall draw so many English antiquaries about our
ears, by these mountain antiquities, that we shall be borne down by the noise, like a
poor fellow with a good cause, whose rich antagonist had fee'd all the Council on the
Circuit against him. Neither truth nor reason can withstand the madness of a mob,
composed of all languages, and all manner of learning. It requires the knowledge of
a Selden or an Usher, to stop the current of such a monstrous stream, and to bring
truth into its old channel. If such a person as you had a paper war with a powerful
party, you can call to your aid old Homer, Hesiod, Pindar, etc. etc., whose very names
would make a London bookseller to tremble. But there is a set of these people in
London engaged in the publication of Camden's Britannia, as rich as Jews, and would
search all the garrets in town for writers, if their darling Diana of the Ephesians was
touched; and they would mind no more to hear of Taliesin, Aneurin Gwawdrydd, and
the Triads, than if they were Hottentots from the Cape of Good Hope, and would get
affidavits inserted in the public papers, that these were three infidels, that came over

† See Appendix xvii.

William Salesbury[1] and Bishop Davies.[2]   In 1620, Bishop Parry,

with the last India Ships, to the great danger of the Church and Constitution. You then, who have such powerful auxiliaries from the coasts of Greece and Italy at your back, should break the ice, in publishing something on this head, and I wish you would. You will see, in reading Camden's Britannia, room enough to animadvert upon him, without any great stock of British antiquities. A Cambro-Briton, with a sharp eye and sound judgment, would make such remarks upon him, as would make an English reader wonder, where his own eyes have been all the while. Attack him with your pen and ink. It is not barking at a lion, it is standing a friend to truth. Attack this great Goliah in his heel, or some vulnerable part, and you will, like little David, give a good account of him bye and bye. The Edition, I think, you have of him is his first, A.D. 1585, where you have him unguarded, and without armour. Begin with his Celtic words, which he endeavours to explain by the Welsh, and you will see that he knew nothing of the matter, tho' positive as he is about our etymologies and antiquities. Why should we bear abuse, if we can defend ourselves and ancient authors ? Ask him how he came to use the fallacy of deriving Servius's Gessi, viri fortes, from Gwâs dewr ; for the comparison is, Gessi and Gwâs, and so on ; and room enough for you to play your great guns against the enemy. Do'nt flinch from attacking Camden : I will send you an account, when I have leisure, of some parts of his body, that are not invulnerable ; not about his heels, but his head. His Britannia is the great oracle of the English, and is swallowed without chewing, because the pill is gilt. Take off the gilding, and you will find sad stuff under it. The design was great, the structure magnificent, but the performance or execution poor and shabby, notwithstanding that it was covered with great learning and industry. But the case is, the foundation was bad, and truth has suffered to serve a national pride. The memory of the ancient inhabitants is endeavoured to be darkened and their names obscured, and every occasion of shadow is taken to revile them, and their writers, and noble actions in war, whilst the Conquerors and ruling Nation are cried up where there is little colour for it."

[1] Salesbury was a Denbighshire man, brought up a lawyer, of Thavies Inn. He had composed and dedicated a Welsh dictionary to Henry the Eighth ; had written a Welsh treatise on Rhetoric, and first published in Welsh the Epistles and Gospels for the whole year, in Edward the Sixth's time. It is a doubt whether an almanac, printed in the time of Henry the Eighth, and the first that came out in Welsh, was by Salesbury or Sir John Price. [Salesbury's Welsh Testament was published in 1567. It is now one of the rarest of books. In 1886, Mr. Quaritch, the well-known bookseller asked 100 guineas for a copy.—Ed.]

[2] [Dr. Richard] Davies was in exile for his religion in Mary's reign, was restored to his country on the accession of Elizabeth, and successively Bishop of St. Asaph, and

with the assistance of Dr. John Davies[1] of Mallwyd, corrected and republished Morgan's bible, which is the version, and a most excellent one it is, with little variation, now in use. A version[2] of the Psalms, in the four and twenty Welsh metres, was made

St. David's. He was of the Tribe of Ednowain Bendew, and was employed, with other eminent scholars, by Elizabeth to translate the Bible into English ; and he translated all that part from the beginning of Joshua to the end of Samuel. He translated also parts of the new Testament into Welsh, particularly some of the Epistles. Ob. 1581. [aged 80. He also translated the Liturgy into Welsh, assisted by W. Salesbury. He was also a good Welsh poet.—Ed.]

[1] Dr. [John] Davies was an universal scholar, the son of a weaver of the parish of Llanferres in Denbighshire, of the Tribe of Marchudd, and brought up under Bishop Parry in the school at Ruthin, and was afterwards his Chaplain. Davies was author of the Welsh grammar and dictionary, and translated the thirty-nine articles and Parson's (the Jesuit's) Resolution into elegant Welsh prose. Thomas ab William,* the Physician, who lived at Trefriw near Llanrwst, had begun a Welsh and Latin dictionary, which Davies, at the request of the Gwydir family, completed and published. In his church of Mallwyd, in defiance of Archbishop Laud, he removed again the Communion table from the east end to the middle of the church, where it still remains.† He built three public bridges at his own charge, and did other charities at Mallwyd, where he resided. He was a Justice of the Peace and an useful Magistrate, and universally beloved and esteemed in his country. Ob. 1644. He left no family. His wife was a daughter of Rhŷs Wynn of Llwynynn, and sister to Bishop Parry's wife.

[2] The metrical version of the Welsh psalms, now in use, was made by Edmund Prŷs, Archdeacon of Merioneth, in the time of Elizabeth. He was an eminent scholar and poet, of the Tribe of Marchudd, and had assisted Bishop Morgan in his biblical Welsh translation. He was Rector of Maentwrog in Merionethshire, where he lies buried. He outlived eighty years, for at that age he addressed some excellent hexameter Latin verses to Dr. Davies of Mallwyd, on the publication of his grammar in 1621. There are fifty-four controversial poems between the Archdeacon and a contemporary Bard,

* Thomas ab William was of the Tribe of Ednowain Bendew. He is commonly known by the name of Sir Thomas ab William, having probably taken his Bachelor's degree. He was born, as he says himself, at the foot of Snowdon. He wrote a book of medical directions and receipts; also a book of Pedigrees, and an Herbal in Latin, Welsh and English, still extant in MS. He was reputed a papist, and is supposed to have known something of the gunpowder plot ; as it is said, he persuaded Sir John Wynn, the historian, not to go up to that Parliament.

† The table has lately been restored to its former place in the east end of the chancel.—Ed.

94

William Myddelton, a younger branch of the house of Gwaenynog, a Captain in Elizabeth's navy, and who had served in her armies. This versification is one of the most· ingenious compositions in the Welsh language, and it may be said of the Captain, in the words of Bishop Fell, that he was a pupil of Minerva, as well as Pallas. It is pleasant a soldier should so well dispose of his leisure hours. Some of his Psalms were penned in the West Indies, some on the Atlantic ocean, and others in his native country. In his Welsh correspondence he stiles himself Gwilym Ganoldref, or Middle-town. He wrote also Barddoniaeth, or the art of Welsh poetry, which is added to the appendix of John Dafydd Rhŷs's[1] grammar.

It was a distinguished family of nine sons and seven daughters ;

.... *longo ordine nati,*
Clari omnes, patria[2] pariter virtute suaque.

called William Cynwal, extant ; both holding a conspicuous seat in the first class of the Welsh poets of that age. It is said moreover that Cynwal fell a victim to the poignancy of the Archdeacon's satire. The last poem of the fifty-four is a most pathetic elegy, composed by the Archdeacon, when the news was brought him of the death of his rival.

[1] John Dafydd Rhŷs took his Doctor's degree in Physic in Italy. He undertook and published his grammar, to assist in understanding Dr. Morgan's translation of the bible into Welsh, then just completed, and he took great pains to preserve and communicate the true sound of the Welsh letters. Had the ancients done the same, we should have been nearer in our pronunciation of the Latin and Greek. To acquire the pronunciation with precision in any language, frequent exercise of the voice, accompanied by frequent corrections of the ear, is necessary. The Doctor has left a treatise on the orthography and pronunciation of the Italian language.

[2] The father, Richard Myddelton, was Governor of Denbigh Castle in the reigns of Edward the Sixth, Mary and Elizabeth. He was descended from Ririd Flaidd, and

From Cynrig come the Williamses of Fron, or Arddynwynt.
They are represented in the Reverend Richard Williams, Rector

was the fourth son of Foulk Myddelton, the third brother of Roger Myddelton,* of Gwaenynog. The eldest son of Richard the Governor, was Richard, whose second son, Roger, married the heiress of Cadogan. This estate had been forfeited by Edward Jones Esquire, but restored to this lady, his descendant. Jones suffered in Babington's plot. The second son of Richard Myddelton the Governor, was Simon ; the third William, distinguished in both elements ; as a sea officer, he had done good service in apprizing his Admiral, the Lord Thomas Howard, in time to avoid the superior force Spain had sent off the Azores to meet him ; and he escaped with the loss of that memorable person, Sir Richard Grenville, his Vice-Admiral. The captain is said to have been the first who smoked tobacco in London, for Raleigh was too good a courtier to have disgusted his Sovereign in that particular. Sir Thomas, the fourth son of Richard the Governor, was bred in London a merchant, traded chiefly with Antwerp, made a great fortune, and purchased Chirk Castle from the Lord St. John of Bletso, in the year 1595. He was Sheriff of London in 1603, and having married a young wife in his old age, gave occasion to the song, " Room for cuckolds, here comes my Lord Mayor." The fifth son, Charles, succeeded his father in the government of Denbigh Castle. The sixth son was that eminent Philosopher and Engineer, Sir Hugh Myddelton, who brought the New River to London, then called Myddelton's waters. He served in six parliaments for Denbigh, and was made a Baronet in 1622, and died in 1631. The seventh son, Robert, was a Master of Welsh prosody, and left a treatise on that subject. The eighth son, Foulk, married the heiress, Wynn, of Bodlith, and was sheriff of Denbighshire in 1610, and the heiress of this branch married Thomas Meredith Esquire of Pentrebychan. Pierce Myddelton was the ninth and last son. The Lord Mayor was father to Sir Thomas Myddelton of Chirk Castle, a distinguished character in the Common-wealth [whose portrait is given in this volume]. The latter was Member for the county of Denbigh and took the field on the part of the Parliament, when he was near sixty years of age, was Sergeant Major General to the forces in North Wales, and in conjunction with Sir William Brereton in 1643 took the Castle of Holt. In 1644 he relieved Oswestry, and beat the King's forces in a sharp action at Mont-gomery, for which he had the thanks of the House. I find him in 1648 among the

* Roger was the eldest son of Dafydd Myddelton of the Myddelton's of Myddelton, descended from Ririd Flaidd. Dafydd his father is styled Receiver of Denbigh, and Valectus Domini Regis, the second year of Richard the Third. As a picture of the barbarous times in which it happened, there is a story of this Dafydd Myddelton, that having gained the affections of Margaret Done of Utkington, in Cheshire, but not her parents consent, she was bestowed upon another ; which Dafydd not brooking, met the groom leading his wife out of church and killed him on the spot. He then carried off his mistress and immediately married her ; so that she was a maid, a wife, a widow, and a wife again, in the same day.

of Machynlleth; a gentleman who has embellished our Welsh

secluded members, and bound in a bond of twenty-thousand pounds not to disturb the government. In 1659 with Sir George Booth, he declared too precipitately for Charles the Second, when his Castle was besieged, and taken by Lambert, and one side demolished, and the trees in his Park cut and sold. He died at the age of eighty in 1666, having survived his son, Sir Thomas Myddelton made a Baronet at the Restoration. The last mentioned Sir Thomas, was father to another Sir Thomas, who by his second wife, Charlotte, daughter of Keeper Bridgman, had an only daughter, Charlotte, first married to the Earl of Warwick, and afterwards to Mr. Secretary Addison, by whom she had a daughter lately deceased, who left her estate to her relations, the Bridgmans. Sir Thomas, leaving no male issue, was succeeded by his brother Sir Richard, repeatedly Member for Denbighshire, and father of Sir William, who died unmarried in 1718. The Baronetage extinguished, but the estate followed the entail to Robert Myddelton, the eldest son of Richard Myddelton of Llŷsfasi, the third son of the old soldier, Sir Thomas the Knight. Robert died without issue, and was succeeded by his brother John, succeeded by his son, Richard, the father of Richard, the last gentleman, who died unmarried in 1796, leaving his three sisters coheiresses.* To return to Sir Thomas Myddelton, the first Baronet. By his second wife, sister to Sir John Trevor of Brynkinallt, Master of the Rolls, and Speaker of the House of Commons, he left a posthumous son, Thomas, born in 1663. This gentleman was bred to the law, and the favourite at the Chancery-bar of his uncle Trevor,† then first Commissioner; but this great lawyer being used to treat the Counsel with extraordinary freedom, something he dropped of this nature to his nephew, was said to go so near his heart, that it brought his life to a period, who for his age was an ornament to the profession. He died in 1696. Among

* Namely Charlotte, Maria, and Harriet. Charlotte, who had the Chirk Castle estate, married Robert Myddelton Biddulph of Ledbury, Herefordshire, and their grandson Richard Myddelton Biddulph is the present owner. Maria, who had Ruthin Castle, married the Hon. Frederick West, third son of Earl Delawarr, and their grandson William Cornwallis West is the present owner.—*Ed.*

† Trevor had been first Commissioner of the Great Seal, Master of the Rolls, and Speaker of the House of Commons, whence he was expelled for corruption. This made the Wits observe, "That Justice was blind, but Bribery only squinted;" for Trevor squinted abominably, as his picture [here given] shews. [So little abashed was he by his expulsion, that soon after, on meeting Archbishop Tillotson, he muttered loud enough to be heard, "I hate a fanatic in lawn sleeves;" to which the Archbishop replied "And I hate a knave in any sleeves." He continued Master of the Rolls for twenty-two years after his expulsion, and possessed a high reputation as a lawyer. He died May 20, 1717, at his house in Clement's Lane, London, and was buried in the Rolls Chapel. His grandson Arthur Hill, was created Viscount Dungannon in the peerage of Ireland. He was also the ancestor of the Marquises of Downshire. On the death of Lord Dungannon in 1862 (when the title became extinct), Lord Arthur Edwin Hill, his kinsman, succeeded to the Brynkinallt estate, and thereupon assumed the surname Trevor in addition to his patronymic Hill.—*Ed.*]

GEORGE LORD JEFFERIES.

Lord Chancellor.

his other virtues Trevor was an economist. He had dined by himself one day at the Rolls, and was drinking his wine quietly, when his cousin Roderic Lloyd was unexpectedly introduced to him from a side door. "You rascal," said Trevor to the servant, "And you have brought my cousin Roderic Lloyd Esquire, Prothonotary of North Wales, Marshal to Baron Price, and so forth, and so forth, up my *back stairs*. Take my cousin Roderic Lloyd Esquire, Prothonotary of North Wales, Marshal to Baron Price, and so forth and so forth ; take him instantly back, down my *back stairs*, and bring him up my *front stairs*." Roderic in vain remonstrated, and whilst he was conveying him down one, and up the other stairs, his Honor removed the bottle and glasses. Another adventure befell Roderic at the Rolls. He was returning rather elevated from his club one night, and ran against the pump in Chancery lane. Conceiving somebody had struck him, he drew, made a lounge at the pump, and the sword entering the spout, the pump being crazy fell down. Roderic concluded he had killed his man ; left his sword in the pump, and retreated to his old friend's house at the Rolls. There he was concealed by the servants for the night. In the morning his Honor, having heard the story, came himself to deliver him from his consternation and confinement in the coal-hole. Trevor was consulted by James the Second and his Ministers, and had the virtue to tell Jefferies, on the very violent proceedings against Cornish,* "That if he pursued that unfortunate man to execution, it would be no better than murder ;" but his advice was not taken. Trevor was first cousin to Jefferies. The latter was certainly a great lawyer, however bad a man ; and the reports† published by Vernon were without doubt the work of Jefferies, but his name was too unpopular to be put to them. He had a vicious profuse way of speaking and debating from the Bench. In the sad business of Mrs. Lisle's trial he throws a sneer at his countrymen. Bullying a witness that he thought would not speak out, he says, "Look thee, if thou can'st not comprehend what I mean, I will repeat it again, for thou shalt see what countryman I am by my telling my story over twice : Therefore I ask thee once again." "Hold your tongue," said he one day to a Counsel, who seemed forward in magnifying his success in untying a knotty point in a cause ; "You are too troublesome : You are exactly like a hen ; if you lay an egg, you must cackle over it." The youngest brother of Jefferies was Canon of Canterbury, and grandfather to Dr. Jefferies now living [1799], the Residentiary of

* This anecdote I had from the late Mr. Lloyd of Tyddyn, whose mother was Cornish's daughter. The anecdote of Jefferies's smiling at Williams, on the trial of the Bishops, I heard from Lord Chancellor Hardwicke.

† We had another of our countrymen a very able lawyer and reporter of that time, Sir John Vaughan, Chief Justice of the Common Pleas ; the ancestor of the Earls of Lisburne, and the friend and executor of the learned Selden. [His portrait is here given. He died in 1674, and was buried in the Temple church, near the grave of his friend, Selden, under a marble monument. His grandson John Vaughan, was created Viscount Lisburne in the peerage of Ireland, and the latter's grandson the fourth Viscount was advanced to an Earldom of Lisburne in 1776.—*Ed.*]

N

98

poetry by his elegant and harmonious English versions. He
is moreover a good Latin poet.[1]

The Kyffins of Maenan, Bodfach, and Glasgoed, descended
from Einion efell,[2] who resided at Llwynymaen [near Oswestry],
was Lord of Cynllaeth, and died in 1196. The surname of
Kyffin was first taken by Madog, the fifth in descent from
Einion, to distinguish him from his father, Madog gôch, then
living. Madog, the son, had been nursed at Kyffin, and thence
the appellation. The male line of Maenan ended, in our times,

St. Paul's. The Canon died young, it is said, broken-hearted with the sad conduct and
character of his brother, the Chancellor. There was a picture at Acton of their father
in mourning for his seventh son, the Canon. The old man outlived all his sons.—*suorum
ultimus.* [George Lord Jefferies, whose portrait is here given, was perhaps the very
worst judge that ever disgraced the English Bench. He was born at Acton, near
Wrexham, in 1648; was created Baron Jefferies of Wem, May 15th, 1685, and died
April 18th, 1689. Macaulay has told the story of his infamous career in words that
make one's cheek burn at the thought that he was a Welshman.—*Ed.*]

[1] Subsequently he became Rector of Llanferres. The elegant translation of "Hirlas
Owain," and others bearing his initials in Pennant's *Tours in Wales,* are by him.
Several pieces of his translation also appear in Jones's *Relics of the Bards.* He died
suddenly, 4th June, 1811, and the estate passed to his wife's family in Cheshire.
(*Cam. Briton,* i., p. 263.)—*Ed.*

[2] Einion bore parted per fess, *sable* and *argent,* a lion rampant, counterchanged of the
field, armed, langued, *gules.* Cynrig bore *gules* on a bend *argent,* a lion passant *sable ;*
whence the arms of their several descendants. Mr. Vaughan, in his "Antiquities
Revived," tells us, "That the illegitimate lines of the Princes of Wales were not generally
tolerated to bear their father's arms ; and if permitted, yet not without difference, as
may be observed," says he, "in the arms of Dafydd gôch, the natural son of Dafydd,
Lord of Denbigh, and in those of Einion and Cynrig, twins, the natural sons of Madog
ab Maredudd, Prince of Powys." [In an old Pedigree at Brogyntyn, the addition is
made to Einion efell's arms of "on a canton *argent* a tower *gules.*" (*Mont. Coll.,* xiii.,
p. 117.)—*Ed.*]

SIR JOHN VAUGHAN.

Chief Justice of the Common Pleas.

in Sir Thomas Kyffin Knight, whose three daughters, coheiresses, were married, Elizabeth to William John Lenthall Esquire, descended from the Speaker of his name; Anne to the Reverend John Wynn, the second son of Maesyncuadd; Ermine to Richard Hughes Kenrick (the younger) Esquire, of Nantclwyd.

The Kyffins[1] of Bodfach ended in an heiress, Elizabeth, daughter of William Kyffin, married to Adam Price of Glan-Miheli; and the heiress of the Prices to the late Bell Lloyd Esquire of Pontruffudd.[2] Glascoed[3] also ended in an heiress, Margaret,[4] daughter of Watkin Kyffin, married to Sir William

[1] Kyffin is nearly the same in sound, but exactly the same in signification, with Confine, and every place of that name is always near some boundary.

[2] He afterwards lived at Bodfach, near Llanfyllin. His son Edward Pryce Lloyd succeeded to a baronetcy on the death of his great uncle, Sir Edward Lloyd, Bart., and was subsequently in 1831, raised to the peerage as Baron Mostyn. He died in 1884, and was succeeded by his grandson, Llewelyn Nevill Vaughan, the present peer. Bodfach was sold about fifty years ago by the late Lord Mostyn, to Sir John Wilson, K.C.B., and by him again in 1854 to John Lomax, Esq., father of the present owner.—*Ed.*

[3] Maurice Kyffin of this house, in 1588, translated Terence's Andria into English, and Bishop Jewell's Apologia Ecclesiæ Anglicanæ into excellent Welsh, in 1595. [He was also a good poet, both in Welsh and English. A poem by him, printed in 1587, entitled *The Blessednes of Brytaine*, was reprinted in facsimile by the Cymmrodorion Society in 1885. According to a Pedigree in *Hist. Powys Fadog*, v., p. 374, he was the direct ancestor of Edward, William, and Frank Lenthall, three brothers living together unmarried at Bessels Leigh Abbey, Berkshire, in 1884, descended paternally from Mr. Speaker Lenthall. Maenan Hall belongs to this family.—*Ed*]

[4] Williams, on one of his Welsh circuits, danced with this lady, and got her leave to propose himself to her father: "And what have you," said the old gentleman pretty roughly to him? "I have, Sir," says Williams, "a *tongue* and a *gown.*" He obtained the lady, and founded the flourishing families of Wynnstay, Penbedw, and Bodelwyddan.

Cedant arma togæ, concedant omnia linguæ.

Williams, Speaker[1] of the House of Commons in the two last short Parliaments of Charles the Second, and Solicitor General to his brother James. To the latter office he was raised in the room of Powys, who had succeeded Sawyer as Attorney General, and for the same purpose, the trial and conviction of the Bishops. Williams used much pains without effect; and on their Lordships' acquittal, there was a great shout in the Hall. Jefferies, then sitting in the Court of Chancery, being told the reason, was observed to put his face in his nosegay to hide a smile, and as if to say, "Mr. Solicitor! I keep my seal;" for he knew it had been promised to Williams, had he carried that cause. Sir William was the son of Hugh Williams, Doctor of Divinity, of Nantanog in Anglesey, a younger branch of the family

---

[1] The Speaker had licensed the votes, which had in them matters of scandal relating to some Lords (Dangerfield's Narrative of the meal-tub plot) so an information was brought against him in the King's Bench ; he was found guilty and fined ten thousand pounds, of which he paid eight. "This was driven against him" says Burnet, "by the Duke of York's party, on purpose to cut off the thoughts of another Parliament, since it was not to be supposed, that any House of Commons could bear the punishment of their Speaker for obeying their own orders." Sir William continued the practice of the law, and to great profit, throughout his life, and I had an opinion of his (which as a curiosity I gave to my Lord Chief Justice Kenyon) after he had left the Speaker's Chair* and the Solicitor Generalship. Pemberton, who had been Chief of both Benches, had done the same ; and his opinion is also to the same case. The late Chancellor, Charles Yorke, had so much respect to the memory of the latter, that he repaired his monument, then in decay, in Highgate Chapel.

* We had three of our countrymen, not distant neighbours, Speakers of the House of Commons, within a short time of each other ; Williams, Trevor, and Hanmer. The last was a stiff man ;
"*Not all were flowers, when pompous Hanmer spoke.*"
Sir Thomas Hanmer left no family : He had married an old woman for love, and a young one for money, and was not very fortunate in either of them. His epitaph by Dr. Freind, Master of Westminster School, was composed in Sir Thomas's life time, and was found in his edition of Shakespeare after his death, and thence supposed to have had his approbation, and was accordingly put on his monument. *Ob.* 1746. [His portrait is given in this volume ; also his epitaph in Latin, and an English paraphrase of it, see Appendix xviii and xix.—*Ed.*

SIR JOHN TREVOR.

Master of the Rolls, and Speaker of the House of Commons.

of Chwaen (descended from Cadrod hardd, or the handsome, the brother of Nefydd hardd, the Tribe) by Emma Dolben, niece to Bishop[1] Dolben of Bangor. Sir William was of Jesus, Oxford; removed to Gray's-Inn; from thence was called to the Bar, and became Recorder of Chester; which city he represented in two Parliaments, when he appeared in opposition, and a warm exclusionist. He sat afterwards for the borough of Beaumaris, and the county of Carnarvon, and died at his chambers in Gray's-Inn in July 1700, at the age of sixty-six, and lies buried at Llansilin in Denbighshire.[2] He left two sons; the elder, Sir William Williams, was grandfather by his third son, Richard, to Watkin Williams Esquire of Penbedw; and great grandfather by his eldest son Sir Watkin Williams Wynn of Wynnstay, to the present gentleman of that place.[3] The Speaker's younger son, John, was an eminent provincial lawyer, practised at Chester, and was great grandfather to the present Sir John Williams of Bodelwyddan.[4]

[1] Dolben was of the family of Segroit, where he was born. He became Vicar of Hackney, which he resigned on his promotion to the Bishopric of Bangor. He died in November 1633 at his Palace in Shoe-lane, and was buried in the Chancel of Hackney church, where is his monument with the Arms of the See of Bangor, empaling his own of Dolben.

[2] His portrait is given in this volume.—*Ed.*

[3] See note. p. 11, *ante.*

[4] He was created a Baronet 24th July, 1798, and on his death in October, 1830, was succeeded by his eldest son, Sir John Hay Williams. He died in September, 1859, and was succeeded by his brother, the late Sir Hugh Williams, upon whose death in May, 1876, the title and estates devolved upon his eldest son, Sir William Grenville Williams, the present Baronet.—*Ed.*

The Maurices of Lloran descend from Einion. They are represented in Edward Maurice Corbet Esquire of Ynysymaengwyn, an estate he inherits in right of his maternal grandmother, a Corbet, the heiress of the place.[1] And here we have an instance of gavelkind; the younger brother inheriting the family house. Jeuaf ab Cyhelyn ab Rhun ab Einion efell, who died in 1242, made this disposition of his estates; Lloran to Madog Gôch, his elder son, and Llwynymaen, the paternal inheritance, to Jeuaf fychan the younger. The house of Lloran was rebuilt in 1230, as we learn from some Welsh verses, which signify, that the years from the incarnation of the Son of God were twelve hundred and three tens, when Cyhelyn founded an huge and high house of wood and stone : " He erected," says the Bard, "on the Banks of Barrog, an house that will outstand the world : Let songs be sung to the amiable Chief in the halls of Lloran."

From Einion were descended the Tanads[2] of Abertanad : Rhŷs Tanad died in 1661, having had by his wife, Margaret, the

---

The Phillips's of Gwern-haulod, also descended from Madog Kyffin. They ended in an heiress, Mary, daughter of William Phillips, married to Thomas Lloyd Esq. of Halchdyn, from whom has descended Phillips Lloyd Fletcher, Esq. of Nerquis Hall. *(Hist. Powys Fadog,* iii., p. 356.)*—Ed.*

[1] The Corbets of Ynysymaengwyn, became extinct on the death in 1878, of Athelstan John Soden Corbet, Esquire. The greater part of the estate was purchased by and now belongs to John Corbett, Esq., M.P. for Droitwich. The late James Maurice, Esq. of Bath (living in 1872), also belonged to the family of Maurice of Lloran.*—Ed.*

[2] They took their name from the river Tanad which falls into the Vyrnwy, near their seat at Abertanad, for the same reason, as the Mostyns, the Glynns, Erddigs, Sontleys, &c., &c., to save the redundancy of Aps.

sister[1] of the memorable Sir John Owen, five sons and six daughters, whereof six survived him; two sons and four daughters. Owen Tanad, the younger of the sons, and the last heir male of the Tanads. died in 1668, in his eighteenth year, and in default of issue to the elder sisters he was succeeded by his youngest, Susannah: She married Colonel Sydney Godolphin, Governor of the Islands and Garrison of Scilly, and Auditor of North Wales. They had issue one son [Francis] Tanad Godolphin, and five daughters. The son died of a fever in Flanders, before he was of age, and when he had served seven campaigns;

Dum numerat palmas, credidit esse senem.

The first, third, fourth, and fifth daughters, died unmarried, and the second, Mary, had the inheritance: She married Dr. Godolphin, Provost of Eton, and Dean of St. Paul's and brother to the Treasurer. They had issue, the last Lord Godolphin and the late Mrs. Owen of Porkington. Lord Godolphin had no family, and gave those estates by will to Lord Francis Osborne, second son of his Grace the Duke of Leeds. Mrs. Owen left two daughters; the elder of Porkington married to Owen Ormsby Esquire, by whom she had a daughter,[2] the right heir and lineal descendant of Abertanad.

---

[1] Her father in some pedigrees is called John Owain Walsingham ; I conclude, as being Secretary to the Great Minister of that name. I remember, Mr. Roberts of Chester, Secretary to Mr. Pelham, was called Pelham Roberts.

[2] Mary Jane Ormsby, whose son John Ralph Ormsby Gore, by her husband William Ormsby Gore, Esq., was in 1876 created Baron Harlech, and upon his death in the same year, was succeeded in the title by his brother, William Richard, the present peer.—See *ante*, p. 17, *note.—Ed.*

The Tanads of Blodwel descended also from Einion. The heiress of the house, Jane, married John Matthews of Court; and the heiress of the Mathewses, Ursula, married Sir John Bridgeman, grandson to the Keeper, Sir Orlando, and Ancestor to the present Lord Bradford, who enjoys the estate.[1]

The Robertses of Llangedwyn descended from Einion: The heiress, Catherine, daughter of Maurice Robert of Llangedwyn, married Owen Vaughan of Llwydiarth; and these estates, with those of the Vaughans of Caergai and Glanllyn (who had married the heiress of Llwydiarth and Llangedwyn), united in Anne, daughter to William Vaughan, who left them to her husband, Sir Watkin Williams Wynn of Wynnstay; and they remain in his grandson, the present gentleman of that place.[2]

The Merediths of Glantanad were of the race of Einion. Margaret, the daughter and heiress of Andrew Meredith, married Edward Thelwal of Plasyward; and the estate was again conveyed by marriage, through the great heiress of that house, to Sir William Williams, the eldest son of the Speaker, and belongs to Wynnstay.

The Lloyds of Aston descended from Einion. The heiress of the house, Elizabeth, daughter of Thomas Lloyd, married

[1] Sir Orlando Bridgeman, whose portrait is here given, was a lawyer of great eminence, having been successively Lord Chief Baron of the Exchequer, Lord Chief Justice of the Common Pleas, and Lord Keeper of the Great Seal. He was created a Baronet, 7th June, 1660. His great great grandson was in 1794 created Baron Bradford, and his son Orlando, second Baron, was created Viscount Newport, and Earl of Bradford in November, 1815. His grandson Orlando George Charles is the present peer.—*Ed.*

[2] See *ante*, p. 11, *note*.

SIR ORLANDO BRIDGEMAN.

Lord Keeper.

Foulke Lloyd of Foxhall, or the hall of Foulke, and was great grandmother to the Reverend John Robert Lloyd, Rector of Whittington and Selattyn, both in his advowson, the present possessor of Aston.[1] The name of the Foxhall family was Rosindale, when they came first from the north. To a younger branch, settled at Denbigh, we owe our learned countryman, Humphrey Llwyd. He was of Brazen-nose, Oxford, studied Physic, and lived as family Physician in the house of the last Earl of Arundel of the name of Fitzalan, the Chancellor of that University. He sat in Parliament for his native town of Denbigh, and died there in the forty-first year of his age, and was buried in the parish church with a coarse monument, a dry epitaph, and a psalm tune under it.[2] He made the map of England for his friend, Ortelius, to whom he dedicates his Commentariolum Britanniæ, and his Epistle De Monâ Druidum Insulâ, antiquitati suæ restitutâ. He left a Chronicon Walliæ a rege Cadwaladero, and the History of Cambria, now called Wales, in MS. He printed a Latin paper De Armamentario Romano, and turned some Medical Treatises from Latin into English. He collected many curious books for Lord Lumley

A.D. 1297

A.D. 1568

[1] The present owner and occupier of Aston Hall is R. T. Lloyd, Esq.—*Ed.*

[2] The character of the "tune" may be judged from the first couplet, which is as follows :—

"The corps and earthly shape doth rest here, tomy'd in your sight,
Of Humphrey Llwyd, Master of Arts, a famous worthy wight."

A copy is here given of the original portrait of him preserved at Aston, near Oswestry. His hair was red, but his countenance was remarkable for its manly beauty, and highly intellectual expression.—*Ed.*

(whose sister he married),[1] which form at this time a valuable part of the Library in the British Museum. One of his sons was settled at Cheam in Surrey, whose great grandson, Robert Lloyd, was Rector of St. Paul's, Covent Garden, and contended, but without effect, for the Barony of Lumley.

From Einion were the Lloyds of Bodlith. The heiress of that house married Foulk Myddelton, the eighth son of the Governor, Richard Myddelton of Denbigh; and the heiress of the Myddeltons married Thomas Meredith Esquire of Pentre-bychan, the grandfather to the present gentleman, Richard Meredith Esquire, of that place.[2]

The Vaughans of Golden-grove, Carmarthenshire, were descended from Einion. John Vaughan, the son of Walter Vaughan of this house, served under Robert, Earl of Essex, Lord Deputy of Ireland, and was knighted by him for his services in that country; was made Comptroller of the house-hold to Prince Charles, and by James the First created Lord Vaughan of Molingar, and Earl of Carbery in that kingdom. He married Margaret, daughter of Sir Gelly Meyrick (who suffered in Essex's

---

[1] Barbara, sister and heir of John Lord Lumley, survived her husband, Humphrey Llwyd, and afterwards married William Williams, Esq. of Cochwillan, Carnarvonshire. (*Dwnn's Vis.* ii., p. 169.)—*Ed.*

[2] He died without issue, whereupon his sister Margaret inherited his estates. She married Joseph Warter, Esq. of Sibberscott, Salop, and had issue a son, Henry, who assumed the name and arms of Meredydd by royal sign manual in 1824. The latter married Elizabeth, a daughter of Mungo Park, the traveller, and by her had a son, the present Lieut. Col. Henry Warter Meredydd of Pentrebychan, Denbighshire. (*Hist. Powys Fadog* v., p. 280.)—*Ed.*

HUMPHREY LLWYD.

rebellion), and was succeeded by his son Richard. Richard was made Knight of the Bath at the Coronation of Charles the First, who created him Baron of Emlyn in England ; and after the Restoration was Lord President of the Marches in Wales, and a Privy Counsellor.[1] His son, Lord Vaughan, who married Rachel, the coheiress of the virtuous Southampton, died without issue before his father. She became after the distinguished wife and pious widow of Lord [William] Russell.

From Owain Brogyntyn, Lord of Dinmael and Edeyrnion, the natural son of Madog, the son of Maredudd, the son of Bleddyn, the founder of the Tribe, descended the Rhŷses of Rug. The heiress of the house, Margaret, married Piers Sales-bury of Bachymbyd, a younger son of Lleweni. Through the Salesburys, the Pughs of Mathafarn, the Prices of Gogerthan (from the alliance of his grandmother of Nannau with the first house), it now belongs to that spirited good Officer, Captain Edward Williames Vaughan Salesbury of the Guards.[2]

---

[1] Jeremy Taylor, afterwards Bishop of Down and Connor, was harboured by this second Earl of Golden Grove during the time of Cromwell, and where it is said he wrote *Holy Living and Dying ; The Golden Grove ;* and other works. The Earldom of Carbery became extinct in 1712, on the death of John third Earl, whose daughter and heiress Anne became Duchess of Bolton, but died without issue in 1751, leaving the Vaughan estates to her kinsman John Vaughan of Terracoed, who bequeathed them to his friend John Campbell, afterwards created Earl of Cawdor, in whose descendant they are still vested. *(Arch. Cam.* 4th *ser.* xii., p. 283.) The late John Lloyd Vaughan Watkins, Esq. of Pennoyre, M.P. for Brecon, was a descendant of the Vaughans of Golden Grove, in the female line, his mother, Susanna Eleanora being the granddaughter and ultimate heiress of the above-named John Vaughan of Terracoed. *(Burke's Landed Gentry.)*—*Ed.*

[2] See *ante,* p. 57, *note.*—*Ed.*

From Brogyntyn were the Maesmors of Maesmor.[1] Their heiress, Catharine, married Peter Morris Esquire of Hafod y maidd, and conveyed the estate into that family,[2] but the male line was continued in Nicholas, her first cousin, and is still extant.

The Lloyds of Dôlglessyn are from Brogyntyn: Their property was not long since alienated to Rug, to which it is contiguous.

The Hughes's of Gwerclas descended from Brogyntyn :[3] Humphrey Hughes Esquire, of that place, living in 1681, was

[1] In the pedigree of this house Robert ab Gruffudd, father of Robert Wynn, marries Margaret Salesbury of Lluesog, and has by her fifteen children ; and it is whimsical to observe the surnames which these adopted, so different from their parents and from each other : Robert Wynn, Ieuan Wynn, Dafydd Llwyd, Morys and Hugh Maesmawr, Sir Rhŷs Wynn, John Llwyd, Gwenhwyfar Llwyd, Lowri, Angharad Wenn, Margaret Wenn, Gwen Llwyd.

[2] Their granddaughter Catherine heiress of Maesmor, married first John Kyffin, Esq. of Ucheldre, who died without issue, and secondly Edward Lloyd, Esq. of Trefnant, County Montgomery, descended from Iestyn ap Gwrgant, founder of the fourth Royal Tribe of Wales, of which marriage there was issue, a daughter and heiress, Catherine Maria Margaretta who married first John Lewis Parry, Esq., Royal Marines, who died 8th May, 1822 ; and secondly Lieut. General John Manners Carr. *(Arch. Cam.* 4th, ser. viii., p. 195.)—*Ed.*

[3] Owain Brogyntyn was the illegitimate son of Madog ab Maredudd by a daughter of the Maer du, or the black Mayor, of Rûg in Edeyrnion. His father granted to him that Lordship, with the honor of Dinmael. Owain had three sons, Gruffudd, Bleddyn and Iorwerth ; Gruffudd, the elder, had one moiety of Edeyrnion, Iorwerth the other, and Bleddyn had Dinmael, Gruffudd ab Owain ab Bleddyn ab Owain Brogyntyn assigned over the Royalty of the Lordship of Dinmael to Lacy, Earl of Lincoln ; that was, all felonies except forfeitures. Prior to this, malefactors were usually executed at a place called Bryn y Crogwr, or the Hangman's Hill, in Maesmor. The children of Gruffudd ab Owain aforesaid were, Owen hên, Llywelyn Offeiriad, Hywel, and a daughter, Generis, who ended her life in retirement at a place since called Muriau Generis in Dwyfaen. The said Llywelyn Offeiriad, or the Priest, in a disagreement with his brothers, Owain hên and Hywel, sold his lands to the Earl of Lincoln, and accepted a grant from the Earl of thirteen pounds of land for the yearly rent of

twelfth in descent from Owain. The heiress of the Hughes's married the Lloyds, the present possessors.[1]

From Cadwgan,[2] the second son of the founder of the Tribe, descend the Nanneys of Nannau. The elder daughter and

thirteen pair of gloves, which parcels of land his descendants still possess in the quality of Freeholders. Owain Brogyntyn married, first, Jonet, the daughter of Hywel ab Madog ab Idnerth ab Cadwgan ab Athelstan Glodrudd, the fifth Royal Tribe, and had no issue by her. He married, secondly, Marred, or Margaret, the daughter of Einion ab Seisyllt of Mathafarn, by whom he had Gruffudd, who married Jonet, daughter of Sir William Say, Knight. From Gruffudd was descended Madog of Hendwr, father of Dafydd, father of Gwion Llwyd, &c., &c. Gwion Lloyd Esquire of Hendwr, in my memory, left Edeyrnion, and bought and settled himself at the lower Gwersyllt, since purchased by my worthy old friend, John Cawley Humberston Cawley Esquire.* Near Porkiugton [Brogyntyn], and far from his own country, is a singular entrench-ment, called Castle Brogyntyn, a fort belonging to Owain Brogyntyn. His dagger and cup are preserved at Rûg. The latter, perhaps, hath been most murderous. [Owain Brogyntyn was a man of distinguished valour. He was made by his father Lord of Dinmael, and after the deposition of his half brother, Elissau, in 1202, he appears to have become Lord of Edeyrnion also. He resided at Brogyntyn, near Oswestry, and was living in 1215. *(Hist. Powys Fadog,* i., p. 125.) His arms were, *argent* a lion rampant *sable,* debruised by a baton sinister *gules (Ib.,* p. 318), though they are generally given without this difference.—*Ed.*]

[1] Dorothea, eldest surviving daughter of Richard Hughes Lloyd, Esq. of Plymog, Gwerclas, Kymmer, and Bashall, was married 6th July, 1832, to her relative, John Hughes, Esq., third son of William Hughes, Esq., representative in the male line of the ancient family of Hughes of Gwerclas, Barons of Kymmer in Edeyrnion—thus uniting the senior with a junior branch of it. The issue of this marriage was one child, Talbot de Bashall Hughes, born 15th December, 1836, an Officer in the Cape Mounted Rifles. The armorial ensigns of this eminent house are those of their ancestors, the Sovereign Princes of Powys, namely, *argent* a lion rampant *sable*—" the black lion of Powys." *(Dwnn's Vis.,* ii., p. 250, *note.)* The account of this family, compiled, I believe, by that learned antiquary, the Rev. Walter Davies, in *Burke's Landed Gentry,* contains a vast amount of genealogical information relating to other Welsh families.—*Ed.*

[2] Cadwgan of Nannau's arms were, *Or* a lion rampant *azure,* armed and langued *gules.* In 1110 he was suddenly attacked by his nephew, Madog, at Welshpool, and

* Subsequently sold to . . . Atherston, Esq.—*Ed.*

heiress of the last of the male line, Hugh Nanney, married William Vaughan Esquire of Corsygedol; but no issue remaining from this match, the estate hath devolved to Sir Robert Williames Vaughan, the grandson of the the twin-sister of his great aunt Mrs. Vaughan. Sir Robert has improved the place (in itself distinguished) by a good family mansion, which is said to have one of the highest situations, of a gentleman's house, in Great Britain.[1]

The Wythans of Trewythan descended from Cadwgan. The line ended in an heiress, Mary, married to Bowen Jones Esquire of Pen yr allt góch, and the issue of the match, the Reverend Evan Jones,[2] is the present possessor of Trewythan.

slain before he could draw his sword and defend himself. According to *Brut y Tywysogion*, he was married *five* times, namely, first, to Gwenllian, daughter of Gruffudd ab Cynan, by whom he had a son, Madog; secondly, to Sanan, daughter of Dyfnwal, by whom he had a son, Einion; thirdly, to Ellyw or Ellinor, daughter of Cadifor ab Collwyn, lord of Dyfed, by whom he had a son, Morgan; fourthly, to "the Frenchwoman," a daughter of Pigot de Say, by whom he had two sons, Henry and Gruffudd; and fifthly, to Euron, daughter of Hoedliw, son of Cadwgan ab Elystan Glodrudd, by whom he had a son, Meredith. *(Burke's Landed Gentry.)—Ed.*

[1] Sir Robert Williames Vaughan, Bart., died without issue in 1859, when the title became extinct, and his estates were divided. The Nannau and Hengwrt properties are now vested in John Vaughan, Esq., and the Rhug estates were devised to the Hon. Charles Henry Wynn, the present owner. The Nanney's bore *Or*, a lion rampant *azure ;* the coat of the Vaughans of Nannau was, *Or* and *gules* four lions rampant counterchanged of the field; on the centre of the field the Nanney escutcheon.—*Ed.*

[2] Mr. Jones by his lady, the sister of Mr. Alderman Combe, has four children, Wythan, Charlotte, Caroline, and Hervey Bowen. [Trewythan, or Trewythen as it is generally called, is in the parish of Llandinam, Montgomeryshire. The Rev. Evan Jones died 10th July, 1827. His eldest son and heir, Wythen Jones, died 16th November, 1855; his only child, Charlotte, having died unmarried before him. By his Will,

From Cadwgan come the Lloyds of Cwmm bychan, still extant. A younger brother of the house was settled, early in this century, at Llanarmon in Yale, and was father to my worthy friend, that excellent historian and Welsh antiquary, the late Reverend John Lloyd[1] of Caerwys.

The Protector Cromwell was descended from Cadwgan. The family name was anciently Williams; Morgan Williams of Nant-church in Cardiganshire married the sister of Thomas Cromwell, the Minister Earl of Essex, and was succeeded by his son, Sir Richard Cromwell of Hinchingbroke in Huntingdonshire, who first assumed the name of Cromwell: He was father to Sir Henry Cromwell, the grandfather by his second son Robert, of Oliver the Protector. I know nothing of Oliver's partialities to Wales; but he encouraged a small octavo of the Welsh Bible,[2]

Wythen Jones devised his estates to his only brother, Hervey Bowen Jones, who died without issue, about the year 1865, having previously sold the estates in 1862. Trewythen now belongs to David Davies, Esq. of Broneirion.—*Ed.*]

[1] My friend Mr. Lloyd was usually called Blodeu; signifying, that he was the Blodeu, or flower of Llanarmon, where he had spent his younger years with his father. [He was the friend also and occasional companion of Pennant in his travels, eighteenth in descent from Bleddyn ap Cynfyn. He was the father of the late Miss Angharad Lloyd, a lady well known among Welsh *literati;* also of the Rev. Robert Watkin Lloyd, who died in 1860, leaving two sons, the Rev. Francis Llywelyn Lloyd of Ty yn Rhyl, and Edward Lloyd, Esq. of Castellau, in the County of Glamorgan. Pennant gives an interesting account of his visit to Cwmbychan in 1776, and of the primitive style of living of its then owner, Evan Lloyd, Esq., whose present representative and descendant is John Lloyd, Esq. of Cwmbychan. The Lloyds of Blaenyglyn, represented by William Wellesley Gordon Lloyd, Esq., and Rev. John Vaughan Lloyd, Vicar of Hope in 1858, are a branch of the same family.—*Ed.*]

[2] William Tyndal, our countryman, had with great cost and labour printed at Antwerp, in 1528, an incorrect impression of the New Testament in English, translated

when that edition (which from its size was thought useful) was scarce; and an act of Parliament passed for the propagation of the Gospel in North Wales. The London Polyglot Bible was produced at the same time, and Cromwell ever appears a steady friend to the Protestant interests.[1] I do not find, that his military occasions brought him to Wales, but he might have

by himself. Whilst mourning the low state of his finances, which would not enable him to amend his book, it chanced that Bishop Tonstal, passing through Antwerp, thought he could do no greater service to the Catholic faith, than by buying up Tyndal's Testaments, and committing them to the flames. Tyndal received the good Prelate's money with rapture, and employed it in printing his Translation correct, which he instantly transmitted to England, where it made many proselytes. Sir Thomas More, in 1529, expressing his surprize at the frequency of these prohibited books, was answered in Council, "That it was owing to the liberal encouragement of Bishop Tonstal."—*Burnet Ref.*

[1] Cromwell had two signal occasions given him so shew his zeal in protecting the Protestants abroad. The Duke of Savoy raised a new persecution of the Vaudois: So Cromwell sent to Mazarin, desiring him to put a stop to that; adding, "That he knew well they had that Duke in their power, and could restrain him as they pleased; and if they did not, he must presently break with them." Mazarin objected to this as unreasonable: He promised to do good offices; but he could not be obliged to answer for the effects they might have. This did not satisfy Cromwell. So they obliged the Duke of Savoy to put a stop to that unjust fury: And Cromwell raised a great sum for the Vaudois, and sent over Morland to settle all their concerns, and to supply all their losses. There was also a tumult in Nismes, in which some disorder had been committed by the Huguenots: And they, apprehending severe proceedings upon it, sent one over with great expedition to Cromwell, who sent him back to Paris in an hour's time with a very effectual letter to his Ambassador,[*] requiring him either to prevail, that the matter might be passed over, or to come away immediately. Mazarin complained of this way of proceeding as too imperious; but the necessity of their affairs made him yield. Cromwell had intended a great design to begin his Kingship with, had he assumed it. He had resolved to set up a Council for the Protestant Religion, in opposition to the congregation De Propagandâ fide at Rome. He intended

[*] Lockhart was employed afterwards as Ambassador to France by Charles the Second, and said, "That he found, that he had nothing of that regard, that was paid him in Cromwell's time."—*Ibid.*

made a friendly visit there; for in the old house at Kinmael, then belonging to Colonel Carter,[1] an officer in his favour, is a room called Cromwell's parlour.

The Vaughans of Wengraig were descended from Cadwgan. The father of Robert Vaughan, the antiquary, married the heiress of Hengwrt,[2] the granddaughter of Lewis Owen, the Baron,[3] to whom the place had belonged. The antiquary died

it should consist of seven Counsellors, and four Secretaries for different Provinces. These were the first; France, Switzerland, and the Valleys: The Palatinate and the other Calvinists were the second; Germany, the North, and Turkey, were the third; and the East and West Indies were the fourth. The Secretaries were to have five hundred pounds salary apiece, and to keep a correspondence everywhere, to know the state of religion all over the world, that so all designs might, by their means, be protected and assisted. They were to have a fund of 10,000l. a year at their disposal for ordinary emergencies, but to be farther supplied as occasions should require it. Chelsea College was to be made up for them, which was then an old decayed building, that had been at first raised to be a College for writers of Controversy.—*Burnet* " *Of his own Time.*"

[1] Carter, before he commenced soldier, was a draper; and marrying after the heiress of Kinmael, a Hollander, the wags said he had chosen (as well he might) the best piece of *Holland* in the country. Kinmael had more anciently belonged to the Llwyds of the tribe of Marchudd. Alice Llwyd the heiress of the place and an old maid, leaves twenty shillings to her ghostly father, Sir John ab Ellis, the parson of Kegidog, or St. George's, the neighbouring church.

[2] She was Margaret, second daughter of Edward Owen of Hengwrt, third son of the Baron, but no heiress. Hengwrt was purchased by the Vaughans of Wengraig, from the Owens. *(Byegones* 1872, p. 99).—*Ed.*

[3] Owen was Vice Chamberlain of North Wales, and Baron of the Exchequer at Carnarvon. "They were called at that time," says old Sir John of Gwydir, "The lawyers of Carnarvon, the merchants of Beaumaris, and the gentlemen of Conway; and," adds the historian, "the records of the King's Court kept at Carnarvon in those days were as orderly and formally kept as those in Westminster-hall." I once passed the place where Baron Owen lost his life. "On the road," says Mr. Pennant, "near Mowddwy, Lewis Owen, Vice Chamberlain of North Wales and Baron of the Exchequer

A.D. 1555

P

in 1667, and by his wife, a daughter of Nannau, left a son
Howel: Howel was succeeded by his son Robert, who married
Jonet, the younger twin-daughter, but eventually the heiress of
Nannau. Her son, Sir Robert Howel Vaughan, by the heiress
Williames of Ystymcolwyn, left three sons; Sir Robert Williames
Vaughan of Nannau, Edward Salesbury Vaughan Esquire of Rug,

at Carnarvon, was cruelly murdered by a set of banditti, with which this country was
over-run. After the wars of York and Lancaster multitudes of felons and outlaws
inhabited this country, and established in these parts for a great length of time a race
of wretches, who continued to rob, burn and murder in large bands, in defiance of the
civil power ; and would steal and drive whole herds of cattle in mid-day from one
country to another with impunity. To put a stop to these ravages, a commission was
granted to John Wynn ab Maredudd of Gwydir (grandfather to the historian Sir John),
and to Lewis Owen of Hengwrt, the Baron, in order to settle the peace of the country,
and to punish all offenders against its government. In pursuance of their orders they
raised a body of stout men, and on a Christmas-eve seized above fourscore outlaws and
felons, on whom they held a jail delivery, and punished according to their deserts.
Among them were the two sons of a woman, who very earnestly applied to Owen for
the life of one of them. He refused ; when the mother in a great rage told him,
opening her bosom, 'These yellow breasts have given suck to those, who shall wash
their hands in your blood.' Revenge was determined by the surviving villains. They
watched their opportunity to way-lay the Baron, as he was passing through these parts
from Montgomeryshire Assizes, in the thick woods of Mowddwy, at a place called from
the deed, Llidiart y Barwn, or the Baron's gate ; where they cut down several trees to
cross the road and impede the passage. They then discharged on him a shower of arrows ;
one of which sticking in his face he took and broke. After this they attacked him with
bills and javelins, and left him slain with above thirty wounds. His son-in-law, John
Llwyd of Ceiswyn, defended him to the last, but his cowardly attendants fled on the
first onset. His death gave peace to the country, for most vigorous justice ensued, and
the whole nest of banditti was extirpated ; many fell by the hand of justice, and the rest
fled never to return." [Baron Lewis Owen lived at Cwrt Plas yn dre, Dolgelley, often
absurdly called " Owen Glyndwr's Parliament House." The old house was pulled down
a few years ago and rebuilt at Newtown, Montgomeryshire, by Mr. Pryce Jones who
had purchased the materials. Evan Lloyd of Blaenglyn, married Mary, daughter of
Robert Owen, sixth in descent from the Baron, and their grandson, Evan Garnons Lloyd
of Erwgoed, was living in 1879.—Ed.]

and Griffith Howel Vaughan Esquire of Hengwrt.[1] Robert, the antiquary, published a small tract by the name of British Antiquities Revived, dedicated to the first Sir Richard Wynn of Gwydir, which was intended to end the controversy, then subsisting, respecting the primogeniture of the sons of Roderic, who on the tripartition of Wales gave the northern parts to Anarawd, the southern to Cadell, and Powys to Merfyn. The South Welshmen contended that Cadell was the elder brother: This is denied with zeal and effect by Mr. Vaughan. He was intimate with Usher; and in the course of their correspondence he tells the Primate, that he had translated into English the annals of Wales, which he had sent him for his perusal, but it does not appear it was ever returned. He left in manuscript the topography of Merionethshire, a tour of Wales, and commentaries on the Triades.[2] He wrote notes also on Gildas [and] Nennius, with an explanatory paraphrase on Welsh Chronology.

In the fifty-third year of his age and the thirteenth of his reign, our founder fell by a fate, familiar to that period, and was murdered by his subjects in South Wales. Bleddyn was

[1] All of whom died without issue. At the time of his death in 1859, the three estates belonged to Sir Robert Williames Vaughan, but after his decease they were divided. See *note*, p. 110, *ante.—Ed.*

[2] These papers are preserved from copies made at Hengwrt by that wayward child of genius, the late Reverend Evan Evans, before that valuable collection was dissipated. This library consisted of 165 MSS. Mr. Vaughan had made an agreement with Mr. Jones [of Gellilyfdy in the parish] of Ysgeifiog, an indefatigable collector of MSS., that the survivor of them should succeed to the other's library. Jones died first, and his collection [which filled upwards of fifty large volumes] came to Hengwrt, [but are now at Peniarth, near Towyn, Merionethshire, having been bequeathed to the late

just and mild in his administration, and framed a system of
laws on the old constitutions of Moelmutius and Hywel.[1] Our
historians condemn him for receiving his crown from Edward of
England, and becoming tributary to that Prince; but the success
of the Confessor's General, Harold,[2] at this period over our countrymen, left little choice in that matter. Bleddyn we are told was
rich: A Welsh distich[3] is quoted to that purpose, but I understand
it means no more than that he was Paramount of Powys, and
that the freehold lands in that principality were held under him
in capite. He had four wives, and issue by them all; Maredudd
by his first;[4] Cadwgan and Llywarch by the second; Madog
and Ririd by the third; and Iorwerth by the last.

W. W. E. Wynne, Esq., by his kinsman Sir Robert Williames Vaughan, Bart., who
died in 1859.—*Ed.*] Vaughan had made many copies of Welsh MSS. from Oxford,
the Tower, and other places : What authority is due to the destruction by one Scholan
of the Welsh MSS. in the Tower, I know not ; nor am I given to believe it. It is
certain, that in the end of Edward the First's reign many Welshmen of rank were
confined in that prison, engaged in the three unsuccessful insurrections after his
conquest. It is said they solicited the favour that their MSS. might be sent them out
of Wales ; that they were indulged in this request, and thence the Tower became the
principal repository of Welsh literature. [Robert Vaughan wrote many works besides
those above enumerated. He died in 1666, and was buried at Dolgelley.—*Ed.*]

[1] According to Geoffrey of Monmouth, Dunwallo Moelmutius was the son of Cloten,
Duke of Cornwall, and reigned in Britain 441 years before Christ. Our Welsh
Justinian, Hywel Dha, died at Rome in 948.

[2] Harold on his success revived the laws of Offa, that no Welshman should pass that
ditch, but under the loss and forfeiture of a limb. Harold had built a magnificent
house at Portyscydd in Monmouthshire, where he entertained his Master, Edward, but
which was soon after pillaged and destroyed by the Welsh.

[3] See *ante*, p. 39, *note.*

[4] His first wife, Haer, was a widow ; very beautiful : She was the daughter and
heiress of Gillyn, the son of Blaidd Rhudd, or the bloody Wolf, of Gêst in Eifionydd.
By Cynfyn Hirdref, her first husband, she was grandmother to Ririd, who took the

appellation of Blaidd, or the Wolf, in descent from his ancestor, Blaidd Rhudd, above mentioned. The famous Hywel y pedolau was the son of Gwenllïan, daughter to Ririd flaidd. There is a Welsh poem extant of Cynddelw Brydydd mawr, the great Bard, who flourished about the year 1160, returning thanks to Ririd for a fine sword, with which he had presented him.

[ADDENDA.]

THE author, it will have been observed, has confined himself to tracing the descendants of two only of the founder's sons, namely, Meredydd and Cadwgan, and he has left many of those unnoticed.

In addition to those already named, the following families are descended from Meredydd:—Pryce of Cyfronydd, Robert Davies Pryce, Esq., Lord Lieutenant of Merionethshire, the present owner of Cyfronydd, being twenty-sixth in direct male descent from the founder of the tribe *(Mont. Coll.* xix., p. 132); the Maurices of Brynygwaliau and Bodynfoel *(Ib.* v., p. 266); Owens, Trefeilir *(Dwnn's Vis.* ii., p. 202); Matthews of Trefnannau *(Hist. Powys Fadog,* i., p. 108); and Rogers of Burgedin *(Ib.),* all three extinct; and Parry of Main, the last representative of which died in 1827 *(Ib.* and *Mont. Coll.* xiii., p. 419). From Cynwrig Efell came the Davies's of Glwysegl and Brynbwa *(Hist. Powys Fadog,* i., p. 128); Griffiths, Gwysanau; Davies, Arddynwent and Marrington; and Parry, Wernddu, near Oswestry *(Ib.)* From Einion Efell, the Wynns of Moeliwrch; and Edwards of Ness Strange *(Dwnn's Vis.,* ii., p. 329); the Maurices of Penybont, Trefedrid, &c.; Swynae of Maenan; Lloyds of Foord and Pentrecoed *(Hist. Powys Fadog,* iv., p. 242); Powells of Park, Whittington *(Ib.,* iii., p. 405); Lloyd's, Moelfre; Hughes, Llanarmon; Daniel, Cefn yr Odfa; Davies, Pentrecae; Maurice, Cwm Blawty; and Hughes, Pentrebach *(Ib.)* From Owen Brogyntyn, the Wynns of Pentre Morgan; and the Lloyds of Ebnall, subsequently merged in the Lloyds of Llwynymaen *(Ib.,* iii., p. 403). Owain Glyndwr *(ante,* p. 53) had six sons, all of whom died without issue, having either fallen in battle, or been taken prisoners and mercilessly put to death. He had also five daughters, namely: Isabel, who married Adam ab Iorwerth Ddu; Alice, who married Sir John Scudamore, Knight, of Kentchurch, in the County of Hereford, whose lineal heir and representative, John Lucy Scudamore, Esq. of Kentchurch Court, was living in 1880; Lucy or Jane, who married Henry Lord Grey de Ruthin, but died without issue; Janet, who married Sir John de Croft, Knight, of Croft Castle, Herefordshire, whose present representatives are Archer James Croft, Esq. of Greenham Lodge, Berks., and Sir Archer Denman Croft, Bart., of Croft Castle; and Margaret, who married Sir Richard

Monnington, Knight, of Monnington, Herefordshire. He had besides these, several illegitimate children. His sister Lowry, married Robert Puleston, Esq. of Emral, to whose family, on failure of Owain's male issue, his arms descended, and they still quarter them, namely, *Paly* of eight *argent* and *gules*, over all a lion rampant *sable.* *(L. Glyn Cothi's Works*, p. 458.) For a long and full account of Owain Glyndwr, see *Pennant's Tours in Wales*, vol. iii., Appendix vii.

Celynin, who flourished during the first half of the fourteenth century, and who bore *sable* a he-goat passant *argent*, was sixth in descent from Aleth, King of Dyfed. Having killed the Mayor of Carmarthen, he fled into Powysland, and according to *Harl. MS.* 1973, fo. 140, married Gwladys, daughter and heiress of Ririd ab Cynwrig Efell, with whom he obtained Llwydiarth, but according to the *Salisbury MSS.* at Wynnstay, she was his mother, which is most probable. Dwnn *(Vis.,* i., p. 294) states that Celynin's wife was Gwenllian, daughter of Meredydd ab Rhydderch ab Tewdwr Mawr. He was the founder of the now extinct families of Llwydiarth and Caergai *(ante,* p. 104), Lloyd of Llanfechain, and Griffiths of Llanfyllin, and of the Lloyds of Dolobran, and Davies of Maesmawr and Fronfelen, Montgomeryshire, both still extant, the one being represented by Sampson Lloyd, Esq., and others, and the other by John Pryce Davies, Esq.

According to Lewys Dwnn *(Vis.,* i., p. 110), Bleddyn by his first wife had, besides Meredydd, a son Gwyn, the ancestor of the Bowens of Llwch-meilir. Catherine, the coheiress of Richard Bowen of Llwch-meilir, married John Scourfield, Esq., from whom are descended the Scourfields of Pembrokeshire.

Cadwgan was also the ancestor of the following families, in addition to those already named by the author, namely, the Wevers of Presteign *(Dwnn's Vis.,* i., p. 258) ; the Nanneys of Cefndeuddwr, whose last lineal male representative died in the present century, when the estates passed, under his Will, to his nephew, David Ellis, Esq. of Gwynfryn, in the County of Carnarvon, who took the name of Nanney, and upon his death without issue in 1819, his nephew, Owen Jones, Esq. of Brynkir, who assumed the name of Nanney after his own, came into the property—*(Hist. Powys Fadog*, v., p. 58) ; the Derwas family of Cemmes, whose present representative in the female line is William R. M. Wynne, Esq. of Peniarth *(Ib.,* p. 109) ; and Matthews of Esgair Foel Eirin, now represented by Oliver Laurence Ruck, Esq. of Pantlludw near Machynlleth. *(Mont. Coll.*, xvii., pp. 58, 63).

Fourth in descent from Cadwgan, was Cynfelyn ab Dolphyn, lord of Manafon, who married Julian, daughter of Roger Mortimer, Earl of March, and was the ancestor of the Wythens of Trewythen *(ante.* p. 111) ; the Merediths of Manafon *(Dwnn's Vis.,* i., p. 285) ; the Maurices of Llandinam *(Ib.,* p. 303) ; the Gwynn's of Llanidloes *(Ib.,* p. 309) ; the Wynns of Gungrog and Trelydan *(Ib.,* p. 320) ; Gilbert Jones *(Ib.,* p. 324) ; Jones, Helygain *(Ib.,* ii., p. 301) ; Jones, Clegyrddwr, Llanbrynmair

(Hist. Powys Fadog, v., p. 54); Pryce, Llanllugan ; Hughes, Llanlloddian ; and Maurice, Llangurig *(Ib.*, p. 63), all of whom appear to be extinct. Cynfelyn gave his name to the Township of Dolgynfelyn, formerly a detached portion of Manafon parish, but a few years ago annexed to the adjacent parish of Llanllugan. His arms were *azure* a lion passant *argent.*

By his second wife, Bleddyn had also two daughters : first, Hunydd, or Gwladys, who became the wife of Rhydderch, second son of Tewdwr Mawr, and a brother of Rhŷs ab Tewdwr, founder of the second Royal Tribe *(ante,* p. 27). Rhydderch was the ancestor of the Lloyds of Forest, Glyn Cothi and Peneint, Carmarthenshire *(Dwnn's Vis.,* i., p. 222); and of the Evans's of Llangeler, in the same County *(Cam. Journal,* 1864, p. 108). Second, Gwenllian, wife of Caradog ab Trahaiarn, by whom she was the mother of Owain ab Caradog. *(Dwnn's Vis.,* ii., p. 99).

Madog and Ririd, the founder's sons by his third wife, were slain by Iestyn ab Gwrgant, prince of Glamorgan, at the battle of Llechryd in 1087. Ririd, however, appears to have left issue, three sons : first, Madog ; second, Cadwgan, the ancestor of, among others, the Davies's of Henblas, Llansilin. John Davies of Henblas, was the author of the well-known *Display of Heraldry,* published in 1716 ; and his sister's son, John Reynolds of Oswestry, also published a book of pedigrees in 1735. Third, Cynwrig, the ancestor of the Foulkes's of Rhiwlas, in the same parish. Both families are now supposed to be extinct. *(Hist. Powys Fadog,* iv., p. 232).

By his fourth wife, Morien, daughter of Idnerth ab Cadwgan ab Elystan Glodrudd (founder of the fifth Royal Tribe), Bleddyn had two sons, namely : first, Iorwerth Gôch, who was slain at Caercinion by his nephew, Madog ab Ririd, in 1109 ; and second, Llywelyn, or, as he is called in some pedigrees, Rhiwallon *(Dwnn's Vis.,* ii., p. 330), the ancestor of the Lloyds of Rhiwlas ; and the Gethins of Glasgoed, Llansilin ; both apparently extinct in the male line ; and the Davies's of Trewylan, Montgomeryshire, still extant. *(Mont. Coll.,* iv., p. 155).

Llewelyn Aurdorchog ("of the Golden Torque,") Lord of Yale, whose arms were *azure* a lion rampant guardant *or,* married Eva, daughter, though some say sister, of Bleddyn ab Cynfyn. Among their descendants were the Evans's of Rhydycarw (ancestors maternally of the Owens of Glansevern); the Lloyds of Berthlwyd ; the Jones's of Garthmyl ; the Hanmers of Pentrepant ; the Lloyds of Conway ; the Owens of Ysgrwgan and Trefgeiriog ; the Lloyds of Nantymyneich, Mallwyd ; the Walcots of Walcot and Bitterley ; and other Montgomeryshire and Border families, mostly extinct in the male line. *(Burke's Landed Gentry.)*

In the description of Bleddyn ab Cynfyn's arms *(ante,* p. 40, *note),* a slight error was made. Instead of " *Or* a lion rampant *gules* armed and langued *or* ;" read " *Or* a lion rampant *gules* armed and langued *azure.*"—*Ed.*

JESTYN AB GWRGANT.

JESTYN AB GWRGANT, the fourth Royal Tribe, was Lord of Glamorgan.[1] He descended in the twenty-ninth generation from our great Caractacus;[2] a sorry slip from such a stock.

The Silurian Prince had defended his country from foreign enemies; his descendant introduced them to enslave it. Fitzhamon divided his conquest (as hath been before observed) among his twelve Knights, and Jestyn fell a just sacrifice to his own treachery and ingratitude; for Rhŷs had raised him to a Royal Tribe.

Of his descendants I find none extant in the male line. The Myttleys of Myttley ended in the Bromleys, and an heiress of the former house was ancestress to the Lord Chancellor Bromley.

The Joneses of Dôl in Edeyrnion descended from a Receiver General of North Wales of this tribe. The last of the family

---

[1] Ultima nunc dicenda venit Morgania tellus,
Pulchra situ, frugumque ferax et amæna locorum :
Regulus hanc tenuit titulo Jestinus avito
Gurganti proles, genus alto e sanguine Cambri ;
Quem nimis incautum, nimis in sua fata ruentem,
Perfidus impellit scelerosis artibus Eynon,
In proprium regem sine re, sine more rebellem.—*Pentarchia.*
His arms were *Gules* three cheveronels in pale *argent.*—*Ed.*

[2] After the captivity of Caractacus the Romans were often defeated by the single state of the Silures. *Romanosque post ejus captivitatem, ab unâ tantum Silurum civitate sæpius victos et profligatos.*—Tacit.

was settled at Llanrhaiadr Dyffryn Clwyd, died early in this [the eighteenth] century, and was buried in the Parish Church with much monumental extravagance. His figure in marble is recumbent at full length in a flowing gown and great Parian periwig, in the bad funebrial fashion of that period.[1] The Newtons of Haethley, extinct in the male line, were of this Tribe. Of this house was the lady of the late Thomas Meredith Esquire of Pentre bychan, who was Chamberlain and Keeper of the King's Original Seal for the counties of Denbigh and Mont-gomery (thence called Baron), and father of Richard Meredith the present gentleman of Pentre bychan, who succeeded him in that office. This honor hath been in the Meredith family for some generations.[2]

[1] This was Maurice Jones, Esq. of Plas Newydd, near Ruthin, who died 10th January, 1702. He left his extensive estates to his cousin, Humphrey Parry, Esq. of Pwll-halawg.—*Ed.*

[2] This office was abolished by the Act of 1830, which did away with the Courts of Great Sessions, and established the present Welsh Circuits. Pentre bychan is now the property of Col. Henry Warter Meredydd, grand-nephew of the above named Richard Meredith. See *ante,* p. 106, *note.—Ed.*

Q

[ADDENDA.]

IESTYN was rejected by his countrymen as Sovereign on the death of his father, Gwrgan, in 1030, owing to his violent and headstrong disposition, and his uncle Hywel was elected instead; on whose death in 1043, however, he succeeded to the throne. In 1088, he waged war with Rhŷs ab Tewdwr, in conjunction with Einion ab Collwyn, and the latter having obtained from England the aid of Robert Fitzhamon, and twelve other Knights, they entirely defeated him at Hirwaen Wrgant (see *ante*, p. 28). A quarrel between the two chieftains immediately afterwards, owing to Iestyn's refusal to give his daughter in marriage to Einion as promised, induced Einion to recall the Normans who had already entered their ships to return home. He shouted to them, and waved his cloak to call them back. They returned, and were easily persuaded by him to wrest the territory of Glamorgan from its prince. They chased Iestyn out of the country, who crossed the Bristol Channel, and fled to Glastonbury, thence to Bath, and ultimately to the Monastery of Llangenys in Monmouthshire, where he died at the great age of 129. His patrimony was divided into nineteen portions:—thirteen were appropriated to Fitzhamon and his Knights, four to Iestyn's sons, one to Einion, and another to Robert ab Seisyllt.

Iestyn was twice married. His first wife, Denis, was, according to some pedigrees, the daughter of Bleddyn ab Cynfyn; but a comparision of dates will shew that this could scarcely have been so. She may have been his elder sister. By her he had eight children,—Rhydderch, Meredith, Cadwgan, Griffith, Rhiwallon, Morgan Hir, Elen, and Gwenllian. His second wife was Angharad, the daughter of Elystan Glodrudd (founder of the fifth Royal Tribe), and by her he had five children, namely, Caradog, Madog, Morgan (who died young), Rhŷs, and Nest. (*Iolo MSS.* 393).

Morgan Hir (or the Tall) was the ancestor of Alo of Trefnant, Caereinion, Montgomeryshire, who came into Powysland in consequence of having killed the Mayor of Ewyas, Monmouthshire, and married Eva, daughter of Einion Ddistain. From him came the Lloyds of Trefnant, and the Pryces of Glwysegl and Llanfyllin, both now extinct. (*Hist. Powys Fadog*, iv., p. 175). The Pryces of Llanfyllin continued steadfast Roman Catholics, and Lord Castlemaine took refuge with them on the abdication of James the Second. The Glwysegl branch ended in two coheiresses—Mary, the wife of Charles Vaughan, Esq. of Llwydiarth; and Elizabeth, the wife of Thomas Maurice Esq. of Lloran.

Caradog was lord of Avan or Aberavan (*vulgo*, Aberavon), which he enfranchised. He married Gwladus, sister [query daughter?] of the Lord Rhŷs, and was the ancestor of the Avans of Avan, Pryces of Briton Ferry, Thomas's of Bettws, Loughors of Tythegston, and Evans's of Gnoll and Eagles Bush. The three first named appear to be extinct; the

Loughors are represented in the female line by the Knights of Tythegston and Nottage Court,and the Evans's are still extant in the male line. The patriotic family of Williams of Aberpergwm, who have resided there for nearly 900 years, and are now represented by Morgan Stuart Williams, Esq., are also descended in a direct line from Caradog ab Iestyn, and bear his arms quarterly with those of Einion ab Collwyn. So also are the Bevans of Fosbury, Berkshire, and Trent Park, Enfield. *(Nicholas's County Families,* pp. 621, 647).

Madog was the ancestor of the Llewelyns of Caerwiggau, and the numerous descendants of Ievan Mady. *(Clark's Land of Morgan,* p. 39). Catherine, sole daughter and heir of Morgan ap Ievan, Lord of Radyr, of this line, married Thomas ab Sir David Mathew of Llandaff, one of the most distinguished men of his age, and Standard-bearer of England to Edward the Fourth. Of this marriage there was issue, five sons, the eldest of whom, Sir William Mathew of Radyr, was knighted by Henry the Seventh on the field of Bosworth ; and was ancestor of the Earls of Llandaff, who became extinct in 1833. *(Burke's Landed Gentry.)* To an Irish branch of this illustrious family belonged the late Father Mathew, the temperance reformer, as does also Mr. Justice Mathew, and several other branches of it are still extant.

Gwenllian or Arddun—according to *Dwnn's Vis.,* i., p. 190—one of the founder's daughters, married Drumbenog, lord of Cantref Selyf, ninth in descent from whom was Sir Roger Vaughan of Tretower, who married Gwladus, daughter of Sir David Gam, and went with his father in law to the battle of Agincourt in 1415, where both lost their lives in saving that of the king, and just before their death, received the honour of knighthood. Sir Roger Vaughan was the ancestor of the Vaughans of Bredwardine, Herast, Tretower, Clyro (now of Courtfield, Monmouthshire), Talgarth, &c. Walter Vaughan, Esq. of Tretower and Talgarth, was a staunch Royalist, and one of the intended "Knights of the Royal Oak," in the time of Charles the Second. His daughter and sole heiress, Bridget, in 1677, married John Ashburnham, Esq., afterwards created Baron Ashburnham, and ancestor of the Earl of Ashburnham. The other branches of the Vaughan family are supposed to be extinct.

Asar, another of Iestyn's daughters, married Sir Payne Turberville, one of Fitzhamon's Knights, and brought to her husband Coety Castle. Turberville afterwards sided with the Welsh, besieged Fitzhamon in his castle of Cardiff, and forced him to abrogate the Norman laws which he had imposed upon his new subjects. *(L. G. Cothi's Works,* p. 100, *note).* This once powerful family failed in the main male line about the close of the sixteenth century, and the cadet lines have since also failed. Cecil, daughter and heir of Edmond Turberville, Esq. of Llantwit Major, married Iltyd Nicholl, Esq. of The Ham, Glamorganshire. From this union have descended the Nicholls of The Ham, of Merthyr Mawr, and of Penlline, and the Carnes of Nash. *(Burke's Landed Gentry.)*

To this tribe belonged Lord Williams of Thame, Lord President of the Marches of Wales, in the first year of Queen Elizabeth, whose daughter and coheir, Margary, was married to Sir Henry Norris, Knight, ancestor of the Earl of Abingdon. *Pennant's Hist. of Whiteford and Holywell, Appendix.*

The only family extant in North Wales, about the beginning of the present century, descended from Iestyn, is stated by Llwyd *(Beaumaris Bay,* p. 51, *note)*, to be the Mealys of Perfeddgoed, near Bangor, an estate possessed by them from a very remote period, and believed to have been granted to them by Llewelyn ap Griffith. The present representative of this family, is the Rev. John Castle Burnett of Bath, who came into the estate upon the death, 22nd February, 1870, without issue of his first cousin, the late Rev. R. R. Parry Mealy, of Perfeddgoed. Of this family was David Daron, Dean of Bangor, who was outlawed for his complicity with Owen Glyndwr's rebellion. He was the Archdeacon of Shakespeare (Henry the Fourth, Act iii., scene 1., the Archdeacon's house at Bangor). This family bears Iestyn's arms, and for a crest, the Holy Lamb carrying a cross, in remembrance of the fact that Christianity was first brought into Wales by Brân the blessed, the father of Caractacus, from whom, as stated, *ante,* p. 120, Iestyn was twenty-ninth in direct descent.—*Ed.*

ATHELSTAN GLODRYDD.[1]

OF this Regulus, the founder of the fifth Royal Tribe, I learn little, but that his country lay between the Wye and Severn, and was anciently called Ferlis: It was independent of the Princes of South Wales. He was the son of Cyhelyn ab Ifor, by Rhiengar, the daughter and heiress of Grono ab Tewdwr Trevor, and from his mother inherited the Earldom of Hereford. He was godson to the Saxon King, Athelstan, who was, it seems, no kind gossip; for at Glodrydd's baptism[2] he marched a strong army against Hereford, and imposed on the country a yearly tribute of twenty pounds in gold, three hundred pounds in silver,

A.D.
933

---

[1] Oftener called *Elystan Glodrudd*=Athelstan "of ruddy fame," Elystan being a corruption of Athelstan. In the Triads he is classed with Morgan Mwynfawr and Gwaethfoed, as " the three band-wearing princes," which insignia they assumed instead of crowns, like the previous Kings of Britain.—*Ed.*

[2] The uncertainty of dates is very perplexing. Mr. Robert Vaughan says, "That Gruffudd ab Cynan, Rhŷs ab Tewdwr, and Bleddyn ab Cynfyn, being the only Royal Tribes then existing, founded two more." As far as this relates to Jestyn ab Gwrgant, the matter may be clear, for these four may be said to have been contemporaries about the year 1073, although Gruffudd at that time had not attained the throne ; but the honor of representing the fifth Royal Tribe must have been given to the sons of Athelstan Glodrydd in the name of their father then deceased ; for our Chroniclers date his birth, as above, in the year 933.* " By Llwyth, or tribe, was meant," says Mr. Llwyd of the Museum, "the descendants from such a person, and not the person himself; so the twelve sons of Jacob are called the twelve tribes of Israel, because from them sprang the twelve tribes of Israel ; and our tribes must be considered in the same sense as Moses called the twelve sons of Jacob tribes, because they represented their posterity, the tribes."

* Some authorities assign 927 as the date of his birth.—(*Dwnn's Vis.*, i., p. 139, *note.*)—*Ed.*

and fine of two thousand five hundred cattle, with a certain number of hounds and hawks.[1]

Of the descendants of Glodrydd were the Powels of Worthen. The male line of this house hath lately become extinct in John Powel Esquire, and the estate and lordship of Worthen hath devolved to John Kynaston Powel Esquire of Hardwick[2] in right of his mother, and sister in half blood to the last gentleman of Worthen. The Powels were anciently seated at Henllan in Denbighshire, and in the Seventh Henry's time their ancestor, Madog, marries Jane, daughter of Dafydd Myddelton of Gwaun-

---

[1] This arbitrary tribute, extorted from the Welsh while under the influence of power, was no longer regarded, than while the Kings of England had the means of enforcing its observance. Edgar, the nephew of Athelstan and son of his brother Edmund, converted into a present of wolves' heads the tribute paid by the Welsh in gold and silver, &c., originally imposed on them by Athelstan. Edgar was rowed on the Dee by eight tributary petty Princes. [Athelstan, or Elystan Glodrudd, married Gwenllian, daughter of Einion ab Hywel Dda, by whom he had three sons, Cad and Madog of whom little is known, and Cadwgan, the father of a numerous family. Elystan was born at Hereford, and was living in 1010, aged about eighty-three years, but was killed in a civil broil at Cefndigoll, and in *Harl. MS.* 1973, it is stated that he was buried at Trelystan, in Montgomeryshire, on the borders of Shropshire. For arms he bore, according to Vaughan the antiquary, two coats quartered, *azure* three boar's heads caboched *sable*, langued *gules*, tusked *or :* his mother's coat parted per bend sinister *ermine* and *ermines :* over all a lion rampant *or*. Cadwgan, who bore for arms, *argent* three boars' heads coupled *sable* tusked *or*, langued *gules*, married Eva, sister of Iestyn ab Gwrgant, founder of the fourth Royal Tribe. He founded the Cistertian Abbey of Cwmhir, and three churches dedicated to St. Michael at Kerry, Cefnllys, and Llanfihangel-bryn-pab-ifan. He was buried at Abbeycwmhir. His great grandson, Hywel ab Ieuaf, lord of Arwystli, resided at Talgarth, Trefeglwys. He bore *gules* a lion rampant *argent* crowned *or* langued *azure* and he obtained Arwystli as a marriage portion with his wife, Merinedd, daughter of Gruffudd ab Cynan, founder of the first Royal Tribe. He died about 1185, and was buried at the Abbey of Strata Florida.—*Ed.*]

[2] See note, p. 86, *ante.*

ynog, the gentleman who obtained his wife (the Done) so roughly, as before related.[1]

The Powels of Ednop, now extinct, were of this Tribe. Powel, the Poet, of this house dedicates his Pentarchia to Charles the First, then Prince of Wales, but it does not appear it was ever printed.[2] He has taken great liberties with prosody and orthography; there are however many good lines, and he is accurate in his facts. He prefaces it modestly enough in the following verses:[3]

> *Non ita sum gnarus, nec in arte peritus* heraldâ
> *Singula ut innumerem, nec enim mihi tanta facultas :*
> *Quod potui feci, quod restat suppleat alter*
> *Doctior, et nostris faveat non invidus ausis.*

I cannot find when he died, or more in relation to him. Could we reach family authorities (certainly abundant), much would be known on the subject in general, and I trust as a good Welshman, that the time may come when that will be the case.

The Owenses of Rhiw saeson descended from Glodrydd: The male line ended in Corbet Owen Esquire, and his sister Anne married Price Maurice Esquire of Lloran, and was mother of Edward Maurice[4] Esquire of Ynys y maengwyn, an estate he

---

[1] See note, p. 95, *ante.*

[2] The original MS. is at Brogyntyn. A literal copy of it was printed in *Arch. Cam.* 1879, p. 267.—*Ed.*

[3] These are wanting in the Brogyntyn MS.—*Ed.*

[4] In the transactions of the Society for the encouragement of Arts is an account of Mr. Corbet's improvement of many hundred acres at Ynys y maengwyn, for which he was presented with a gold medal.

possesses in virtue of the marriage of Anne Corbet, the heiress, to Athelystan Owen Esquire of Rhiw saeson, his mother's father.[1]

The Pryces of Newtown, Bodfach, and Glan Miheli,[2] descended from Glodrydd: They were settled at the first place about the time of Henry the Sixth, and the two last families were branches of Newtown. Their ancestor, Rhŷs, was an Esquire of the Body to Edward the Fourth. The male line of Newtown ended in Sir Edward Manley Pryce, who died a bachelor some few years since.[3] His father, Sir John Powel Price, married a Manley of Manley. This gentleman was accustomed to follow his hounds many years after he had totally lost his sight, and would run the risk of some dangerous leaps. The grandfather (Sir John Pryce) to the last Baronet was a gentleman

[1] Under the entail created by Mrs. Owen, the estate, after the death of Mr. Maurice (afterwards Corbet), eventually vested in Athelstan Corbet (previously Maurice), Esq., who died 26th December, 1835. After his death, it was held in trust for his niece, Henrietta, wife of John Soden, Esq., whose son, Athelstan John Soden, came into the property, on attaining his majority in 1870. He died unmarried about ten years ago, and the estate was sold. The greater portion of it was purchased by John Corbett, Esq. M.P. for Droitwich, the present owner.—*Ed.*

[2] Anne, daughter and heir of Edward Pryce of Glanmiheli, married Bell Lloyd, Esq., whose son, Edward Pryce Lloyd, was created Lord Mostyn. See *ante*, p. 99, *note.*—*Ed.*

[3] He was found dead in a field at Pangbourne, near Reading, on the 28th October, 1791. He was so destitute, it is said, as not to have left even the means to pay the expense of his interment. His body, therefore, remained unburied for *forty five weeks*, when at last some benevolent persons had it buried at their cost. Some say that he had married the daughter of a Mr. Flinn of Norfolk Street, London, and had by her an only son, who died an infant in his father's lifetime. Some years afterwards, a coffin enclosing the remains of a child were discovered in the roof of a house at Chiswick, to which a plate was nailed, with an inscription stating the body to be that of Edward Manley Powell Pryce, only son and heir of Sir Edward Manley Pryce, Bart., who died April 28th, 1788, aged five years and a half.—*Ed.*

of worth, but of strange singularities. He married three wives; his first, a Powel, the granddaughter of Sir John Powel, one of the Justices of the King's bench (in the reign of James the Second), who eminently signalized his integrity and resolution in the case of the seven Bishops. To the memory of his second wife, a Morris, Sir John Pryce wrote an elegy of a thousand lines, still extant; in which he affirms, that with his latest breath he would *lisp* Maria's name.[1] But he forgot his vow, and was soon smitten with the charms of a widow Jones. This lady would not give her hand to Sir John until he had entombed her predecessors, who had, till that time, lain in state and chemical[2] preparations in his bedchamber. He survived this wife also, and on her death writes to Bridget Bostock,[3] the Cheshire Pythoness, to this purposes; [4]"Madam,—Being very well informed by very creditable people, both private and public, that you have done several wonderful cures, even when physicians

[1] She died August 3rd, 1739. On the 6th July, 1741, Sir John wrote a very singular letter to the Rev. William Felton, Curate of Newtown, then lying dangerously ill, and who died the very next day; beseeching him to convey several loving messages from him to his "two dear wives," especially to the latter of them. On the 19th December following, he married his third wife.—*Ed.*

[2] We had a later instance in John Vanbutchel's wife (the spring-band and garter man) pickled by William Hunter, and more highly preserved by an epitaph of great humour and of fine taste and latinity, attributed to the first perhaps of our modern Physicians.—Appendix xxi.

[3] During this season of miracles worked by Bridget Bostock of Cheshire, who healed all diseases by prayer, faith, and an embrocation of fasting spittle, multitudes resorted to her from all parts, and kept her salival glands in full employ.—*Pennant.*

[4] The copy of Sir John Pryce's letter here given, is taken from *Arch. Camb.*, second series, vol. v., p. 108; that given in the original edition of this work being inaccurate.—*Ed.*

R

have failed; and that you do it by the force and efficacy of your prayers mostly if not altogether (the outward means you use being generally supposed to be inadequate to the effects produced), I cannot but look upon such operations to be miraculous, and if so, why may not an infinitely good and gracious God, enable you to raise the Dead, as well as to heal the Sick, give sight to the Blind, and hearing to the Deaf? For since He is pleased to hear your prayers, in some cases so beneficial to mankind, there's the same reason to expect it in others, and consequently in that I have particularly mentioned, namely, raising up the Dead. Now, as I have lost a wife, whom I most dearly loved, my children one of the best of stepmothers, all her near Relations, a friend whom they greatly esteemed, and the Poor a charitable benefactress; I entreat you, for God Almighty's sake, that you wou'd be so good as to come here if your actual presence is absolutely requisite, or if not, that you will offer up your prayers to the throne of Grace on my behalf, that God wou'd graciously vouchsafe to raise up my dear wife, Dame Eleanor Pryce, from the Dead,—this is one of the greatest acts of charity you can do, for my heart is ready to break with grief at the consideration of the great loss—this wou'd be doing myself and all her Relations and friends, such an extraordinary kindness, as would necessarily engage our daily prayers for your preservation, as the least gratuity I could make you for so great a benefit, tho' were any other compatible with the nature of the thing, and durst we offer, and you accept it, we should think nothing too much to the utmost of our abilities, and I wish the bare mention of it is not offensive both to God and you. If your immediate presence is indispensably necessary, pray let me know by return of the Post, that I may send you a Coach and Six and Servants to attend you here, with orders to defray your expenses in a manner most suitable to your own desires. If your prayers will' be as effectual at the distance you'r from me, pray signify the same in a letter directed by way of London, to, good Madam, Your unfortunate afflicted petitioner and humble Servant,—John Pryce.—Buckland, 1st December, 1748. P.S.—Pray direct your Letter to Sir John Pryce, Bart., at Buckland in Brecknockshire, South Wales. God almighty prosper this undertaking, and others intended for the . Benefit of mankind, and may He long continue such a useful person upon Earth, and afterwards crown you with Eternal Glory. in the Kingdom of Heaven, thro' Jesus Christ.—AMEN."[1]

[1] Sir John Pryce intended a *fourth* marriage as appears by his Will, a very curious document (see copy in *Mont. Coll.*, xvi., p. 283). He died at Haverfordwest, on the 28th October, 1761, and was buried there. He was comparatively poor when he died, and his son and grandson squandered nearly all that remained of his once very fine estate. On the failure of male descendants of Sir John Pryce, on the death of Sir Edward Manley Pryce in 1791, the remnant of the estate came to the Rev. George Arthur Evors (Sir John Pryce's grandson in the female line), who died without issue in 1844. He devised it to his nephew, Arthur Brisco, Esq., who died a bachelor and intestate in the lifetime of his father, the late Wastel Brisco, Esq., who therefore inherited it. He died April 18th, 1878, and thereupon his second son, Wastel Brisco, Esq., the present owner, came into the estate.—*Ed.*

[ADDENDA.]

THE descendants of Elystan Glodrudd were at one time very numerous, especially in Radnorshire, Cardiganshire, and Montgomeryshire; and although most of the main lines have failed, the alliances in past ages with families belonging to other tribes, such as those of Brochwel Ysgythrog, Cadivor, Gwaethfoed, and Einion ab Seisyllt, were so frequent, that there is little difficulty, even at the present day, in tracing the descent of very many families in Central Wales and the English borders, indirectly to the founder of this tribe. The Blayneys of Gregynog, for instance, who were of the tribe of Brochwel, were closely connected by marriage with both the Owens of Rhiwsaeson, and the Pryces of Newtown.

The following families directly descended from Elystan, are I believe still flourishing :— Lloyd of Dinas, Breconshire; Lloyd, Pentrathro; Jenkins, Cilbronau, Cardiganshire (represented by Col. Heyward of Crosswood, Montgomeryshire, only son of the late Rev. John Jenkins of Kerry); Jenkins of Trefigin; Lloyd of Coedmore; Campbell Davys of Neuaddfawr; Thomas of Llwynmadog, Breconshire; Thomas of Wellfield, Radnorshire; Blayney of Evesham; Evans of Ash Hill, Limerick and Milltown Castle, Cork; Lloyd of Ferney Hall, Salop; Morrice of Betshanger, Kent; Lloyd of Gilfachwen; Morris of Hurst, Pentrenant and York; the Earl of Cadogan; Williams of Pentremawr, Llanbrynmair (some of this family are in America); Pugh of Cwmrhaiadr (represented in the maternal line by Williams of Wallog, Cardiganshire); and Thomas of Coedhelen, Carnarvonshire and Trevor Hall. Sir William Thomas of Coedhelen, ancestor of the present Rice William Thomas, Esquire, of that place, was Member of Parliament for the County of Carnarvon, in the fifth Parliament of Queen Elizabeth. He subsequently commanded two hundred Welshmen in the Low Countries, under the Earl of Leicester, and was slain at the battle of Zutphen, where Sir Philip Sidney also fell.

Dr. John Lloyd, Bishop of St. David's, who died in 1687, was a lineal descendant from Einion of Mochdre (ancestor of the Pryces of Newtown), and so to Elystan. (*Dwnn's Vis.*, i., p. 301).

Eva (or, according to some, Mabli), daughter and heiress of Henry ab Gwilym of Court Henry, eleventh in descent from Elystan, married Sir Rhŷs ab Thomas, K.G., one of the most distinguished and powerful men of his time, who was related to Henry the Seventh and was a great favourite of Henry the Eighth. He died in the year 1527, at the age of seventy-six, and, as well as his wife, was buried in the Priory Church at Carmarthen, their monumental effigies being afterwards removed to St. Peter's Church in that town. His arms were *argent* a chevron *sable* between three ravens *proper*. (*Dwnn's Vis.*, i., p. 210, *note.*) Sir Rhŷs ab Thomas, whose illustrious grandfather,

Gruffudd ab Nicholas, was also maternally descended from Elystan, was the ancestor of the noble families of Pembroke and Powis. Some authorities (see *L. G. Cothi's Works*, p. 170) say that Eva had a sister, Jonet, who was married to Sir William Matthew of Radyr, ancestor of the Earls of Llandaff. See *ante*, p. 123.

The following families appear to have become extinct :—Lewis of Gernos, Cardiganshire ; Lloyd of Porthykrwys, Llanynys, Breconshire, whose heiress, Margaret, about the commencement of the seventeenth century, married John Stedman, Esq. of Strata Florida *(Dwnn's Vis.*, i., p. 242) ; Vaughan of Beguildy *(Ib.*, 251) ; Pryce of Mynachdy *(Ib.*, 252) ; Lloyd of Rhayader ; Phillips of Llandewi Ystradeny, and Powel of Cwmtoyddwr *(Ib.*, 260); Vaughan of Linwent *(Ib.*, 261) ; Powel of Cascob *(Ib.*, 262) ; Miles of Harpton, Old Radnor *(Ib.*, 263) ; Price of Radnor *(Ib.)* ; Owen of Machynlleth, Morben, and Peniarth *(Ib.*, 272) ; Broughton of Lower Broughton or Owlbury *(Ib.*, 329) ; Parry of Llanerchydol *(Ib.*, 332) ; Kerry of Binweston ; Clun of Clun ; Oliver, Neuaddwen ; Oliver, Llangyniew ; Wynn, Gellidywyll and Llanfendigaid ; Meredith, Llanafan ; James, Croesgynar ; and Matthews of Blodwel. *(Pennant's Whitford and Holywell, Appendix.*

The Pryces of Plas yn y Rofft (now called Esgairweddan), Towyn, Merionethshire, were maternally descended from Elystan *(Dwnn's Vis.*, ii., p. 239) ; but this line failed in the male line, on the death of Sir John Edwards, Bart. of Machynlleth, in 1850. The present Dowager Marchioness of Londonderry is his only child and heir. The estate of the Pryce's, however, belongs to another branch of the family, the Thrustons of Talgarth Hall.

Margaret, daughter and heiress of Owen ap Griffith of Gorddwr Linwent, fourteenth in descent from Elystan, married Owen Vaughan of Llwydiarth *(Dwnn's Vis.*, i., p. 291). His descendant, Anne Vaughan, heiress of Llwydiarth, married Sir Watkin Williams Wynn, the third Baronet, whereby the Llwydiarth and Llangedwyn estates were conveyed to the Wynnstay family. See *ante*, p. 104.

Elizabeth, daughter of Matthew Pryce of Newtown, sometimes called Matthew Goch, married Edward Herbert, Esq., of which marriage there was issue, four sons and seven daughters. Three of the sons became ancestors of peers, namely, of Edward first Lord Herbert of Chirbury, of Sir Henry Herbert of Ribbesford, afterwards Lord Herbert of Chirbury, of the second creation, and of the Earls of Powis of the present line. Bridget, daughter and heiress of Arthur Pryce, Esq. of Vaynor, Matthew Goch's great grandson, married George Devereux, the ancestor of the Viscounts Hereford, to whom she conveyed the Vaynor estate, but which was subsequently sold, and now belongs to William Corbett Winder, Esq.

For a more full account of Elystan Glodrudd and his descendants, see *Mont. Coll.*, i., p. 235.—*Ed.*

APPENDIX.

No. I.

William Morgan, Bishop of St. Asaph, to Sir John Wynn of Gwydir.

SALUTEM IN CHRO.

YOURE motyves that I shold confyrme youre Lease upon the Rectorye of Llan Rŵst are dyverse, vz.

1. Youre greeffe to mysse, havynge neaver fayled before of anie attempte.

2. That you had rather forgoo 100l. landes a yeare.

3. That the rent reserved ys as much as the Rectorye ys worth.

4. That youe purchased the Lease deere.

5. That yᵉ. world may thynke youre love to me ward unkyndlye rewarded.

6. That others, by my example, wyll lesse esteme youe.

7. That youe hope to finde me such to youe, as youe are to me.

8. That the adioynyng of Tybrith did cost you much.

9. My sundrie promysses that youre Lease shold be the fyrst. And one thynge moveth me agaynst all these, vz. my conscience, wᶜʰ. assureth me that youre request ys such, that in grauntyng yt I shold prove my selfe an unhonest, unconscionable and irreligiouse man ; ye a sacrilegiouse robber of my church, a perfydiouse spoyler of my Diocesse, and an unnaturall hyndrer of preachers and good scholers ;—the consyderatione whereof wold be a contynual terror and torment to my conscience. And to com to youre motyve reasons :

1. I pray God that youre greeffe of myssynge be not Achab's greeffe for Nabothe's vineard.

2. 100l. landes are worth 200l. tyth.

3. I credyblie heare that Rectorye to be worth twyse the rent reserved ; the wᶜʰ. youre seconde reason confyrmeth.

4. Youre 4 reason confyrmeth the same ; for youe wold not purchase deere a Lease worth lytlc more then the rent.

5. Youe have shewed to me much kyndnesse, but no unhonest kyndnesse ; neather do I ever meane to denie youe in youre honest requestes.

6. You shall not be the better estemed by gettynge ungodleye requestes, but worse thought of ; for to fayle of badd attemptes ys no shame, but to relynquysh them wylbe greate credyt.

7. Youe shall finde me, such as I desyre to find youe, in omnibus licitis et honestis, youre assured.

8. I do not counte the adioynyng of Tybrith to be eather hurtfull or beneficiall to me or the church.

9. My promysse was and ys, that I wylle do nothing for anie subject wth. I wyll nott do for youe, and that I wyll not confyrme anie such Lease as youre's before youre's. Neather am I nowe mynded to confyrme anie lease at all. But the Chaptre do meane to revyve one lyff in a lease of theare's.

Amongest other youre kyndnesses, you gave good testymonie of me. I pray youe lette me continewe worthie of yt. So manie chypps have bene allreadye taken from the church, that yt ys readye to fall. God hath blessed youe so well, that youe are bownde rather to helpe hys poore church then to hynder yt.

Thus wth. my hartiest commendationes to youre selfe and good Mystres Wyn, I reast

Eveare youre owne in y^e. Lorde,

Willm. Asaphen.

15°. *Ffebr,*
1603.

Verte Folium.

I knowe of syxe or seaven suters for confyrmationes of Leases upon presentatyve benefyces, wth. meane to brynge the landes of Pryvye Counsellers, yff not Hys Maiestye's owne lande. And at the next Parliament, I look to be layde to. But I trust y^t. God wyll defende me and hys church.

W. A.

One wold open the doore for all the reaste.

[To the Right Wor. his
veary lovying Frend,
John Wyn of Gwedur,
Esquicr.]

No. II.

Answer to the Above.

HOMINIBUS ingratis loquimini, lapides. The sower went out to sowe; and some of his seede fell in stonie ground, where hitt wythered, because hitt could take noe roote. The seede was good, but the land nought. I may justly say soe by you. I have in all shewed my selfe your ffreinde, in soe much as yf I had not pointed you the waye with my finger (whereof I have yett good testimonye) you had beene styll Vycar of Llanrhayder. You pleade conscience when you should geve, and make no bones to receave curtesie of your ffriends. But I appeale to him that searcheth the conscience of all men, whether you have used me well, and whether hitt be conscience (wth. you ever have in your mouth) be the sole hinderance of my request. I wyll avowe and justiffie hitt befor the greatest Dyvyns in England, that it hath beene, nowe ys, and ever wylbe, that a man may wth. a salfe conscience be farmour of a lyvinge, payeing in effect for the same as much as hitt ys woorth ; and soe ys this, surmyse you the value to be as you layst. Nether was the losse of the thynge that I regard a dodkyn, but your unkinde dealinge. Hitt shall leson me to expect noe sweete fruite of a sower stocke. Your verball love I esteeme as nothinge ; and I make noe doubt (wth. God's good favour) to lyve to be able to pleasure you, as much as you shall me, et é contrà. You byd me thank God for his meny benefytts towards me. God graunt me the grace ever soe to doe. In truth, I did much thanke Him in mynde to see you preferred to the place you are in, as yf you had beene my owne brother ; but that I recall, for I never expect good wyll of you, nor good torne by you.

John Wyn,
of Gwyder.

Gwyder, the house that
did you and your's good.
24*th February*, 1603.

[To the Reverend Father, The
Lord Busshop of St. Asaphe.]

———◆◇◆◇◆———

No. III.

Sir John Wynn to Mr. Martyn.

MR. MARTYN,

SIR,

NO greefe to the greefe of unkyndnes : They rewarded me yll for good to the great dyscomfort of my sole. I may say so, and justly complaen unto you of my L. of St. Asaphe, who (besydes what hys ancestors receved by myen) ys dyversly, and in great matters, behouldynge unto me, whereof (beynge schooled by hys late letter, of wth. I send you a trew coppy) thoghe I expect no rent, yett yt easethe my wronged mynd muche, to lay open hys hard dealyngs towards me, and my benefyts towards hym, befor you, who are not ignorant that I delyver but a truethe, in most of them havynge been an ey wytnes.

Hyt squarethe therefor wth. a good method in a narration to begyn wth. my deserts, wth. I wyll run over breefly ; wth. I wold have you to put hym in mynd of : 1. in that he protested to hys late servant Tho. Vaghan, that he remmbred no more therof, then that I had lent hym my geldyngs to go to Llandaff, and had sent hym a fatt oxe att hys fyrst comynge to St. Assaphe. W^ch. ys to strayne a gnatt, and swallow a camell.

Fyrst, I let hym have a Lease uppon hys farme of Wybernant, parte of the township of Doluthelan for forty years, for forty poundes in money. The farme he hathe sett att the yerly rent of twenty foure poundes per ann : and yeldethe of the Kyng's rent viijs. too pence yerly, as farre as I remember.

In measurynge the sayd farme wth. my farme of Penannen, I let hym have, in Pant yr Helygloyn, land to the valew of iijl. yerly ; for wth. my uncle Owen Wyn reprooved me muche.

I bare the hatred of Jeuan M'dythe, and hys nephew Ed. Morice, the lawyer, durynge hys lyfe ; for that I was a daysman, and agaenst hym ; I mean, Jeuan M'dythe, and appointed my frends commyssyoners agaenst hym.

Was hyt not I that fyrst delt wth. Mr. Boyer to make hym Bushopp, and made the bargen, S^r ? Mr. Boyer was nether knowen to hym, nor he to Mr. Boyer ; ergo, yf that had not beene, he had contynued styll Vycar of Llan Rhayder. I know you do not forgett what was obiected against hym and hys wyf to stopp his last translation, and how that my certyfycatt and my frends quitted hym of that imputation, and so made hym prevayle ; for the wh^ch. both they and I wear worse thoght of by those we have good cause hyghly to respect.

I labored, as yf hit had had beene to save the lyf of on of my chyldren, to end the cause of dylapidations between hym and my coosin Dd. Holland ; knowynge hit wold have beene his great hynderance to be so matched att first dashe. How sufficyent a man, how well ffrended, and what a toothe-man in hys suets my cousin Holland ys, every man that knowethe hym, knowethe that also.

My L. of St. Assaphe I knew to be but poore (hys translation havynge stood him in muche) yett wylfull and heddy to run into law suets ; therefor I was as muche trobled to reclaeme hym to reson and consyderation of hys owen estate as I was to bringe the adversse part to reson and conformyty. My L. Bushopp's cheefe lyvynge was the tenth of the Paryshe of Abergele, where my coosin Holland comandeth absolutely. Yf they had gone to suet of law, he would so have wronged hym in the gatherynge of

S

the tythe, as hit shold have beene lyttell worthe unto hym. My self excepted, was ther on Jent. in the contrey wold once have shewed hym self for hym agaenst my coosin Holland? and that knew he well. But my L. can make use of Jent. when they serve hys torne, and after decarde them upon pretence of conscyence ; wch. may appere by the coppye of hys letter unto me, whereof, I avowe on my credyt this ys the trew coppye. Thus much touchynge that matter of my desert ; and now touchynge fny request.

M^r. Sharp, my L. Chancelor's Chaplen beynge by hys L. collated parson of Llanrŵst, leased hys benefyce to on Robt. Gwyn of Chester, who appointed a ffrend of myen, on Robt. Vaughan, brother to my brother Tho. Vaughan, his under farmor. Doctor Elice, somtyme a great comander in theese quarters, in favor of Doctor Meryke (who rewarded him wth. a township of teythe whear his mansyon house was in 'Spytty) dyd geeve lev to dysmember the parsonadge of Llan rŵst of Tybrithe tythe, and to joyne hit to Corwen. Whearuppon, pyttyinge to see Llan rŵst churche dysmembered by unlawfull practyse, acqueanted my L. of S^t. Assaphe, that I ment to stand for the right of Llanrŵst agaenst Doctor Meryke, wth. an intent to do more for that churche, as I then made knowen to my L. The suet prooved, by Doctor Meryke's weywardnes and hope in his fautors, more chardgeable and troblesom then was expected. Wheruppon I eftsons acquainted my L. Bushop, that I ment to buy Robt. Gwyn's lease into my hands, that, surrendringe hit, Mr. Sharp (in consyderation of my great chardge in the suet) myght grant me a lease of the lyvynge for iij lyves, the only mean in some part to quit my chardge ; wth. he promysed me to confyrme, and that hit should be the fyrst of all other that should receve confyrmation. Havynge to my chardge and troble compased Robt. Gwyn's lease of 10 years, and by surrender of the same gott a new lease of three lyves of Mr. Sharp, I sent hyt to be shewed my L. by my servant W^m. Lloyd ; who then seemed to myslyke hit, and answered doutfully touchynge the confyrmation, wth. all chidd Mr. Sharp in suche sort, as givynge cause to have my lease new made, he made me pay 10l. more then was att fyrst, by reson my L. Bushop had chidd hym. In end, hearynge of a Chapter appointed for the confyrmation of the other leases, I sent myen also by my son Mostyn, and my letter to my L. the contents whearof you shall fynd in my Lord's answer. To wch. I receved this answer, wth. whether hit be fyttynge my desert ys your's to judge, as also to expostulat wth. hym, beynge oure ffrend, common to us bothe.

I am not of nature to put up wronge ; for as I have studyed for hys good, and wrought the same, so lett my L. be assured of me as bytter an enemye (yf he dryve me to hit) as ever I was a stedfast frend ; nether ys he com to that heyght, or wantethe enemyes, that he may say, Major sum, quám cui possit fortuna nocere. For as Honores mutant mores, so mores mutant honores. I am ashamed for hym, that he hath geeven herby cause to his enemyes and myen to descant of his ungrate dysposition ever aggravated towards hym. Hys answer att lardge I pray you retorne me, yf nothynge els.

Your lovynge ffrend,

GWYDER, this xiijth of Marshe, 1603.

John Wyn,

of Gwyder.

He promysed me an advowson of the lyvynge by Tho. Robts, when he denyed the confyrmation. I sent unto hym the same man, wth. in too dayes after for the same, and my coosin Elice Vaghan wth. all; and he denyed me eny, saynse he had provyded no preferment for his wife, and that he myght overlyve Sharpe, and have that lyvynge in Comendam. So, to conclude, I must have nothynge but a scornefull, chetynge letter, in leu of all my good indeavors.

No. IV.

Bishop Morgan, to Mr. Martyn.

SALUTEM IN C.HRO.

I Fynd that Mr. Wyn hath acquaynted you wth. the unkyndnes wch. he conceaveth in me; and I am glad to have so indyfferent an arbytrator. Hys requeste was, that I wold confyrme a Lease for three lyves upon the Rectorye of Llanrŵst (being a presentatyve benefyce, fytt to be some preacher's lyvynge) at the yearelye rent of 50l. the thynge being worth 140l. and beinge of my patronadge. Thys requeste much perplexed my mynde, for that yt greved me to denye Mr. Wyn anye thynge, and my conscyence reclaymed agaynst the grauntynge of thys thynge, being so preiudiciall to preachers, speciallye to the next incumbent and to the church yt self, wch. wanteth competent mayntenance for preachers.

To com to the pleasures that Mr. Wyn dyd unto me, they are not so greate as he accounteth them; for I payd for hys time upon Wybernant, and hys uncle Rob^te^. 40l. or more att one tyme, beinge a greater some then they had of anie of the other tenantes that held lyke landes in that township. I pray God forgeve Mr. Wyn hys harde dealynge wth. these tenantes, whose tenementes he could not covett w^th^oute impiety.

In measurynge of Pant yr Helygloyn, I had lesse then some affyrmed to be due unto me, and more then others wyshed ; in leue wheareof I was to erect a stone wall, or a dytch of earth, betweene me and hym to my greate charges.

Jeuan Meredydd and I weare ffrendes, when, upon Mr. Wyn hys request, I gott to hys brother Robt. Wyn his nowe wyf; wth. caused such hatred and sutes betwene me and the sayd Jeuan, that yt cost me from 6ol. to 1ool. more than I had. Mr. Wyn in deed procured to me two commyssioners, Mr. Morys Johnes once, and Mr. Morys Lewys, an other tyme ; and was my dayseman to ende that cause. I sustayned all those broyles and obloquyes for hys sake and hys brother's.

He wrote unto me allreadye, that yff he had not bene, I had contynued yet Viccar of Llan Rhayadr. How much he ys deceaved herein, youe and others do knowe. But yff I had contynued Vicar of Llan Rhayadr, I had bene in better case then nowe I am. I had testymonials inough bysydes that wth. he procured ; and I had prevayled, yff I had had none, as my Lo. of Canterburye and my L. Treasurer beleved. Yet I confesse that Mr. Wyn thearein shewed great love (as then I thought) to me ; but (as nowe I fynde) to hym selfe, hopynge to make a stave of me to dryve preachers partryges to hys netts. I thanke Mr. Wyn for hys paynes in daynge betwene me and Mr. Holande ; although he gott me but 15ol. wheare I shold have had 1oool, But I may not requyte thys paynes wth. the spoyle of anie church. Yt seemeth that Mr. Wyn thynketh that I do but pretend conscyence. But I assure youe, in verbo Sacerdotis, that I think in my harte, that I weare better robb by the hygh waye syde, then do that wth. he requeasteth. And I knowe that as to serve an errynge conscyence ys a falt, so to do agaynst con-scyence, though yt be errynge, ys a synne. Yff my ffathere and mothere weare lyvynge, and made the request that Mr. Wyn maketh, I hope that I sholde have the grace to say them nay. I fynde farther that Mr. Wyn is in two errors ; the one ys, that I promysed to hym a confyrmatione of that Lease; and the other ys, that I promysed hym by John Robtes an advowson ; wheare in truth I promysed neather of both, but told Mr. Wyn that I wold be veary loath to confyrme anie Lease upon anie presentatyve benefyce ; that I wold do for hym as much and more then anie other ; and that yff I wold confyrme anie such, hys shold be the fyrst. I neaver confyrmed anie, nor meane to do. But the Chapter and I graunted, not iij lyves, but one lyff, not upon a presen-tatyve benefyce, but upon an impropriatione, wth. is a dyvydent amongst manie, and can not be occupyed by anie of us, for that we are farr of and thearefore must be letten for one terme or other ; and the incumbe ys for the church, and not for a lay man. But Mr. Wyn thoughe he knoweth that theare ys dyfference betwene grauntynge a lease of oure owne and confyrmynge the lease of an other man ; betwene a presentatyve benefyce and an impropriatione ; betwene one lyff and iij lyves ; betwene a publyke use and a pryvate, styll exclaymeth, that I have confyrmed a lyke lease, and wyll not according to promyse confyrme hys. My answeare to John Robtes was, that a Bushopp's advowson wold not bynde the successor ; and when he asked, whyther Mr. Wyn shold have yt, yff yt dyd bynde, I told hym, that, yff yt dyd bynde, he shold have yt and myne eares also ; for that I dyd well knowe that yt can not bynde. And when he cam next to aske, yf I wold graunt yt de bene esse, whyther yt wold bynde or not, I told hym, I wold not, and that yt was no part of my promyse or meanynge. John Robtes mystooke my wordes concernynge my wyff ; for I dyd not say that she must be fyrst provyded for, meanynge that I wyll gett for her anie such lease. For though she be my wyff, and thearefore one flesh, yet shall she be neaver provyded for by me rather then by such leases ; I wyll not spoyle y'. church. Thys was the effect of my then speach, whearby Mr. Wyn myght have understoode that nothynge dryveth me to thys resolutione, but my conscyence. Of my Commendam, I dyd and do say, that yff I weare so lewde as to confyrme all the leases in the Diocesse, yet I wold not be such a foole as to confyrme anie, before I weare better provyded for my Commendam. Yff I dyd, tell Mr. Sharpe, that he shold do well to leave hys lyvynges to hys successors as ffree as he founde the same, I dyd but my duetye. Yff thys weare not a case of con-scyence, you shold not neede to perswade me to gratifye Mr. Wyn ; for hys owne requeste ys of great force w'. me. Youre two reasons, or rather hys reasons (for he used the lyke in hys letters to my selfe) do lytle move me. For yff I shall fynde hym as bytter an enemye, as ever I founde hym my frende, yt wylbe a comfort to me to suffer in so good a cause. I knowe that God, whose church I wold defend, ys able to defende me agaynst all enemyes, and wyll defende me so farr, as he shall see yt to be expedient for me ; that Mr. Wyn can not kyll my soule, nor do to my bodye more then God wyll permytt. And my confydent trust ys, that God wyll not permytt anie thynge to be commytted agaynst me, but that w'^th. shalbe for my good, either in thys worlde or in the worlde to com. And yff dyverse men wyll dyversely descant of thys unkyndnes ; What? ys thys to move a man that shold be setled in conscyence, to do agaynst con-scyence ! I knowe that some do blame me in hys presence, and blame hym and commende me in his absence. And yt may be that others do use me in lyke sort. Inconstans eu mutabile vulgus. Auxilium meum in nomine Dui.

Thus resolved to do neather thys nor anie other act that shalbe preiudiciall to the church,

I rest,

Amicus usque ad aras,

[To llys very lovynge Frende, Mr. Thomas Martyn at hys house over agaynst St. An-drewe's, in Holborne.]

Willm. Asaphen.

[My L. Bushopp, being in London at the Parliament, wrote this unto me.
Thomas Martyn.]

No. V.

William Morgan, Bishop of St. Asaph, to Sir John Wynn of Gwydir.

SALUTEM IN C.HRO.

SEEINGE you can better agree wth. my tithe in Langustenyn then wth. me, and have, as I heare, taken order for the gatheringe of it ; I am loath to contrarie you therin, soe that you send me money by this bearer for the same, although I knowe my tithe to be worthe twise as much as you pay for it.   But I pray you to cause the tithe of Bodescallan to be gathered in kind ; for yo'. cosen Hugh Gwynne Gru : hath written to me that he would tithe it in specie this yeare.

Thus wishinge you in all thinges the direction of the Holy Ghost, I rest,

Yo'. sickly neighbour,

Willm. Asaphen.

At ST. ASAPH, the 24th of July, 1604.

[To his wors. neighbour,
John Wynne of Gwydir,
Esquire.]

————⟨⟩————

No. VI.

Richard Parry, Bishop of St. Asaph, to Sir John Wynn of Gwydir.

GOOD MR. GWYN.

YOU needed not this paynes to remoove anye conceite of myne. Before y'. letters, I never heard of your refusall of Subscription unto myen certificate ; and now havinge heard of it, I conceave no woorse of you then of a very wyse and sufficient gentleman, whose love in anye good and honest cause I shall be glad to deserve.   Touchinge my certiefcate, I did sufficientlye knowe, y'. no one man in my countrey subscribinge wold much further me, nor anye one man wantinge wold anye thinge hinder me.   I am farr from imagininge y'. a gentleman of your place and woorth eyther doth flatter me, or expect benefite by me. You have no cause to use y*. one, and I have no meanes to afforde y*. other ; for as you truelye write, all I have is litle enough for y*. support of mye owne estate.

Your hard censure of my predecessor I am verye sorye to heare ; for I willinglye embrace nothinge : De mortuis nisi sanctum. Domino suo stetit aut cecidit. And so doe we. God graunt we may stand unto the Lord, unto whose defence I commend us ; and with my verye hartye commendations to y'selfe, I rest

Your lovinge frend,

Ric. Asaphen.

GRESFORD, 24to. Febr. 1604.*

[To the R. Woor. mye Lovinge frend
John Gwyn of Gwyder, Esquier, these
at Gwyder.]

◆◇◆◇◆

No. VII.

John Williams (afterwards Abp. of York) to Sir John Wynn.

WORSHIPFULL. SIR,

MY dutie and most heartye comendations remembred. The continuance of your lovinge kindenes towardes me, by howe much the lesse worthylye, by soe much the more must I account my selfe for the same bounde and obliged unto your Worship's service.

Concerninge that money my brother owes me (wth. I cannot tell well whither it be 7 or 8l.) if your Worshippe will this next terme see it convayed to be delivered to my Lord of London's Stewarde, Mr. Griffyn, or to my Tutour Mr. Gwynne, I shall rest bounde unto you. I have written acquittaunces both for the yeare 1604 and the yeare 1605, the owne from Cambridge, and the other from London, in the presence of William Lloyd ; and therefore it is not in my over sight that your Worshippe hath not received them. In place of them this letter may serve your Worshippe.

* This date is, of course, according to the Old Style whereby the year ended 24th March. Bishop Morgan, the writer of the preceding letter, died 10th September, 1604, and was succeeded by Dr. Richard Parry, the writer of this letter. This will explain the apparent contradiction in the dates.—*Ed.*

I have gotten of late a small benefice, wch. will do well, being ioyned to my place in Cambridge ; and therefore if your Worshippe could procure me for this yeare's rent but 7l. before hande, I would give William Lloyd a generall acquittaunce for this yeare ; or if I have two yeares more to expire of my lease (as indeede I do not knowe) I would be contente to take 12l. for both yeares, if your Worshippe could procure me soe much. Howesoever I must and will acknoweledge my selfe æternallye bound to praye for your Worshippe, for your Worship's kinde love and care of me this last yeare ; and soe desiringe oportunitye to make uppe my gratefull wordes wth. thankfull deede, I committ your Worshippe to the Almightie's tuicion.

Your Worshippe's poore kinsman,

bounde in all dutye,

John Williams.

LONDON HOUSE this 5 of Decemb. [1605.]

To the worshipfull, his approved
lovinge kinsman Mr. John Gwynne
Esquier, at Gwydder, deliver these.
Wth. speed.

————◦◦◦◦————

No. VIII.

Mr. Holland to Sir John Wynn.

RIGHT WOOR.

I Doe understand by yor. lres that you purpose to send yor. sonnes to this universitye, soe soone as you cane be resolved in what colledge, and wth. what tutor to place them. Ffor my part I hould S^t. John's colledge to be omni exceptione majus ; not inferior to any colledge for the bringinge up of yonge gentlemen, but the ffyttest and best house that you cann send yor. sonnes unto. And for the choise of a good tutor (yf I may presume to advice you) yor. beast course wilbe to cause yor. good brother Mr. Rychard Gwyn for to commend them by his ltres unto Mr. Dr. Clayton, the master of our colledge, whoe, I ame well assured, will at my cosen Rychard his comendacione be redie to nominate such a tutor for them, as will for his sake be verie respective and carfull of their good.

Touchinge the proportione of allowance that wilbe requisyte for them, I can say lytle ; ffor I doe not know whether you will have them to be in the ffellowes' commons ore not, of wth. rancke yf it be yor. pleasure to have them to be, then cann you allowe noe lesse then threescore pounds yearly for bothe, ov^r. and besyde the apparell ; but yf you purpose to have them to be in the schollers' commons, then halfe the former allowance will serve, ther apparell beinge noe part therof. The tuicione for every ffellow comoner is 4lb. per annum, and a pentioner paythe 40s. yearly to his tutor for readinge to him. Ffurther it wilbe requisyte that they have beddinge, wth. such furniture as shalbe needfull, sent from home. And when they doe come, they shall find me redy to the uttermost of my power, to performe all good offices towards them. Yf my cosen Mr. Owen Gwyn had not beene a discontynewer from the colledge, he, I conffesse, might have donn them greater pleasure then I can doe ; but howsoever yf my cosenes come to St. John's, they shall want noe ffrends in the howse. And thus humbly takinge my leave, I rest ever,

Y^r. woor^{pp}. poore kinsman,

most assured to use,

Wyllm: Hollande.

St. John's Coll. in Cambr.
November the last, 1606.

[To the right woor. my assured
good cosen Sr. John Wynn,
Knight, de: these at Gwyder.]

No. IX.

John Williams (Abp.) to Sir John Wynn.

RIGHTE WORSHIPFULL,

My dutie remembred. I hope by this time your wor. hath received two letters, answeringe in effecte those doubtes propounded in your letter, wch. I receiv'de by this bearer. Since my last ill newes, there hath happen'd here noe occurrence worthe the relatinge ; our feare is noe lesse, and the daunger noe more then it was at firste. Sithence your son's goinge into the countrey (wch. was at this daye se'nighte.) I have heard in a letter from my curate of his well doinge, his abode beinge within a mile of my poore benefice. When he returnes unto the colledge, I will

T

putte that stratagem in practice, wch. you mencion in your letter, and send your wor. the coppye of his theame. For my likinge of his proceedinges, bonâ fide I like his learninge well for his yeares ; his witte better, especiallye when yeares of discretion shall season it. If I listed to find faulte (althoughe truelye no greate cause) I doe sometimes call more egerlye on him to keep his studye, wch. nowe (his gaudye dayes beinge spent) we may more boldlye doe then heretofore ; and he must (as surelye he dothe) daylye amend. Scholler he is for Mr. Price his place ; and so is my man to, Mr. John Lloyd's sonne, for one Sir Dolben's· His tutour, I hope, doth certifye the receipte of such thinges as the bearer broughte him ; onlye his token, beinge five shillinges from my ladye, I have taken uppe, and will deliver it to him at my next goinge to my benefice. I doe hope our colledge shall meete agayne before Christmasse ; for as yeate there is more causeles feare then apparent daunger of any infection. Thus with my heartiest comendacions and bounden dutye to my good Ladye, I commend both your Wor. to God's protection.

Your Wor. in all dutye,

John Williams.

ST. John's Coll. in Camb.
  this 20th. of Novemb. 1608.

Postsc.

I will, by God's leave, either provide him a studye to his full contentement, or make him profer of a studye in myne owne chamber. A dieu.

> [To the righte worshipfull my
> ever approved good freynde, Sir
> John Wynne at Gwydder,
>   deliver these.]

━━━◆◇◆◇◆━━━

No. X.

John Williams (Abp.) to Sir John Wynn.

RIGHT WORSHIPFULL,

M Y moste true love ever remembred. My coz. Robin, who wth. the helpe my serchers hath furnishte you for your provision, doth promisse me to sende you at this time a complete note of his former expences. My mechanique buisinesses at the Fayre are such as I cannot take that paynes therein I otherwise wolde doe. Truelye I cannot excuse either him or his brother, for absence from theyre studyes at extraordinarye howres, or any neglect of theyre Tutor's lectoures. And yeat they are nowe (as formerlye they were) my under-neighboures.

How the proiecte of hasteninge his beinge felowe failed, I list not to enquire ; but I am sure, after your departure there was nothinge donne. And the yssue noe other, but that the Juniour Proctour was sharpelye rebuked, that he, contrarye to the statute, wolde offer to bringe in one by his Majestie's mandate. Who replied, He never went about any such matter ; as resolved, if once he hadd showne himselfe in the buisines, to effecte it, or have line in the dust for it. Marye, he added, that if the youth him-selfe compassed any such matter, he thoughte that he hadde deserv'de that favowre at the Colledge, as to accepte thereof without such grudginge.

What you were enformed of my troubles and oppositions wth. the heades of our colleges, I knowe not ; but this I am certayne, I rest much obliged to your Wor. for your most kind and lovinge counsaile, wch. could proceede from noe other heade, then that well-springe of your former and never-failinge affection. But Mr. Th. Edwards my felowe could have gonne nere to enforme you of all the buisines.

The opposition twixte the maisters of Colleges and the bodie of the Universitye, wch. is the companye of our Regent and Non-regent Maister of Artes, hathe beene soe longe a foote, as any Cantabrigian can enforme you thereof ; but it is most of all perceived in that twixt the vice-chauncelour and the proctoures, who are in a maner Tribuni Plebis, and represente the bodye, as the vice-chauncelour dothe the heades of Colleges. In former yeares, as the vice-ch^{rs}. were allwayes grave old men and Divines by profession (noe yonge, servinge-man lawier, as this yeare) soe the proctours for want of other meanes did over-shoote themselve soe farre in takinge of under-hande considerations ; as that lienge allwayes in the vice-chauncelour's lurche, they never durste shewe themselves either for the maintenaunce of theyre owne places, or the statute-freedom of the Universitye.

My selfe being by God and my good M^r. soe well provided for (to myne own con-tentement at leaste wise) as that my mynde scorn'de to be obnoxious to any man for the leaste bribe or fee due by statute, grewe by soe much the more boulde to stande upon myne owne place and the libertie of the Universitye graunted in statute, and conseqentlye to overthwart the new-fanglednes of this vice-ch^r. endevouring by all meanes possible to reduce our Aristarchie to a Monarchie (as they terme it) but, as we understand, an absolute Tyrannie.

This was soe well taken for the firste parte and moytie of the yeare, that not onelie the M^{rs}. of Artes, who graced me with as many and those extraordinarye favoures, as they laded my adversarye with shame and ignominie ; but the heades of Colleges themselves encouraged with all applause my just and academicall cariage and proceedinges. For you must knowe Dr. Cowel and Dr. Clayton, the two greateste maisters in towne, and my extraordinarye deare freyndes to be as yeat alive ; in whose places......ded two other, defective, thoughe not in affection, yeate in pare.........action.

Afterward falls in the interim our Heade-shippe of St. John's in wch. busines I, servinge my turne abroade, with the good opinion conceiv'de of me at home, was thoughte to have donne such service, as procur'de the hatred of two of the cheefe m^{rr}. Dr. Carye beinge one of them ; who, as they thinke, hadd it not been for me, hadd gott the maistershippe of St. John's There was the first opportunitye the vice ch^r. hadd againste me.

In the weeke of this, falls the death of the L. Treasurer and Chauncelour ; by consequence greate canvasinge who should succeede him. All the heades (two excepted) expectinge bushopricks and deanries, came upon the Archbp. of Canterburye. My selfe, still reposinge great trust in the bodye of the Universitye, and fearinge if his Grace were our Chauncelour, any complaynte of the Vice-chaunc. wolde be hearde against me, who was, both for my buisines of Llanrhayader, and this late of our maistershippe, growne more distastefull unto his Grace, putt all my force togeither, and by many voices, against the heades, chose the L. Privie seale twice to our Chancelour ; thoughe I knewe Googe the vicech^r. to be a servant to his nephewe the L. of Suffolke. You see then a second oportunitie for the Vicech^r. to ioyne wth. the heades to putt somme disgrace upon me.

And yeate all this while, thoughe buisines were in hammeringe, nothinge coulde be donne, while it was terme time, and that the m^{rr}. of Artes hadd occasion of meetinge, my strengthe encreasinge still in the bodie. After the Commencement, all occasions of meetinge for this yeare ended, the vicech^r. desirous to revenge somme p^{rr}. of his disgraces, upon me, whom he hadd envied for the love of the Universitye shewed me, then for any other cause hated, ioynn'de wth. these heades, and summon'd me to appeare before them ; yeate not soe suddenlye, but I was given to understand, that yf I appear'de, he wold de facto committ me to prison. Whereupon, one of these inconveniences, either to incurr by submission a disgrace nev^r. heard of in a proctour of an Universitye, and most unbeseeminge my person (having soe nere a dependaunce upon soe Honourable a P^{r}sonage) or els by resistinge a suspicion to be the authour of a riot and tumulte, into wch. I sawe all the m^{rr}. so readye to enter ; hereupon I gave place to this Bedleme felowe, whom I knewe arm'de with authorityc, and appeal'de to our newe-chosen Chauncelour, where I had an honourable and noe disgracefull releese.

Here indeed we have stucke these ten weeks. The vicech^r. desirous of somme disgrace on me before my going out of this office, and I on the contrarye endevoured to gett of the stage without any hishinge. True, the E. of Suffolke hath dealte ernestly for him and many of the Heades of the Universitye : the L. Chancelour as ernestlye for me, and the whole bodie of the maisters ; and I thinke we are at an ende.

This is all that suite in lawe your Wor. heares of. So as my prosperous succes in that first enterprize you speake of, hathe beene the source and ofspringe of the second. It was spoken of olde in the comendacion of Traiane, Nec bella times, nec provocas. I confesse I am not soe valourous ; for I protest I feare troubles, and am contente with any losse of money to redeeme my quietnes. My farmour in Northamptonshire can witnes it well, of whom (as Mr. Johnes my best freynde can testifie) I was gladde, for quietnes' sake, to take 5ol. where a 100l. was due ; and that but thise laste winter. Marye, a man's creditte once loste cannot be soe well supplied as his money. Profligatissimi homuncionis est (saithe Tullic) negligere famam et diligere pecuniam. Creditt and virginitie are seldomme recover'd. And especiallie for a scholler, it is the ayre he breathes in and deprive him of that he hath noe longer beinge. But I take your common Barrestours to be plainetifes, not (as my case is) mere passive defendaunts. It was helde a disgrace to Claudius the Emperour, that he was to readye to putte uppe :

> Non faciendo fuit, sed patiendo, nocens.

And the greatest credit that ever Cato hadde, that, being cal'de in question two and fourte severall times, he ever assoilde himselfe, and was clear'de by the judges. I hadd leifer be quiet indeede, if it were possible for one and the same man to be imployed in actions of this nature as to make a freynde Mr. of soe great a Colledge, and receive noe envie afterward. Thus much of that busines, because I wolde in your Wor. accompte be freede, non solum a crimine, verum etiam et a criminatione.

Now, Sir, I pray you give me leave to request you to take somme   to congratulate your coz. our maister his fortunes, and to thanke him for   paste and desire his futherance for futures, in the behaulfe of your sonne. He hath (upon my suyte) bestowed a chamber on them. And I do not knowe, whither (upon these occasions of difference we heare of betwixt your Wor. and his brother) he expecte somme complementes.

> Sæpe rogare soles qualis sim, Prisce, futurus,
> Si fiam locuples, simque repente potens.
> Quenquam posse putas mores narrare futuros ?
> Dic mihi, si fueris tu leo, qualis eris.

> *Martial, lib. 12. Epigr. 94.*

Not that I finde the gentleman a whit altered ; but that I knowe your Wor. beinge putt in mynde not to be backeward in these ceremonies.

My coz. Robin, for his shorte time of absence, was but at Sir Thom. Tresham, my wor. good freynde, invited thither by his sonne and heyre, one of his companions.

Thus most most thankefull for your Wor. greater care of soe poore a kinsman as my selfe, I will ever rest

Your Wor. much obliged

John   Williams.

... R'S BOOTH in STURBRIDGE,
the 13th of Sept. 1612.

> [To the r. worshipfull his most
> approved lovinge Coz. Sir John
> Wynne Knight Barronett at
> Gwyder.]

No. XI.

John   Williams   (Abp.)   to   Sir   John   Wynn.

SIR,

MY dutye and heartiest love and service remembred, I have received your money, wth. puttes me in mynde of God's usurye, ubi (as Sct. Gregorie writes) fænvs triplicat mutuum, the interest trebles the principall ; and yeat, not withstandinge the rigour of the statute, your Worshippe is like to receive no other returne, then of a fewe thanks ; wth. Simonides, once tossinge up and downe his cofer, found to be nothinge. But your Wor. may well remember that sentence (wth. we Academickes would gladlye disperse as farre as we maye) once observ'de by Seneca, often usurpte by Traiane : Beatius est dare, quam accipere.

I have by good chaunce, satisfied your Wor. requeste for a chamber for my coz. Robin, at leaste wise for this winter ;—ne obtentu frigoris muniretur negligentia, as Plinie Speakes.

I am sorye everye waye to heare your Wor. reporte of my brother in lawe's disastrous courses, but the more pacientlye sorye, because I ever expected it. Marrye, this moves me a newe, to heare that my brother should soe unadvisedlye and unfortunatelye (for I can never beleeve he would doe it willfullye) be an occasion of the leaste discontentement or disopportunitye to your Wor. especiallye busines cominge nowe to that passe ;

.....................................non *quiret.*
Ut si ipsa salus servare hunc hominem vellet,

Your Wor. knowes in parte, and should more clerelye, if you sawe my letter to him *Quam consilio, non meo, hoc fecerit.* And I most humblye intreate your Wor. to impute it rather to an unexperienced indisscretion, wch. I finde to pregnaunt in all his proiectes, then to any obstinate and heady wilfulness. Howesoever, I must still continue my suyte unto your Wor. *ex visceribus misericordiarum,* to remember my poore sister.

.........................., Nihil illa nec ausa est ;
Nec potuit.

And soe I commend your Wor. to God's protection, wth. thankes for all your love and courtesies,

Your Wor. in all dutye,

John Williams.

St. John's Coll. in C. Nov. 3.

[To the righte Wor. his ever
approved lovinge Coz. Sir John
Wynn at Gwyder.
deliver these.]

No. XIa[1].

Sir John Wynn of Gwydir's Instructions to his Chaplain, John Price, how to govern himself in his service.

FIRST.—You shall have the chamber, I shewed you in my gate, private to yourself, with lock and key, and all necessaries.

In the morning I expect you should rise, and say prayers in my hall, to my household below, before they go to work, and when they come in at nygt—that you call before you all the workmen, specially the yowth, and take accompt of them of their belief, and of what Sir *Meredith* taught them. I beg you to continue for the more part in the lower house : you are to have onlye what is done there, that you may inform me of any misorder there. There is a baylyf of husbandry, and a porter, who will be comanded by you.

[1] This, and the following No. xi. (b) were not included in the Original Edition, but are copied from the Appendix to Pennant's *Tours in Wales.—Ed.*

The morninge after you be up, and have said prayers, as afore, I wo⁴. you to bestow in study, or any commendable exercise of your body.

Before dinner you are to com up and attend grace, or prayers if there be any publicke; and to set up, if there be not greater strangers, above the chyldren—who you are to teach in your own chamber.

When the table, from half downwards, is taken up, then are you to rise, and to walk in the alleys near at hand, until grace time ; and to come in then for that purpose.

After dinner, if I be busy, you may go to bowles, shuffel bord, or any other honest decent recreation, until I go abroad. If you see me voyd of business, and go to ride abroad, you shall command a gelding to be made ready by the grooms of the stable, and to go with me. If I go to bowles or shuffel bord, I shall lyke of your company, if the place be not made up with strangers.

I wold have you go every *Sunday* in the year to some church hereabouts, to preache, giving warnynge to the parish to bring the yowths at after noon to the church to be catekysed ; in which poynt is my greatest care that you be paynfull and dylygent.

Avoyd the alchowse, to sytt and keepe drunkards company ther, being the greatest discredit your function can have.

⎯⎯⊃✦◦✦⊂⎯⎯

No. XIb.

Inventory of Sir John Wynn's Wardrobe.

A NOATE of all my clothes : taken the eleventh day of June, 1616.

IMPRIMIS. i. tawnie klothe cloake, lined thoroughe with blacke velvett ; one other black cloake of cloth, lined thoroughe with blacke velvett ; another blacke cloake of velvett, lined with blacke taffeta.

Item.—ii. ridinge coates of the same colour, laced with silke and golde lace ; i. hood and basses of the same ; one other olde paire of basses.

Item.—ii. blacke velvett jerkins ; two clothe jerkins laced with goulde lace, of the same colour.

Item.—One white satten doublett, and black satten breeches ; one silke grogram coloured suite ; and one suite of blacke satten cutt, that came the same time from *London.*

Item.—One other blacke satten suite cutt; and one blacke satten doublett, with a wroughte velvett breeches.

Item.—One leather doublett, laced with blacke silke lace; one suite of *Pteropus*, laced with silke and golde lace; another suite of *Pteropus*, laced with greene silke lace.

Item.—One old blacke silke grogram suite cutt; two blacke frise jerkins.

Item.—One blacke velvett coate for a footman.

Item.—One redd quilte waskoote.

Item.—ij. pare of olde boothose, toppes, lined with velvett in the topps.

Item.—ij. pare of blacke silk stockins; and two pare of blacke silke garters, laced.

Item.—One pare of perle colour silke stockins; one pare of white *Siterop* stockins; three pare of wosted stockins.

Item.—ij. girdles, and one hanger, wroughte with golde; one also blacke velvette girdle; one blacke cipres scarfe.

Item.—Nine blacke felte hattes, whereof fowre bee mens hattes; and five cipres hatbands.

Item.—One guilte rapier and dagger, and one ridinge sworde with a scarfe, with velvet scabbards.

Item.—ij. pare of *Spanishe* leather shooes.

Item.—One russet frise jerkin.

Item.—Two pare of leather *Yamosioes*, and of one clothe.

Item.—ij. pare of white boots; one pare of russet boots.

Item.—iij. pare of newe blacke boots, and five pare of old blacke boots.

Item.—ij. pare of damaske spurres; iij. pare of guilte spurres.

No. XII.

Contract between Bernard Lyndesey and Richard Wynn Esqrs.

M'd.

Y_F Mr. Bernard Lyndesey Esquier Groom to his Matie. Bed-chamber procure a pardon for Sir John Wynn Knight and Baronet and some of his servants of their fynes and offences inflicted upon them by the Counsell of the Marches, upon the sealing of the said pardon he is to receave from Richard Wynn Esquier sonne and heire to the said Sir Jo: Wynn the somme of three hundred and fiftye pounds. In witness of this agreement between us we have both sette our hands the sixteenth of January 1615.

Signed in the presence   *B. Lyndesey.*

of me,   *Rich. Wynn.*

Amb: Thelwall.

No. XIII.

Inscription on Sir Richard Wynn's Monument.

HIC JACET

RICARDUS WYNN de GWYDIR

In comitatu de Carnarvon, M. et Baronettus, Thesaurarius,

Nec non Conciliarius honoratissimi principis et Henriettæ Mariæ Reginæ,

Qui linea parentali ex illustri illâ familiâ et antiquissima stirpe

Brittannica, North-Walliæ principum oriundus.

Denatus 19 die Julii 1649,

Æt: 61.

No. XIV.

Inscription on the Vicarage House at Gresford.

Dr. Robert Wynne, Chancellor of St. Asaph and Vicar of Gresford, elder brother to the Welsh historian William Wynne, put on the house the following inscription.

Reverendus Vir HUMPHREDUS LLOYD.

Episcopus BANGOR: hujus Eccl: Vicarius,

Ædem hanc lapsam proprio sumptu

Ex fundo struxit:

Hoc qualecunque pii Præsulis monumentum

Posuit ROBERTUS WYNNE D.D.

A: D: 1702.

No. XV.

Character of Mr. Blayney.

ARTHUR BLAYNEY of Gregynog Esquire was descended from Brochwel Ysgithrog a Prince of Powys in the seventh century, but he valued himself on his pedigree no otherwise, than by taking care that his conduct should not disgrace it. In the early part of his life he had applied to the study of the law, not with any professional view, but merely to guard himself, and those who consulted him, from chicane and injustice, to which many who made the profession their livelihood, were in his opinion so strongly tempted and inclined, that he seldom mentioned a lawyer without expressive marks of dislike ; but this could be humour only. He read much and had a good collection of books, but was more disposed to conceal, than to obtrude his knowledge. He was a firm adherent to the Constitution under which he lived, and never spared his zeal and support when the public stood in need of it. At the same time his loyalty did not preclude him from using that invaluable privilege of a British subject in freely censuring, upon proper occasions, both the measures and instruments of Government. Uncorruptible himself, he detested venality in others. He was of no party, but that of honest men. Whether he supposed that the Peerage was degenerated, and that some degree of contagion dwelt near a Court, or whether he had gathered the prejudice from history, in which he was conversant; but certain it is, he was by no means partial to Lords or Placemen. No man thought more highly of Parliaments, but pertinaciously he declined the honour of representing his native county, though often invited to it by the unbiassed suffrages of his countrymen. The active part he took in behalf of other candidates was so pure in its motives, that his support gave a decided superiority over the highest rank and influence; most of the neighbouring freeholders only waited to know his opinion, to make up their own. Few gentlemen were better qualified for the magistracy, or more sensible of its importance, but from an unaccountable diffidence he could never be prevailed upon to act in the commission, though always ready to applaud and second the just efforts of those who did. Of the established religion he was a steady member; defended its rights and respected its ministers, where they respected themselves. There is scarce a church, in which he had any concern, but what in its repairs and ornaments bears witness to his munificence. His tenants, from their relation, he considered as friends, and not only allowed them ample profit from his estates, but encouraged and assisted them in every rational attempt to improvement. In his farm houses and their offices, beyond what was necessary, he was always studying convenience and comfort, according to the situation, and even taste of the occupier: He did so much in this way, and did it so well, that it is easy to trace his premises, which were very extensive, by the condition in which he left them; and although he possessed an uncommon quantity of the finest wood, he generally bought his timber. To his small tenants he was a bountiful master, and he complained of the bad state of a cottage he shewed me, which in any other place might have been thought a good one. He applied a little land to each, to keep their cow in the summer, and in the winter he gave them hay to support it. Nor was it his own property that he was desirous of improving only; the county at large he looked upon as having a peculiar claim upon him, and no undertaking was proposed, but met with his countenance and liberality. The roads in particular for many miles round, owe their creation almost entirely to him, and when his land was wanted to widen them, he would give it on one condition only, "That they took enough." You had only to convince him of the utility of a design, to be sure of his purse and protection. He always took time to consider and enquire; but from the moment he was decided, he wanted no subsequent instigation. His charity was liberal and diffusive; but instead of confining it to the idle vagrant and clamorous poor, his chief aim was to put deserving objects in the way, to afford them the means of providing for themselves. There are many respectable tradesmen and gentlemen too, whose embarassments have been removed by his friendly assistance. He was undoubtedly an œconomist on system, which enabled him to do what he did: when the object of expense was a proper one, he never regarded the sum; of course, nothing sordid or niggardly could be imputed to him, even when œconomy was most conspicuous: He would never be persuaded to keep a carriage, and very seldom hired one, performing, till his infirmities disabled him, his longest journies on horseback. His constant

residence was at Gregynog, except occasional excursions to his other house at Morvill
near Bridgnorth. One of the most prominent features in his character was his
hospitality, of which there are but few such instances now remaining. His table was
every day plentifully covered with the best things the country and season afforded, for
unless it was to do honour to particular guests, he never indulged in far sought delicacies
(preferring the ducks and chickens of his poor neighbours, which he bought in all
numbers, whether he wanted them or not, and I remember in the summer of 1793, a
small pond near the house swarming with the former kind) but he was very choice in
his liquors, which were the best, that care and money could procure. His place, not
happy in situation, was neither elegant, nor ornamented, but comfortable in the most
extended sense of the word ; inasmuch that it would be difficult to find another house,
where the visitor was more perfectly at his ease, from the titled tourist to the poor
benighted way-worn exciseman, who knew not where else to turn in either for refresh-
ment or lodging ; for Mr. Blayney's hospitality reached every traveller known or
unknown who could decently make any pretentions to it. In his conversation he was
affable, polite, instructive, and cheerful ; seldom brilliant, but never dull, and appeared
always to enjoy the innocent sallies of humour and wit from others, though they seldom
originated from himself. To his domesticks, he was a kind and indulgent master ;
their services were easy, but expected to be prompt and exact, not only to himself, but
to the humblest of his company. They always looked sleek and happy, and might grow
rich if they would. In truth, no animal in his possession, from the stable to the poultry-
yard, had cause to complain, and I knew him once vexed with a servant for sending, as
he said, a thin dog from Gregynog. His hounds too fat for speed, were fed and
followed by a running huntsman : His partridge were set, and his woodcocks shot on
the ground with a pointer, and stalking-horse. Order and regularity pervaded his
whole household. He was never married, but was remarkably pleased with, and
pleasing to the ladies, who visited him, and they were not a few. He carried his notions
of independence to a pitch, that bordered upon excess ; always ready to confer reasonable favours ; he reluctantly accepted them ; several worthy Bishops of the Diocese
have lamented, that he would never put it in their power, to use their patronage, in
favour of his recommendation. In his temper, he was constitutionally warm ; What
true Welshman is otherwise ? His resentments, generally well founded, were consequently
strong, and sometimes permanent. He could forgive an injury, but if his confidence
was forfeited, it was nearly impossible to retrieve it. His dress was plain and studiously
neat and becoming, and he made a London suit every year, and his constant direction
to his taylor (whom he had not seen for forty years) was, that he made the present coat
as the last : His shoe buckles were very small, and he had a dressed pair ; they were
of the old form and fashion ; and he wore his breeches' garters very high. Mr. Blayney
died at Gregynog, the first of October, 1795, in the eighty-first year of his age, and was
buried by his particular directions, very privately, in the church-yard at Tregynon. He

was uuiversally and justly lamented ; an advantage which amiable men possess ovei great ones.

[THE directions for his funeral left by Mr. Blayney, referred to above, were as follows :—

" It is usual for people in this Country (out of a pretended respect but rather from an Impertinent Curiosity) to desire to see persons after they are dead. It is my earnest request that no person, upon any pretence whatever, may be permitted to see my Corpse, but those who unavoidably must.

I desire to be buried in the North side of the Church-Yard of Tregunon, somewhere about the Centre, my Coffin to be made in the most plain and simple manner, without the usual Fantastical Decorations, and the more perishable the Material the better.

I desire that no Undertaker, or professed performer of Funerals, may be employed : But that I may be conveyed to the Church-Yard in some Country Herse, which may be hired for the Occasion : And my Corpse to be carried from the Herse to the Grave immediately, without going into the Church, by six of the Chief Tregunon Tenants, to whom I give two Guineas each for their Trouble. It is my Earnest request and desire to have no upper Bearers, or any persons whatever, invited to my Funeral, which I desire may be at so early an Hour, as will best prevent a Concourse of People from collecting together. The better sort, I presume will not Intrude, as there is no Invitation.

I have been present at the Funerals of three of my Unkles at Morvil. I was pleased with the privacy and decency, with which all Things were conducted, no strangers attended. All was done by the servants of the Family. It is my Earnest desire to follow these examples, however unpopular ; and that no Coach, no Escutcheon, and no pomp of any kind may appear. I trust that my Executor will be well justified against the clamour and obloquy of Mercenary people, when he acts in performance of the last request of a dying Friend ; who solemnly adjures him in the name of God, punctually to observe these directions.

AR: BLAYNEY.

I likewise give to all my Servants, five Guineas each, in lieu of all Mourning, which it is my desire no person may use on my account."

The uncles referred to, were members of the family of Weaver of Morville. near Bridgnorth ; Mr. Blayney's mother being Ann Weaver. Henry, eighth Viscount Tracy, married Susannah Weaver, Mr. Blayney's first cousin, and to whom he devised his estates. Lord Tracy died 27th April, 1797, leaving an only surviving child and heiress, Henrietta Susanna, who married her cousin, Charles Hanbury, Esq., who assumed by royal licence, the additional surname and arms of Tracy ; and in 1838, was raised to the peerage as Baron Sudeley. The present peer, the third Baron Sudeley, is his second son, the second Lord Sudeley (his brother) having died unmarried. The Blayney arms were those of Brochwel Ysgythrog: *Sable* three nags' heads erased *argent*. Arthur Blayney was the last of a long line of Blayneys (extending back at least three centuries), who had dwelt at Gregynog. The name is still born by several persons in Montgomeryshire, descendants of collateral branches, but Arthur Blayney, it appears, left no direct male heirs. The Lords Blayney of Ireland, who were related on the female side, became extinct some years ago.—*E'1.*]

No. XVI.

Some Observations on the Crown Manors in Wales.

IN Norden's Survey at the British Museum, may be seen the map of the lordship of Bromfield and Yale, consisting of seventeen manors, with their several members or townships, as there enumerated. This extensive tract in its present state is of little use to the Crown or the subject, when it might be made advantageous to both ; and to this purpose let a bill pass for the sale of this and other Welsh lordships, since the power of the Crown goes, at present, to a limited lease only. And might not the several manors, composing the whole, be separated from the mass, and sold distinctly and by themselves ; and by valuing in the sale of every of them, the divisional allotments due to the Crown, as Lord, from each, together with the other manorial rights, excepting the mines and minerals, long since alienated, might not an handsome sum be expected ; and in the case of some of the manors, where there may be little waste, still something may be looked for from the consideration of game and sporting objects. And might not the Crown in this course avoid the difficulty (in an ugly moment of a Welsh revenue question once experienced) of negociating themselves with the freeholder, in the first instance, who if brought to terms of inclosure, may more readily agree with the new, than the old proprietor ? It is apprehended that other paramountships in North Wales, now in the Crown, have in them many of these aggregated manors, accumulated by conquest, succession or forfeiture, and heretofore granted out of the Crown, and as this, returned into it again. And might it not tempt the rich and zealous Antiquary to purchase and restore the venerable remains of our castles, many yet renewable, if the Crown brought them to the market, also, and discharged them, as I have little doubt it can, from such claims, as by payments of small acknowledgments certain individuals make upon them, but which, I conceive, give not to those persons power to alienate them themselves. Thus, and what was the state of Warwick and Alnwick once, their magnificence might be restored, and a good price might be obtained by the Crown for them, whilst at present they are incumbrances to it from the payment of sinecures to their governors. North Wales has not had the attention it merits; it possesses sea and land, as other countries, but systems have interposed to check these advantages. The uses of the first are, in a manner, forbidden to us by an heavy coal coast duty, of small profit to the state (which might be relieved by commutation) which renders our vast depôt of lime half useless; and the same shores of the same island seem to front each other, not as natural friends and fellow subjects, but as rancorous rivals and jealous enemies;

Litora litoribus contraria, fluctibus undas :

To our land then; much is cold, savage, and unprofitable,

......................Mons undique et undique cœlum.

Cultivation is checked from the reasons just given, and the mountain starves again a third of what it breeds; it fattens none. Large plantations would be probably made if it was once appropriated; hence in time, wood would warm the waste, and bring habitation into it. At present, its best produce is peat, without which much of the surrounding country would not be habitable.

The plan to be pursued and the learning necessary to an effective practicable bill of this nature, delicacy and consequence, might be assisted, from a review of the acts of Parliament respecting Wales; from the annexation under Henry the Eighth (the parent and prototype of a greater Union since effected, as acknowledged by Lord Somers, and long before suggested by Chief Baron Doddridge) to the time of William the Third; which with the speech of Mr. Price in the House of Commons, and of Sir William Williams, before the Council, might give the Legislature light in such a business. Some slight and humble hints are here only offered.

No. XVII.

Bishop Goodman's Will.

In the Name of the FATHER, and of the SON, and of the HOLY GHOST, our Creator, our Redeemer, our Sanctifier, three Persons and one God. Amen:

THIS Seventeenth day of January, in the year of our Lord 1655, I Godfrey Goodman bishop late of Gloucester, being weak in body, but of perfect memory and understanding, I praise God for it, do here make and declare this my last will and testament, and thereby revoking all former wills and testaments by me made. And first of all I give and bequeath my sinful soul to God, hoping by his mercy and by the death and passion of my dear Lord and Saviour Jesus Christ, dying a member of his Church, that he will take me into the number of his Elect. I do humbly thank God that he hath given me a penitent and contrite heart, as an earnest of my repentance and reconciliation to himself; and here I profess that as I have lived, so I die most constant in all the articles of the Christian Faith, and in all the doctrine of God's holy Catholick and Apostolick Church, whereof I do acknowledge the Church of Rome to be the Mother Church, and I do verily believe, that no other Church hath any salvation in it, but only as far as it concurs with the faith of the Church of Rome : And for my Body I do leave to christian burial in the parish Church, near the font, in the meanest manner, according to the due deserts of my sins. And touching such worldly goods, that it hath pleased God to bestow upon me, for which I give him most humble thanks and due acknowledgement, that he hath plentifully supplied me, and that I never had any wants. In the first place I desire, that my executor should give towards the adorning of the font, either by way of painting or otherwise, as the church-wardens shall think fit, the sum of 40s. and I do humbly thank God for the benefit of my Baptism. Item, I do give a hundred poor housekeepers of this parish 12d. a piece. Item, to all my poor parishioners of Stapleford, 12d. a piece. Item, to all my poor parishioners of West Ildesley in Berks,. 12d. a piece. Item, I do give the tenement in Yale and the two tenements in Carnarvonshire, viz. Coed mawr and Tŷ dû, to the town of Ruthin in Denbighshire, where I was born, the tenements are purchased in the names of others in trust, and "are to be disposed of by the Lords Bishops of Bangor and St. Asaph, when it shall please God that they shall be restored, and by the Chief Justice and second Justice of Chester and the Warden of Ruthin, and by the heirs of brother Gabriel, who is now William Salusbury of Rùg, and by the heirs of my sister Susan, being now William Parry of Llŵyn Ynn, and by the heirs of Charles Goodman of Glanhespin, to the heirs of my sister Jane, who is Gabriel Goodman of Nantglyn and his heirs male, and to the heirs of my sister Martha, who married Justice Prytherch in Anglesey, and until such time as the bishops of Bangor and St. Asaph shall be restored, it shall be in the power of those to nominate two churchmen, incumbents upon their benefices, not dwelling eight miles from Ruthin, to supply the places of those bishops, who shall have the same power as the bishops should have had ; and I desire all the lands may be at the letting out and disposal of them in this manner : That the rent of the tenement in Yale shall be weekly given to the relief of the poor of Ruthin ; yet so that it shall not continue in the same course above three years together ; for the tenements in Carnarvonshire, which amount to forty pounds yearly, I desire that five pounds thereof might be spent at their meeting, which I desire wholly at the appointment of the Chief Justice of Chester, and I wish it might be one day in Michaelmas Assizes, and for the other five

v

and thirty pounds, I desire that fifteen pounds thereof may be paid for the binding out two apprentices, yet that they may not be bound within the principality of Wales, where we have not any working trade in its full perfection, and for the other twenty pounds, I desire that choice may be made of some gentlemen who shall desire to travel, and that together with good security shall undertake within the compass of two years, to live two months in Germany, two months in Italy, two months in France, and two months in Spain; I desire that my own kindred should be chosen before others, and such as have had their breeding in the school of Ruthin, and for want of those, such as have been born within the principality of Wales, and the house of Talar in Flintshire may be preferred before others, and in the choice of the gentleman I desire that no relation should be had to his poverty, but pulchrior doctior nobilior cæteris paribus anteferendus, and so I do repose the trust in the Chief Justice and others for the letting out of the tenements; so I desire them to take special care for the preserving and planting of wood, and I do give all there now, or that hereafter shall grow there, except the necessary timber to be used about the ground or houses, towards repairing or building of churches within that county by the appointment of the Chief Justice and others, yet so that in one year they shall not give above the twentieth part of it, and what is so given shall appear under the hands of the greater part of the feoffees, in whom I have reposed trust for that purpose; and whereas I have purchased the perpetual patronage of Kemerton, and have settled it upon the hospital of St. Bartholomew's in Gloucester, with this condition, that unless I have a kinsman of my own, descended from my grand-father Edward Goodman, who shall be of my name and capable of it, and shall make means within three months after the vacancy; this kins-man must be nominated long before by the feoffees in trust, for if he omits his three months, he is made incapable to demand it; and as for the rest of my estate, being so small as it is, having had those great losses that I have had, I must intreat my friends to accept of small legacies; Item, I give and bequeath to my sister Jonnet Goodman of Rûg. the sum of five pounds, and to her daughter my cousin Mary Salusbury,* being my heir at common law, I give a hundred marks; Item, to my sister Martha Prytherch of Anglesey I do give five pounds; Item, I give to my cousin Charles Goodman of Glanhespin five pounds; Item, I give to my cousin William Parry of Llŵyn Ynn and his sister five pounds; Item, I do give to my cousin Ellin Goodman of Nantglyn, with

* Mary Goodman, alias Salusbury, sole daughter and heiress of Gabriel Goodman of Abinbury, Prothono-tary of North Wales, married October the 28th, 1635, Owen Salusbury of Rûg, by whom among other issue she had Dorothy her eldest daughter, born 16th November, 1636. The said Dorothy married John Wynne of Melai, the 16th of April, 1651, by whom she had issue William Wynne of Melai, also Dorothy and Barbara. Dorothy married Thomas Wynne of Dyffrynaled, by whom she had Robert Wynne of Dyffrynaled: Robert married Elizabeth Foulkes of Merriadog and Carregfynydd, and had issue Pierce Wynne and Dorothy. Pierce Wynne married Margaret, daughter to Robert Wynne of Garthewin, and had issue Diana Wynne of Dyffrynaled. Dorothy married William Thomas of Coedhelen, and left issue.

many thanks for her care in educating her children, five pounds ; Item, I do give my cousin Charles Goodman, glazier, forty shillings, and to his brother John Goodman, virginal-maker, forty shillings ; Item, to Mrs. Slatyr I give three pounds, in regard of the great care she hath with her aged father. These legacies I desire might be paid out of those bonds which are due unto me and undoubtedly good debts, but of such money as I have in the house I leave to Gabriel Goodman, my sister's grand-child, for his pains in the time of my sickness and his care at my funeral ; Item, I have placed trust in Mrs. Sylla Aglomby, I leave her five pounds, and give her the bed and blankets which are in her house ; Item, I leave her a box and a key which I desire may not be opened, and if I have any other small things in her house I do freely give her, in hope and confidence that she will discharge the small trust which I have reposed in her ; Item, after all church duties and funeral expenses being paid, I desire that what is now left in the house may be distributed according to the discretion of my executor among those ministers that were deprived of their benefices by that long and most unjust parliament, God forgive them and their committees, which will be sixteen pounds ; and further, whereas I am to receive some money upon bonds, the 6th day of May next, from Sir Benjamin Agliffe, I desire that one hundred pounds thereof may be given amongst those poor distressed churchmen according to the good discretion of my executor. Item, the books I intended for Chelsea College (the college being now dissolved) I do bestow them upon Trinity College, Cambridge, with this condition, that, if ever Chelsea College be restored, the books shall likewise be restored. Item, whereas I have taken a great deal of pains in writing of notes, my desire is, that some scholar may be employed to peruse them all over, and if any thing should be found worthy the printing, that then some course may be taken for the publishing of them ; and the scholar, when he hath so taken pains, shall be rewarded with ten pounds ; and I repose the whole care of this business to Mr. Francis Westby, and he is to find the scholar and to order things accordingly. And here I do from my soul ask forgiveness of God and of all others whom I have offended, and I heartily forgive all men, and do confess, that if I was guilty to myself, that if I had wronged any man to the value of one farthing, I would make satisfaction with recompence : And I do hereby constitute and appoint my sole executor Gabriel Goodman, one who now lives with me, to whom I give all the rest of my goods, chattels and debts whatsoever, in hope and confidence that he will be careful of his brothers and sisters, and so beseeching God to bless all the estates of men, and to send times of peace and quietness in this church, and to restore her to her just revenues and honor, and to send peace in the christian world for the sparing of the effusion of christian blood, and I do hereby conclude with my last words, into thy hands O Lord I recommend my soul ; Lord Jesus receive my soul !

In witness hereof I have hereunto subscribed my hand and seal,

Godf. Goodman.

Sealed, subscribed and declared this to be my
last will and testament in the presence of

$$R. H.—S. A.—L. P.—M. S.$$

This will was proved in London before the Judges for probate of wills, and carefully
authorized the 16th of February, in the year of our Lord 1655, by the oath of Gabriel
Goodman, kinsman to the deceased and sole executor, named in the said will, of all and
singular the goods, chattels and debts of the said deceased, being first legally sworn
truly to administer the same.

Thos. Wetham.
<small>Reg. Dep.</small>

━━●◦◉◦●━━

No. XVIII.

Sir Thomas Hanmer's Epitaph.

EPITAPHIUM in Thomam Hanmer, Baronettum.

Honorabilis admodum Thomas Hanmer Baronettus
Wilhelmi Hanmer armigeri, e Peregrina Henrici North
De Mildenhall in Com. Suffolciæ Baronetti Sorore & Hærede,
Filius,
Johannis Hanmer de Hanmer Baronetti
Hæres Patruelis,
Antiquo Gentis suæ et titulo et patrimonio successit.
Duas Uxores sortitus est ;
Alteram Isabellam, honore a patre derivato, de
Arlington Comitissam,
Deinde celsissimi principis ducis de Grafton viduam dotatam ;
Alteram Elizabetham Thomæ Folks de Barton in
Com. Suff. Armigeri
Filiam et Hæredem.
Inter humanitatis studia feliciter enutritus,
Omnes liberalium Artium disciplinas avide arripuit,
Quas morum suavitate haud leviter ornavit.
Postquam excessit ex ephebis,
Continuo inter populares suos fama eminens,

SIR THOMAS HANMER.

Speaker of the House of Commons.

Et Comitatus sui legatus ad Parliamentum missus,
Ad ardua regni negotia per Annos prope triginta
Se accinxit ;
Cumq : apud illos amplissimorum virorum ordines
Soleret nihil temere effutire,
Sed *probe* perpensa diserte expromere
Orator gravis et pressus,
Non minus integritatis quam eloquentiæ laude
commendatus,
Æque omnium utcunq ; inter se alioqui dissidentium
Aures atque animos attraxit ;
Annoque demum MDCCXIII, regnante Anna,
Felicissimæ florentissimæque memoriæ Regina,
Ad prolocutoris Cathedram
' Communi senatûs universi.voce designatus est :
Quod Munus,
Cum nullo tempore non difficile,
Tum illo certe negotiis
Et variis et lubricis et implicatis difficillimum
Cum dignitate sustinuit.
Honores alios, et omnia, quæ sibi in lucrum cederent, Munera
Sedulo detrectavit,
Ut rei totus inserviret publicæ,
Justi rectique tenax,
Et fide in patriam incorrupta notus.
Ubi omnibus, quæ virum, civemque bonum decent, officiis satisfecit,
Paulatim se a publicis Consiliis in Otium recipiens
Inter literarum amœnitates,
Inter ante actæ vitæ haud insuaves recordationes,
Inter amicorum convictus et amplexus,
Honorificè consenuit,
Et bonis omnibus, quibus charissimus vixit,
Desideratissimus obijt.

No. XIX.

Sir Thomas Hanmer's Epitaph Paraphras'd:

THOU, who survey'st these walls with curious eye,
Pause on this tomb—where Hanmer's ashes lie.
His various worth, thro' varied life attend,
And learn his virtues, while thou mourn'st his end :
His force of genius burn'd in early youth,
With thirst of knowledge and with love of truth,
His learning join'd with each endearing art
Charm'd every ear, and gain'd on every heart ;
Thus early wise th' endanger'd realm to aid,
His country call'd him from the studious shade ;
In life's first bloom his public toils began,
At once commenc'd the senator and man ;
In bus'ness dextrous, weighty in debate,
Thrice ten long years, he labor'd for the State ;
In every speech persuasive wisdom flow'd,
In ev'ry act refulgent virtue glow'd ;
Suspended faction ceas'd from rage and strife,
To hear his eloquence and praise his life ;
Resistless merit fix'd the senate's choice,
Who hail'd him Speaker with united voice.
Illustrious age! How bright thy glories shone,
When Hanmer fill'd the chair, and Anne the throne!
Then—when dark arts obscur'd each fierce debate,
When mutual frauds perplex'd the maze of state ;
The moderator firmly mild appear'd,
Beheld with love, with veneration heard.
This task performed, he sought no gainful post,
Nor wish'd to glitter at his country's cost ;
Strict on the right, he fix'd his stedfast eye,
With temp'rate zeal and wise anxiety ;
Nor e'er from virtue's path was turn'd aside
To pluck the flow'rs of pleasure or of pride ;
Her gifts despis'd, corruption blush'd and fled
And fame pursu'd him, where conviction led :
Age call'd, at length, his active mind to rest,

With honor sated and with cares opprest ;
To letter'd ease retir'd and honest mirth,
To rural grandeur and domestic worth,
Delighted still to please mankind or mend,
The patriot's fire yet sparkled in the friend.
Calm conscience then his former life survey'd
And recollected toils endear'd the shade ;
Till nature call'd him to the gen'ral doom,
And virtue's sorrow dignify'd his tomb.*

* See the Gentleman's Magazine for May 1747.

———◦◦◦———

No. XX.

Inscription on Sir William Williams's Monument in Llansilin Church, in Denbighshire.

H. S. E.

HONORATISSIMUS Vir GULIELMUS WILLIAMS
De Glascoed—Miles et Baronettus :
Omnibus ingenii animique dotibus illustris ;
In foro civili inter primarios suæ Ætatis
Togatos, semper præclarus,
Et tantum non purpuratis adscriptus,
Quippe qui in facultate sua opus
Potius quam honores, aut magistratum, amavit ;
Ac prodesse quam præesse, maluit ;
Adeo in consiliis sagax, in dicendo promptus,
Ad negotia habilis,
Ut dignus habitus est, qui in altera Senatus
Domo, sæpius sedem, bis Cathedram teneret,
Orator peritissimus.
In his publicis et amicorum rebus
Dum esset occupatus,
Nihil interim de propriis remisit,
Quod familiæ suæ dignitatem aut censum augeret.
Ex uxore meritissima,

Filios habuit duos, Filiam unicam ;
Quos omnes tam larga, et quod rarius,
Viva manu, ditavit,
Ac si eorum quemlibet hæredem
Adscripserat.
Obiit Londini x—die Julii MDCC Æt: 66.
Hic magno sumptu, licet meritis impari sepultus,
Expectat immortalitatem.

——————

No. XXI.

Epitaph on Mary Vanbutchell.

IN reliquias MARIÆ VANBUTCHELL
Novo miraculo conservatas
et a marito suo superstite,
Cultu quotidiano, adoratas.
Hic, exsors tumuli, jacet
Uxor Johannis Vanbutchel,
Integra omnino et incorrupta ;
Viri sui amantissimi
Desiderium simul et Deliciæ ;
Quam gravi morbo vitiatam,
Consumptamque tandem longa morte,
In hunc quem cernis nitorem,·
In hanc speciem et colorem viventis
Ab indecora putredine vindicavit,
Invita et repugnante natura
Vir egregius Gulielmus Hunterus
Artificii prius intentati
Inventor idem et Perfector
O fortunatum maritum
Cui datur
Uxorem multum amatam
Retinere una, in unis ædibus,
Affari, tangere, complecti ;

SIR WILLIAM WILLIAMS BAR.[T]

Recorder of Chester.

Speaker of the House of Commons, and Solicitor General.

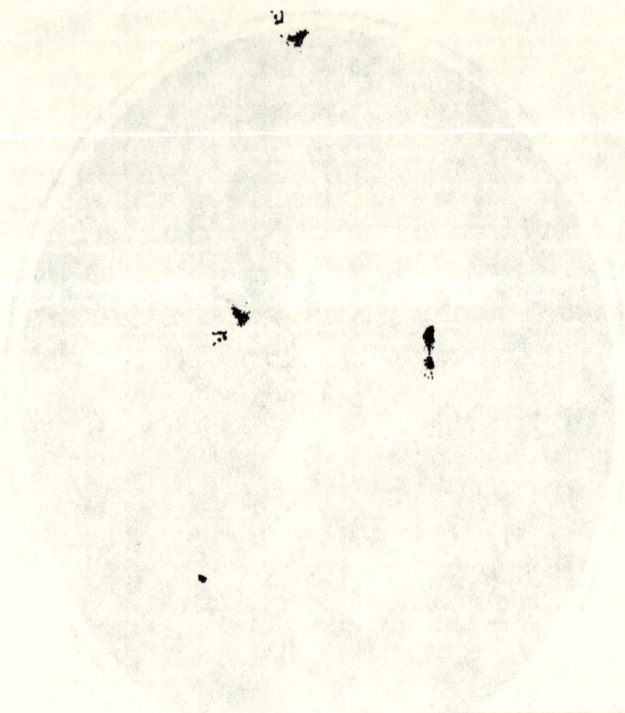

Non Fatis modo superstitem
Sed (quod pluris æstimandum,
Nam non est vivere, sed placere vita)
Etiam suaviorem,
Venustiorem,
Habitiorem,
Solidam magis, et magis succi plenam
Quam cum ipsa in vivis fuerit !
O fortunatum virum ! et invidendum !
Cui peculiare hoc, et proprium contingit,
Apud se habere fœminam
Non variam, non mutabilem,
Egregie taciturnam,
Et horis omnibus eandem.

————◆◦◆◦◆————

No. XXII.

A literal translation for the Benefit of the Ladies,
By a Noble LORD.

HERE covered not by earth or stone,
Lies John Vanbutchell's wife alone :
His pleasure, joy, and sole desire,
Quite uncorrupted, and entire :
Who was preserved by Hunter's art,
When death had shot his fatal dart.
Behold her now 'gainst nature's will,
With face so fair, and blooming still.
O Husband blest ! who in one house,
Can still retain one charming spouse,
Can speak to, kiss, and with her toy,
And sleep close by ; if such his joy :
Who now exists, not as you see,
The Fates would choose to have her be ;
But what's more wond'rous, is much sweeter,
More perfect too in limb and feature ;

W

More firm her flesh, more full of juice,
And fitter for domestic use.
O fortunate and envy'd Van!
To keep a wife beyond life's span ;
Whom you can ne'er have cause to blame ;
Is ever constant and the same ;
Who qualities most rare inherits,
A wife that's dumb ; yet full of spirits.

No. XXIII.

Note to the House of Caergai.

OF the House of Caergai was Rowland Vaughan, who flourished in the middle of the last century, called Rolant Fychan y Cyfieithydd, or the translator ; because he translated several pious books into Welsh, particularly Bishop Bailey's Practice of Piety, and Dr. Brough's Manual of Prayer ; which last was at the request of Colonel William Salusbury, of Bachymbyd, commonly called Blue Stockings, the sturdy governor of Denbigh castle, in the civil wars of the last century [17th] ; at whose expence it was printed and distributed among the poor. Salusbury was also active in repairing several churches that were defaced, and he founded and endowed the chapel at Rûg. Vaughan, besides being a translator, was an author in Welsh prose of good credit.

No. XXIV.

Note to Humphrey Hughes.

HUMPHREY HUGHES of Gwerclas, was born in 1605, married Maudlen Rogers, aged thirteen, in 1615, was Sheriff in 1620, ut patet by his own memorandums and the roll of Sheriffs. He married afterwards Eleanor Savage of Chester, in 1659. In 1662, he married Sarah Franklin, of Cambridgeshire, and in 1666, Eleanor Mutton.*

* The British pronunciation of the letter *y* in Mylton is the same with that of *u*, in Mutton after the English, and both a local name, as should appear by the termination *ton*, but where the place so called is situated I know not. [Mytton is now generally pronounced as if written Mitton.—*Ed.*]

THE FIFTEEN TRIBES OF NORTH WALES.

—————•—————

THE origin of these Tribes, which belong exclusively to North Wales, and the grounds for the selection of some of their founders for such a distinction, while others of greater merit have not been so honoured, have given rise to some difficulty. Several of these chieftains lived as early as the ninth, and some as late as the twelfth century, but it has been suggested that many difficulties will be explained if we assume that the Tribes were constituted subsequently to the reign of Owain Gwynedd (1137-1169), and were limited to the districts which remained unconquered. The following account of the Fifteen Tribes is taken from the *Cambrian Register* for 1795, p. 145; and appears to have been compiled by Robert Vaughan, the antiquary, about the middle of the seventeenth century, and annotated for the *Cam. Reg.* by either Dr. Owen Pughe, or the Rev. Walter Davies. An account almost identical, exclusive of the Notes, but including catalogues of extant and extinct families descended from each tribe, was published by Pennant in 1796, as an Appendix to his *History of Whiteford and Holywell;* and this with an Introductory Preface, by W. Trevor Parkins, Esq., has lately been reprinted as an Appendix to the recent edition of *Pennant's Tours in Wales* (Carnarvon 1883). The tribe of March or Tudor Trevor is of a later date, and has no connection with the rest— Pennant calls it the Sixteenth Tribe. It includes a number of families belonging entirely to Powys.—*Ed.*

A Brief History of the FIFTEEN TRIBES OF NORTH WALES (Y Pymtheg Llwyth Gwynedd), *from which the chief families of that part of the Principality trace their pedigrees. Extracted from a manuscript written about the middle of the last century* [the 17th].

I.—HWFA AP CYNDDELW.[2]

THE first of the tribes of North Wales was Hwfa ap Cynddelw, who lived in the time of Owain Gwynedd, Prince of North Wales, and, as some will have it, was steward to the said prince. His office, by inheritance, was to bear the prince's coronet, and to put it upon his head when the Bishop of

[1] They are likewise frequently called the fifteen Peers of North Wales, being, I presume, certain nobles who held their lands by Baron service, being bound to particular ministerial attendances on their princes, besides what they were in general obliged to, as subjects, by homage and fealty.

[2] Rowlands in his *Mona Antiqua*, says that Hwfa ap Cynddelw of Presaddfed, held his estate in fee, by attending on the prince's coronation, and bearing up the right side of the canopy over the prince's head at that solemnity, and cites the following extract from a manuscript of one Lewis Dun, out of the Gloddaith Library.—" Yr Hwfa hwn a'i Etifeddion hynaf a wiscant y Dalaith am ben y Twysog, gyda ac Escob Bangor, ac ar y dydd cyntaf y cyssegrid y Twysog yn y Dalaith, yr oedd i Hwfa y par dillad a fai am y Twysog wrth wisco y Dalaith am ei ben. A hyn oedd wasanaeth Hwfa ap Cynddelw." [This Hwfa and his eldest heirs placed the coronet on the head of the prince with the Bishop of Bangor, and the first day the prince was consecrated in the province, to Hwfa belonged the suit of clothes worn by the prince when the coronet was placed on his head. And this was the service of Hwfa ab Cynddelw.]

Bangor anointed him as Nicholas,[1] Bishop of Bangor affirmeth. His house was Presaddfed in Anglesey.[2] What lordships he had besides that, is mentioned in the Extent of North Wales,[3] to have been divided between his five sons, Methusalem, Cyfnerth, Ievan, Iorwerth, and Blettrws. Sir Howel y Pedolau was a famous man in his time, and descended from him, as being the son of Gruffudd ap Iorwerth, ap Meredydd, ap Methusalem, ap Hwfa ap Cynddelw. Sir Howel's mother was King Edward the Second's nurse, and he being foster brother to the king, was in great favour with him. He was a very strong man, insomuch that he could break or straiten[4] horse shoes with his hands. Llewelyn ap Hwlkin was a very famous gentleman descended of him: he left four sons to inherit his manors, as

[1] Nicholson Robinson, Bishop of that See, A.D. 1566. [He was a native of Aberconwy, and a very learned man. Among other works written by him, was a translation from Welsh into Latin of the Life of Gruffudd ab Cynan (see *ante*, p. 23, *note.)* He died February 13th, 1584-5, and was buried on the south side of the high altar in his Cathedral church of Bangor.—*Ed.*]

[2] Rowlands *(Mona Ant. Res.,* p. 106) derives this name from *Præsidii Locus=* the President's habitation ; and surmises it to have been originally the Roman Governor's residence. It is in the parish of Bodedeyrn, about eight miles east of Holyhead, and is still a fine old mansion.—*Ed.*

[3] This *Extent,* or Survey of North Wales, is a very fine folio MS. in the *Harleian Collection,* bearing date 1352, and has been printed in the *Record of Carnarvon.* It only relates to the Counties of Anglesey, Carnarvon, and Merioneth. It appears to have been begun in the time of Edward the First, continued by Edward the Second, and completed in the twenty-sixth year of Edward the Third.—*Ed.*

[4] And therefore called Howel y Pedolau. A few years ago there was a mutilated tombstone in the church of St. Peter's, Carmarthen, with the effigy of a warrior on it, holding a horseshoe, with both his hands, seemingly in the act of exercising his strength thereon. Quære, if that might not have been the tomb of Sir Howel y Pedolau.

Meuric, of whom the Owens[1] of Bodeon in Anglesey, and and Orielton in Pembrokeshire are descended, and also the Owens of Bodsilin, of whom comes Sir John Owens of Clynnenney; (2) Hugh ap Llywelin[2] (alias Hugh Lewis), of whom come the Lewises of Presaddfed; (3) Griffith, of whom come the Griffiths of Chwaen; and (4) Rhys, of whom Wynn of Bodowyr and others are descended. His arms he beareth *gules* between three lioncels rampant a chevron *or*.

[1] The houses of Bodeon and Orielton are now united, since the marriage of Sir Hugh Owen of Orielton, with Catherine, daughter and sole heiress of . . . Owens, Esq. of Bodeon. The first of that family, who came into Pembrokeshire, was Sir Hugh Owen, Knight, Barrister at Law, and Recorder of Carmarthen, who married Elizabeth, daughter and sole heiress of George Wyrriott, Esq. of Orielton, who lived in the reign of Queen Elizabeth. [The Bodeon estate has long since passed into other hands. Sir Hugh Owen Owen, Bart. of Orielton, County of Pembroke, now represents these united families.—*Ed.*]

[2] Of him likewise was descended the late . . . Lewis, Esq. of Llanddyfnan, in Anglesey, a gentleman as generally known by the title of King of Spain, a title which I never could learn how he obtained; but from which that of Prince of Asturias, naturally resulted to his eldest son, and of infantas to his daughters. Nay, when one of the infantas had cast her affections on a robust country curate, and had honoured him with her hand in marriage, the Puisne Judge of the North Wales circuit, the facetious Thomas Potter, Esq., desirous of collecting all the Spanish dignities into the family, with that ready humour which he is so remarkable for, styled the happy parson Archbishop of Toledo.

[ADDENDA.]—Hwfa ab Cynddelw, often styled lord of Llys Llivon, was a direct descendant of Cunedda Wledig, "King of Britain," and flourished about 1150. By his wife, Ceinfryd, daughter of EDNOWAIN BENDEW, founder of the thirteenth Noble Tribe of North Wales, he had in addition to the five sons above named, three daughters, namely, Avandrog, Gwerful, and Gwladus *(Dwnn's Vis.*, ii. p. 236). An old MS. quoted by Dwnn *(Vis.* ii., p. 83) states that "he was chosen by Owen Gwynedd to be heir apparent, because he was gallant and brave."

Sir John Owen of Clenneneu, the famous Royalist referred to above, was the son of John Owen of Bodsilin, who was Secretary to the great Sir Francis Walsingham, and married the heiress of Clenneneu and Brogyntyn, with whom he obtained those estates. Sir John, whose portrait is at Brogyntyn (the seat of his descendant, Lord Harlech), was a Colonel in the army, and Vice Admiral of North Wales. He greatly distinguished himself at the siege of Bristol, where he was desperately wounded, and in other actions. Near the close of the war he was taken prisoner, and condemned to death, but his life was spared through the humane exertions of Ireton, who told the House of Commons " that there was one person for whom no one spoke a word, and therefore requested that " he might be saved by the sole motive and goodness of the house." After a short imprisonment he was set at liberty, and retired into his own country, where he died in 1666 (*Pennant's Tours*, i., 337). Among his lineal descendants are Baron Harlech, and on the mother's side Baron Kenyon (*ante*, pp. 17 and 103, *notes.*) The estate of Bodsilin was sold towards the close of the seventeenth century, by John Owen, page to the Prince of Condé (*Dwnn's Vis.*, ii., p. 164, *note.*)

The Wynns of Bodychen, a once powerful family, belonged to this tribe. Of them Rhys ab Llewelyn ab Hwlcyn, a powerful chieftain, went to Bosworth with a company of foot, to assist Henry the Seventh, and in return was sworn Sheriff of Anglesey for *life*, being the first Sheriff appointed for that County. He made his house the County Gaol ; and Pennant (*Tours*, iii., p. 75) says that " the dungeon was lately to be seen." The *Arch. Camb.* for 1871, p. 238, gives an account, accompanied by a view of an old building, supposed to be part of the original residence. Jane, daughter of John Bodychen, left the Bodychen estate, which she inherited, to her second husband, John Sparrow, Esq. of Red Hill, Sheriff of Anglesey in 1708 (*Arch. Camb.* 1871, p. 335.) There was no issue of this marriage, but Mr. Sparrow married again and had issue, and the estate has since continued in his family. His grandson, John Bodychen Sparrow, Esq., married Anne, daughter and heiress of Ambrose Lewis, Esq. of Trysglwyn, who was the last male representative of a younger branch of the Bodewryd family, belonging to this tribe. Of this marriage there was issue, five sons and nine daughters. One of the latter (Barbara), married Hugh Robert Hughes, Esq., and their son Hugh Robert Hughes, Esq. of Kinmel Park, is the present Lord Lieutenant of Flintshire (*Burke's Landed Gentry.*) The Gwyn's of Baron's Hall, in the County of Norfolk, claim descent from the Wynn's of Bodychen (*Ib.*)

William Lewys, Esq. of Presaddfed (Sheriff in 1549, 1557, and 1572, and who represented Anglesey in two Parliaments), married first, Margaret, daughter of Sir John Puleston, Knight, Chamberlain of North Wales, and Constable of Carnarvon Castle, by whom he had several children ; the last male representative of whom, John Lewys, Esq. of Presaddfed, left an only daughter and heiress, Anne, who was twice married—her first husband being John, eldest son of Sir Hugh Owen, Bart. of Orielton ;

her second, Mark Trevor, Lord Viscount Dungannon, after whose death she sold Presaddfed to John Owen, Esq. of Cromlech. The said William Lewys married secondly, Elin, daughter of Edward ab Hugh Gwyn of Bodewryd, descended from GWEIRYDD AP RHYS GOCH, chief of the third Noble Tribe (see *post.*) The eldest son of this marriage, was Robert Lewys of Cemlyn, whose last lineal male descendant, Robert Lewys, Chancellor of Bangor, died in 1738, leaving three daughters and coheiresses, namely, Sydney, who married Love Parry, Esq. of Wernfawr ; Anna Maria ; and Mary, who married the Rev. Edward Hughes of Kinmael, father of the first Lord Dinorben, and grandfather of the above named Hugh Robert Hughes, Esq., Lord Lieutenant of Flintshire *(Dwnn's Vis,* ii., p. 199 ; and *Hist. Powys Fadog,* v., pp. 281-6.)

The Griffiths of Chwaen ended in an heiress, Anne, only surviving child of John Griffith, Esq., Sheriff of Anglesey in 1709, and of Carnarvonshire the following year. She was born in 1724, and was married to William Lewis, Esq., of Trysglwyn, father of the above named Ambrose Lewis, Esq. *(Dwnn's Vis,* ii., p. 147, *note.)*

Another old family of this tribe, named by Dwnn *(Vis.,* ii., p. 258), that of Arianell Goch, ended in an heiress, who married John Pritchard, Esq. of Dinam, near Gaerwen, of whom the Rev. H. Pritchard of that place is a lineal descendant.

The Nanney's of Cefndeuddwr and Gwynfryn, also trace their descent from Hwfa, through the Ellis's of Bodychen. Elizabeth Ellis, the eventual heiress of that house, married John Jones, Esq. of Brynkir, and their eldest surviving son, Owen Jones, Esq., assumed the surname of Ellis-Nanney, on succeeding to the estates of his maternal uncle, David Ellis Nanney, Esq. The present representative is H. J. Ellis Nanney, Esq. of Gwynfryn, in the County of Carnarvon *(Burke's Landed Gentry.)*

The following families appear to be extinct, or only existing in the female line :— Williams of Llanbedr *(Pennant's Tours,* iii., p. 429) ; Bould of Trerddol *(Ib.)* ; Owen of Llanfaethlu *(Ib.) ;* Morris of Treiorwerth *(Ib.);* Wynn of Bodowyr *(Ib.) ;* Owen of Twrcelyn *(Dwnn's ·Vis.,* ii., p. 192) ; Owen of Treddafydd, Malldraeth *(Ib.,* p. 201) ; Llachylched *(Ib.,* p. 259) ; Talebolion *(Ib.,* p. 262) ; and Niwbwrch *(Ib.,* p. 266.)—*Ed.*

II.—LLYWARCH AP BRÂN.

HE lived in the time of Owen Gwynedd, and was the prince's brother in law, for both their wives were sisters, the daughters of Gronw ap Owain ap Edwyn, Lord of Tegaingyl, as Griffith Hiraethog,[1] and Sir Thomas ap Ievan ap Deicws, and also an old parchment manuscript, written about four hundred years ago, do testify. What office he bare under the prince I do not know, but some say he was his steward, as in a book of Sir Thomas ap William[2] of Trefriw, I found. He dwelt in the township which from him is called Tref Llywarch, which hath in it Caergybi,[3] and three parcels bearing the name of his three sons, Wele[4] Iorwerth ap Llywarch, Wele Cadwgan ap Llywarch, Wele Madoc ap Llywarch, as in the Extent of North Wales is manifest. He had a grandchild by his son Iorwerth, called Meredydd, who for his good service had the freehold of the township of Escynniog, given him and his heirs for ever, by prince Llywelin ap Iorwerth, whose posterity, Ievan Wyddel and Tudur ap Hywel ap Tudur, held the same by virtue of the grant aforesaid, in the twenty-sixth year of King Edward the Third. Ievan Wyddel's mother was the daughter of the Lord of Cywchwr in Ireland, descended of the Earl of Kildare,

---

[1] A noted bard and herald who flourished about the year 1530.

[2] An eminent physician and antiquary in the reign of Queen Elizabeth.

[3] Holyhead.

[4] Wele, i.e. seat, or family, into many of which most trefs or townships were divided.

X

of whom the gentlemen of Mwsoglen, Porthamal,[1] and many other houses are descended. He beareth *argent* between three crows, each bearing a Queen of Ermin in their bills, a chevron *sable*, by the name of Llywarch ap Brân.

[1] Houses now extinct, or in the possession of men of yesterday, such is the mutability of property !

.... " You see it alter,
From you to me, from me to Peter Walter ;
Or in a mortgage prove a lawyer's share,
Or in a jointure vanish from the heir."

[ADDENDA.]—Llywarch ab Brân was lord of Cwmmwd Menai in Anglesey, and flourished about 1137. He was eighth in descent from Rhodri Mawr.

Iorwerth ab Llywarch, according to Rowlands *(Mona Antiqua)*, lived at Porthamel uchaf, Anglesey. His descendant Ievan Wyddel had two sons, namely, Rhys, who settled at Bodowyr; and Howel, who founded the ancient house of Berw (so called, possibly, from the *cresses* which abound there) which descended to his granddaughter Elinor. She married an Englishman named John Holland, who claimed descent from the Dukes of Valence. The Hollands continued owners of Berw for many generations. Several of them represented Anglesey in Parliament, and they formed alliances with some of the best families in the country. The last of the name was the Rev. Thomas Holland who died about 1750. On his decease, the property descended to his niece and heiress, Elizabeth, wife of Richard Trygarn, Esq., whose daughter, in 1755, married John Griffith, Esq. of Carreglwyd, "a worthy and convivial gentleman," as Pennant calls him, whose descendants still hold it *(Arch. Camb.* 1868, p. 97.) The ancient and interesting mansion of Berw is still preserved intact. The Anglesey Central Railway passes close to it.

Ievan ab Ednyved, in the time of Henry the Fourth, married the heiress of Jenkin ab Llewelyn ab Iorwerth of Myvyrian, a descendant of Llywarch, and from this union came the Prytherchs of Myvyrian, who became extinct in the male line about two hundred years ago, and by marriage were closely related to the families of Berw, Bodowyr, and the Trevors of Denbighshire. Their matrimonial connections were indeed so complicated, that Sir Edward Trevor of Brynkinallt, wrote the following epitaph on Eva, his grandmother :—

"Here lyes by name the world's mother,
  By nature my aunt, sister to my mother ;
  By law my grandmother, mother to my mother ;
  My great grandmother, mother to my grandmother ;
  All this may be without breach of consanguinity."—*(Arch. Camb.* 1848, p. 293.)

From Cadwgan ab Llywarch came the Hughes's of Plâs Côch, Anglesey. The old house of Porthamel isaf, where they resided, was rebuilt in 1569 by Hugh Hughes, Attorney General for North Wales, and was thenceforth called Plâs Côch from the colour of the stone used on that occasion. The late William Bulkeley Hughes, Esq. of Plâs Côch and Bryndu, was lineally descended from Hugh Hughes. He was for many years Member of Parliament for the Carnarvon Boroughs, and died in March, 1882, leaving an only daughter married to Captain Hunter. The family is also represented by his brother's son, Rice William Thomas, Esq. (formerly Hughes) of Coed-helen, Carnarvon *(Hist. Powys Fadog,* v., p. 311.) The Hughes's of Plascoch intermarried with the Bulkeleys of Bryndu and Beaumaris, the Owens of Clenneneu, and the Trevors of Denbighshire.

From Cadwgan were also descended the Meyricks of Bodorgan and Goodrich Court, by the marriage of their ancestor Einion Sais, with Eva, daughter of Meredydd ab Cadwgan *(Hist. Powys Fadog,* v., p. 312.) Dr. William Lloyd, successively Bishop of St. Asaph, Lichfield, and Worcester, was also descended from Cadwgan.

Owen Wynn, only son of Hugh Gwyn of Mwsoglen, was eleventh in descent from Ievan Wyddel. He married in 1628, Grace, daughter of Sir William Glynne of Glynllifon, but died without issue, and the male line of that family became extinct. His sister, Elizabeth, by her marriage with Hugh Owen, Esq. of Bodeon, conveyed the Mwsoglen estate into that family *(Dwnn's Vis.,* ii., p. 208.)

Eva, daughter of Llywarch ab Brân, became the second wife of the celebrated Ednyfed Vychan, minister of Llewelyn the Great, and by whom he had six sons, namely Sir Tudor, who had Plas yn Nant and Llangynhafal ; Rees, who had Garth Garmon ; Howell, who became Bishop of St. Asaph ; Llewelyn and Cynfrig, who had the Creuddyn ; and Iorwerth, who had Abermarlais *(Dwnn's Vis.,* i., p. 331.)

The latter was the ancestor of the renowned Sir Rhys ab Thomas of Dinevor (see *ante,* p. 132.) David Goch, his contemporary, another redoubtable warrior and a famous swordsman, who was killed by Sir Rhys's father, Thomas ab Griffith, in a desperate hand to hand encounter at Pennal, Merionethshire, also belonged to this tribe *(L. G. Cothi's Works,* p. 141.)

Tangwystl, another daughter, married Llywarch Goch, lord of Rhos and Meiriadog, and had issue, Llywarch Fychan the ancestor of Jones of Llyfnant, Ddol and Ruthin in Denbighshire *(Hist. Powys Fadog,* iv., p. 323.)

The old family of Meredith of Monachdy Gwyn, Clynog fawr, Carnarvonshire, now extinct were of this tribe. Meurig Meredith the last heir male, left an only daughter and heiress, Anna Maria, who married first, John Mostyn, Esq. of Segrwyd (of which marriage came the Mostyns of Llawesog) ; and secondly, Watkin Edwards Wynn, Esq. of Pengwern, Merioneth, and Llwyn, Denbighshire, by whom she had no issue. She died in 1828 (*Hist. Powys Fadog*, iv., p. 382.)

Catherine, daughter and heiress of Ellis Lloyd, the last male representative of the old family of Rhiwgoch, Trawsfynydd, of this tribe, married Henry Wynn, son of Sir John Wynn of Gwydir (see *ante*, p. 9), and was the mother of Sir John Wynn, Bart. of Wynnstay, in whom, dying without issue, the title ended.

The following families also extinct, according to Pennant, belonged to this tribe :— Lloyd of Maesyneuadd ; Wynn and Lloyd of Hendre'r mur, Merionethshire ; Lloyds of Brynhir or Brynkir, Coed y rhygyn, Llandecwyn, Cefnfaes and Cae Adda ; Meredith of Hafod Lwyfog ; Parry of Bodafon, Anglesey (*Dwnn's Vis.*, ii., p. 264) ; and Owen of Ruthin ; also the old families of Garregfawr, Amlwch (*Dwnn's Vis.*, ii., p. 264) ; Rhosgolyn (*Ib.* 266); Twrcelyn (*Ib.* 267) ; and Lloyd of Tymarian Heilyn, Llanddyfnan (*Ib.* 268.)—*Ed.*

III.—GWEIRYDD AP RHYS GOCH.

HE was of the hundred of Talybolion in Anglesey, and dwelt at Cardegog: The hamlets and tenements thereof to this day bear the names of his children and grandchildren, as Gwely Madoc ap Gweirydd, Gwely Llywarch ap Gweirydd, Gwely Howel ap Gweirydd, Gwely Meuric ap Gweirydd, whose great grandchild Howel ap Ievan ap Ednyfed ap Meuric ap Gweirydd enjoyed Gwely Meuric in the twenty-sixth of Edward the Third, as appears by the Extent of North Wales, of whom are descended Pierce Lloyd of Gwaredog, Esq. ; Edward Wynn of Bodewrid, Esq. ; and Owen Hughes of Beaumaris, Esq. ; and many more. He beareth *argent* on a bend *sable* three lions heads caboshed of the first. He lived in the time of Owen Gwynedd.

[ADDENDA.]—Gweirydd ap Rhys Goch flourished about the commencement of the twelfth century.

The families above named are stated by Pennant to be all extinct, or extant only in the female line, in his time, but he names one, namely, that of Foulkes of Gwernygron, Flintshire, as still extant in the male line. Pierce Lloyd, Esq. of Gwaredog, was Sheriff for Anglesey in 1595 and 1603. His first wife was Maud, daughter of William Hanmer, Esq., great grandson of Sir David Hanmer, Justice of the King's Bench (1383-1386), whose daughter, Margaret, married the renowned Owen Glyndwr. His son, Pierce Lloyd, Esq. of Llugwy, was Sheriff in 1612. His descendant, Thomas Lloyd, Esq., died without legitimate issue, and the estate was sold after his death to Sir William Irby, Bart., afterwards Lord Boston. *(Dwnn's Vis.*, ii., p. 198.) The estate of Bodewrid became united in the latter half of the seventeenth century to that of Penrhos, by the marriage of Ann, daughter of Edward Wynn to Hugh Owen, Esq. *(Ib.)* Margaret, daughter of Iorwerth ab Ieuan Lloyd (eighth in descent from Gweirydd) married William ab Ieuan of Bryn Gwallanog, Anglesey, the ancestor of Sir William Williams, Speaker of the House of Commons *(ante*, p. 101), and through him of the Williams's of Bodelwyddan, and the Wynns of Wynnstay *(Ib.* p. 266.)

IV.—CILMIN TROED-DU.

He lived in the time of Merfyn Frych, King of Man, being his brother's son, with whom he came from the North of Britain, when Merfyn married Esyllt, the daughter and heir of Conan Tindaethwy, King of the Britons. His posterity were wise and discreet men in all their ages, and many of them learned in the laws and judges under the kings and princes of Wales, as Morgene Ynad ap Gwydr, and Cyfnerth his son, whose lawbook is yet extant, fairly written on parchment, Morgeneu Ynad ap Madog, Morgan Ynad ap Meuric, and Madog Coch Ynad.[1] Robert ap Meredydd ap Hwlcyn Llwyd, a wise gentleman, lived in the time of Henry the Seventh, and of him are descended the Glynns of Nantlle; Sir William Glynn, Knight. of Glynllifon, father of Thomas Glynn of Glynllifon, Esq., and of Sir John Glynn,[2] Knight, Serjeant at law, now living; the Glynns of Lleyar, &c. Cilmin dwelt at Glynllifon, from whence the gentlemen aforesaid took the name of Glynne. He beareth quarterly, first, *argent*, an eagle displayed with two heads *sable;* second, *argent*, three fiery ragged sticks *gules;* the third as the second, the fourth as the first. Over all upon an escutcheon *argent*, a man's leg[3] couped a-la-cuise *sable*.

[1] A judge.

[2] He was of Bicester, of Oxfordshire, and of Hawarden in Flintshire, and one of the Judges (if not Chief Justice) of the Common Pleas. Prior to him there occurs a William Glyn, Serjeant at Law, of the house of Glynllifon [near Carnarvon], now the seat of Lord Newborough.

[3] Hence arose the whimsical mistake in representing the sign of the principal Inn at Carnarvon, which is now painted and called the Boot; whereas, without doubt, it was originally meant to hold out this armorial bearing as above blazoned, the house having always belonged to the estate of Glynllifon. The family arms have at all times been used as the signs of Inns; and this alone can account for such appearances as Dragons, Bears, Lions, Spread Eagles, &c., hung out over doors, so little indicatory of what is expected within.

[ADDENDA.]—Cilmin Troed-du or ("the black foot") flourished about 830. His foot became so discoloured, according to the legend, in escaping from an evil spirit, whose books he had assisted a magician to steal. In leaping over a brook, which was to be the limit of the pursuit, Cilmin's left leg plunged into the water and assumed its black colour *(Pennant's Tours*, ii., p. 391.) He is said to have been supreme judge of North Wales.

The wife of Robert ab Meredydd ab Hwlcyn Llwyd, the ancestor of the Glyn's, was Catrin, daughter of William ab Jenkin, descended from Osbwrn Wyddel *(Dwnn's Vis.,* ii., p. 149, and *ante*, p. 16, *note.)* Extracts are given from Robert ab Meredydd's Will in *Arch. Camb.*, 1883, p. 14.

Thomas Glyn, Esq. of Nantlle, was sheriff for Carnarvonshire in 1627, and died in 1659. He had several children, but the family is supposed to be now extinct *(Dwnn's Vis.*, ii., p. 149.)

The Glyn's of Bryngwdion, were another branch. Richard Glyn, Esq. of Bryngwdion, was Sheriff for Carnarvonshire in 1634, and his Will was proved in 1642. His son, William Glyn, married Margaret, daughter and heiress of Richard Evans of Eleirnion, descended from RHYS AB TEWDWR (founder of the second Royal Tribe.) This family became extinct in the male line about the close of the seventeenth century *(Arch. Camb.*, 1876, p. 180.)

The fine old church of Clynog, Carnarvonshire, contains monuments to several members of the family of Glynne of Lleuar. William Glyn, Esq. of that place, died in 1660. His daughter and heiress, Mary, married Col. George Twisleton, and their granddaughter and eventual heiress of the estate, became the wife of Captain William Ridsdale, who sold the estates of his wife to Sir Thomas Wynn of Glynllifon, and was killed at Dettingen in 1743 *(Dwnn's Vis.*, ii., p. 150.)

The Glyns of Glynllifon, ended in an heiress, Frances, daughter of John Glyn, Esq., who married Thomas Wynn, Esq. of Boduan, and conveyed to him the Glynllifon estate. He was created a Baronet in 1742, and was the great grandfather of the present Lord Newborough.

The distinguished lawyer, Sir John Glynne, Serjeant at Law above referred to, was born at Glynllifon in 1602, and by his ability, gained a prominent position at the bar. He took the popular side, and was one of the most active in prosecuting Strafford. In due time he was appointed Chief Justice during the Commonwealth. After the Restoration, being "wise and discreet," he managed to gain favour with Charles the Second, who not only knighted him, but bestowed on him the honour of prime Serjeant, and created his eldest son a Baronet. Sir John Glynne purchased the Hawarden Castle estate. He died in 1666. The late Sir Stephen Richard Glynne, the ninth Baronet, was his lineal descendant. He died in 1874 without issue, when the title became extinct, and the estates came into the possession of his sister, Catherine, wife of that distinguished statesman, orator, scholar, and writer the Right Hon. William Ewart Gladstone, M.P., the late Prime Minister.

The Glyns of Ewell, Surrey (now represented by Sir George Turbervill Glyn, Bart.), and of Gaunts, Dorsetshire (whose present representative is Sir Richard George Glyn, Bart.), are both descended from the Rev. Richard Glyn, Rector of Llanfaethlu in 1587, a younger son of William Glyn of Glynllifon *(Burke's Peerage and Baronetage.)—Ed.*

V.—COLLWYN AP TANGNO.

HE is said to be Lord of Eifionydd, Ardudwy, and part of Llŷn, and it is true that his progeny and posterity do to this day, possess and enjoy most of the said country. His grandchildren Asser, Meirion, and Gwgan, the sons of Merwydd ap Collwyn, lived in the beginning of Griffith ap Cynan's reign, as by the life of Griffith ap Cynan is manifest, whereby may be known what time he lived and flourished. It is said he dwelt some time in Bronwen's tower at Harlech, calling the same town from his own name Caer Collwyn. But his said children, when Griffith ap Cynan first challenged the principality of Wales, lived in Llŷn, as in the said book of his life is extant. Collwyn's posterity were always the noblest and best men in Eifionydd and Ardudwy, next to the Princes and their issue. His heir, from eldest son to eldest, is hard to be known, in regard that by the British laws, every man's inheritance was to be divided between his children, and the youngest had the principal house, whereby every one having an equal portion of their parent's lands, their posterity was forgotten. Collwyn ap Tangno beareth *sable* between three flower-de-luces, a cheveron *argent*. Sir Hywel y Fwyall descended of Collwyn, was a noble warrior and was in the battle of Poictiers with the Black Prince, when the French King was taken prisoner, where with his pole-axe he behaved himself so valiantly that the prince made him a Knight, and allowed a mess of meat to be served before his axe or partizan for ever in perpetual memory of his good service; which mess of meat after his death, was carried down to be given to the poor for his soul's sake, and the said mess had eight yeomen attendants found at the King's charge, which were afterwards called yeomen of the Crown, who had eight·pence a day of standing wages, and lasted to the beginning of Queen Elizabeth (as by the relation of Serjeant Roberts of Hafod y Bwch, near Wrexham, and Robert Turbridge of Cae'r Fallen, near Ruthin, Esq., is recorded in the history of the noble house of Gwydir). Besides this he had the constableship of the Castle of Cricciaith,[1] where he kept house, and the rent of Dee Mills at Chester, for the term of his life. His father was Gruffudd ap Howel ap Meredydd ap Einion ap Gwganen ap Merwydd ap Collwyn. His arms were *sable* between three flower-de-luces a pole-axe *argent*.[2]

[1] Cricciaith, though a contributory borough to Carnarvon, and governed by a Mayor and two Bailiffs, consists of a few miserable houses. The ruins of the Castle, which is boldly situated on a tongue of land jutting out into the sea, alone can claim the traveller's attention, and hereafter to any person who reading this may connect it with the history of Sir Howel, his mess and his pole-axe, it may, perhaps, become an object of more curious enquiry. [Criccieth has lately become a favourite watering place on account of the mildness and salubrity of its climate. The Commissioners appointed in 1876 to inquire into Municipal Corporations, reported that Criccieth had long ceased to be one.—*Ed.*]

[2] To the head of this tribe, Sir John Vaughan, Knight, of Crosswood or Trawscoed in Cardiganshire, Chief Justice of the Common Pleas, traced his lineage, as thus: Sir John Vaughan ap Edward ap Evan ap Richard ap Morris ap Ievan ap Llewelin ap Adda ap Meredydd ap Adda ap Llewelin ap Griffith ap Eynon ap Kadifor ap Collwyn ap Tangno. The present Lord Lisburne is a descendant of Sir John Vaughan [see *ante*, p. 97, *note.*]

[ADDENDA.]—Collwyn ab Tangno was descended from Cunedda Wledig, and flourished about the beginning of the eleventh century. He married Modlan Benllydan, granddaughter of Gwaethfoed Fawr of Powys, gread grandfather of Bleddyn ab Cynfyn,

Y

by whom he had five sons, Ednowen, Merwydd Goch, Einion, Ednyvet, and Cadifor. He had also a son, Cynan, by another wife. Einion was the ancestor of the famous poet, Rhys Goch Eryri, who flourished about the year 1400, and lived on his own estate at Hafod Garregog, Beddgelert; also of Robert of Lygun, another eminent bard. Cadifor was, as already stated, the ancestor of the Vaughans of Crosswood, now represented by the Earl of Lisburne. The following are some of the chief families, besides those already mentioned, belonging to this tribe.

Wynn of Bodvel and Gwydir. John Wynn, Esq. of Bodvel, for his distinguished services as standard bearer in the battle of Norwich in 1549, obtained a grant of the Isle of Bardsey (which still belongs to his descendants), and of the Abbot of Bardsey's demesne house near Aberdaron. His son Hugh assumed the name of Bodvel or Bodville, and his great granddaughter, Sarah Bodville, coheiress of the estate, on failure of the male line, married Viscount Bodmin, son of John, Earl of Radnor. Mary, the other coheiress, married Hugh Cholmondeley, Esq., and their son, Robert, was raised to the peerage of Ireland as Viscount Cholmondeley of the second creation. From him is lineally descended the present Marquess of Cholmondeley. Sir Thomas Wynn, Bart. (Equerry to George the Second), descended from Thomas Wynn, Esq. of Boduan or Bodvean, youngest son of the above named John Wynn, married Frances, daughter and at last heiress of John Glynn, Esq., and so acquired the Glynllifon estate (see *ante*, p. 184). His grandson Sir Thomas Wynn, Bart., was, in 1776, created Baron Newborough in the peerage of Ireland. The present peer is his third son *(Burke's Peerage)*.

Bodwrda of Bodwrda. The male line of this family became extinct on the death of Hugh Bodwrda, Esq., Sheriff for Carnarvonshire in 1687. His daughter and heiress, Mary, carried the estate to her husband, George Coytmore, Esq. of Coytmore. Their granddaughter and heiress, Mary Coytmore, married Edward Philip Pugh, Esq. of Penrhyn, and had an only son, James Coytmore Pugh, Esq., who died without issue, and whose sister and heiress, Bridget, married in 1766, Col. Glynne Wynn, brother of the first Lord Newborough *(Dwnn's Vis.*, ii., p. 248), by whom she had three sons who died issueless, and one daughter, Bridget, who married John Percival, fourth Earl of Egmont.

Wynn of Pennardd. Mary, daughter and heiress of Hugh Wynn, Gent. of Pennardd, married Love Parry, Esq. of Cefn Llanfair, whose descendant, Sir Thomas Love Duncombe Jones Parry, Bart., now represents this family *(Ib.*, p. 172).

Ellis, Bronyfoel and Ystumllyn. Margaret, the heiress of this family, married Griffith Wynn, Esq. of Penyberth, whose family also belonged to this tribe. She died in 1712, and he in 1719. Their descendants for three generations held the property, but it has since repeatedly changed hands *(Ib.*, p. 93). In 1837, the Ystumllyn estate was sold to the late Rowland Jones, Esq. of Broom Hall, to which place the portrait and coat of arms of Sir Howel y Fwyall was removed from Ystumllyn (*Camb. Journal* 1860, p. 261.) It now belongs to Owen Lloyd Jones Evans, Esq., also maternally descended from Collwyn.

Wynn of Gwynfryn. This family ended in an heiress, Mary, daughter of John Wynn, Esq., who, about the middle of the seventeenth century, married David Ellis, Esq. of Bodychen, descended from HWFA AB CYNDDELW, fourth in descent from whom was David Ellis Nanney, Esq., named *ante*, p. 176 (*Dwnn's Vis.*, ii., pp. 96 and 171.)

Vaughan, Aberkin. John Vaughan, Esq. of Aberkin, the last male representative of this family, died in 1730, leaving a daughter and coheiress, Ellen, who married the Rev. Griffith Williams, and their daughter, Ellinor, inherited the estate. She, in 1744, married William Wynn, Esq. of Wern, and their grandson, William Wynn, Esq. of Peniarth, succeeded to the property. He sold the Aberkin estate about 1821, to Lord Newborough's Trustees (*Ib.*, p. 182.)

Vaughan of Talhenbont and Plas hên. Of this family was Dr. Richard Vaughan, Bishop of Bangor, Chester, and London, who died in 1607. By the marriage of Ann, daughter and heiress of Richard Vaughan, Esq. of Plas hên, with William Vaughan, Esq. of Corsygedol, the two estates were united. The Vaughans of Corsygedol, became extinct in the male line (see *ante*, p. 17), upon the death in 1791, of Evan Lloyd Vaughan, Esq., M.P. for Merioneth. They are now represented in the female line by Lord Mostyn (*Ibid.*) Of this family also was Dr. Henry Rowlands, the eminent Bishop of Bangor, 1598-1615; whose munificent charities included the founding of a grammar school at Bottwnog, and of two fellowships at Jesus College, Oxford (*Ib.* p. 183.)

Owen, Plasdu or Pencoed, Llanarmon, Lleyn. Of this family was John Owen, the famous Epigrammatist, who died in 1622, and was buried in St. Paul's Cathedral (*Ib.* p. 180.)

Jones, Castellmarch, Lleyn. Sir William Jones, Knight, Chief Justice of the King's Bench, Ireland, and afterwards Justice of the same Court in England, was of this family. He died 6th December, 1640, and was buried in Lincoln's Inn Chapel. His granddaughter, Margaret, heiress of Castellmarch, married Sir William Williams, Bart. of Vaenol, whose grandson, in a drunken fit, bequeathed both estates to Sir Bourchier Wrey and his brother for life, with remainder to William the Third. They were granted afterwards by Queen Anne to the Right Hon. John Smith, Speaker of the House of Commons, in whose family they still remain (*Nicholas's County Families.*)

Edwards, Nanhoron, claim descent from Sir Howel y Fwyall. Captain Timothy Edwards, great grandfather of the present owner of Nanhoron, Francis William Lloyd Edwards, Esq., was a very distinguished naval officer (*Nicholas's County Families.*)

Evans, Tanybwlch. Catherine, eldest daughter and eventually heiress of Evan Evans, Esq., married Robert Gruffudd, Esq. of Bach y saint, Carnarvonshire. Their descendant, Evan Gruffydd, Esq., left a daughter and heiress, Margaret, who married William Oakeley, Esq., from whom the present owner is descended *(Dwnn's Vis.*, ii., p. 224.)

Rhydderch, Tregayan, Anglesey. John Prytherch, Esq., the last male representative of this family, married Ann, daughter and heir of John Roberts, Esq. of Cwmister, and · left an only daughter and heir, Ann, who, by her marriage with the Rev. Dr. Edmunds of Aber, left an only daughter, Margaret Edmunds, who married Robert Lloyd, Esq. of Gunys, Carnarvon. Their son, Robert Lloyd, Esq. of Tregayan, Vice Admiral R.N., left an only daughter, Margaret Hooper, who married Thomas Jones Parry, Esq. of Llwynon *(Burke's Landed Gentry.)* Their grandson, Thomas Edward John Lloyd, Esq., the present owner assumed the name of Lloyd, on succeeding to his great grandfather's property *(Nicholas's County Families.)*

Madryn of Madryn. William Madryn, Esq. of Madryn, sold this estate about the close of the seventeenth century, and this family has long been extinct in the male line *(Dwnn's Vis.*, ii., p. 177.)

Pennant speaks of Williams of Aberarch, Carnarvonshire, as being extant in his time. Also of the following as being extinct besides those above named : Wynn, Pant du ; Wynn, Bodsannan ; Lloyd, Bodfari ; Lloyd, Gardd; Lloyd, Dol penrhyn *(Dwnn's Vis.*, ii. p. 281) ; and Owen, Maentwrog.—*Ed.*

VI.—NEFYDD HARDD.

HE was of Nant Conway, and lived in the time of Owain Gwynedd, who gave Idwal his son to be foster'd by him ; but he, for what reason I know not, caused Dunawt his son to kill the young prince at a place called of him, Cwm Idwal ; wherefore Nefydd and his posterity were degraded, and of gentlemen were made bondmen. His son, Rhyn, to expiate that foul murther, gave the lands whereon the church of Llanrwst was built, whose grandchild[1] was steward to Llewelin ap Iorwerth, prince of Wales. Doctor William Morgan, Bishop of St. Asaph, who assisted in the translation of the Bible, was lineally descended of him. He dwelt at Cryg-nant, Llanrwst. He beareth *argent* three spear's heads, imbrued *sable* pointed upwards.[2]

---

[1] In the Churchyard of Llanrwst there is this inscription on his grave-stone : "Yma rwyfi yn gorwedd Madoc ap Iorwerth ap Gwrgeneu Pen Ystiwart Arglwydd Cymru." [Here I lie, Madog ap Iorwerth ap Gwrgeneu, Chief Steward of the Lord of Wales. This Madog is generally called Madog Goch.—*Ed.*]

[2] Other authorities give, *argent* a chevron between three javelins *sable* pointed upwards *gules.—Ed.*

[ADDENDA.]—Nefydd Hardd, or "the handsome" flourished about the middle of the twelfth century, and was lineally descended from Cunedda Wledig. He dwelt at Crygnant, Llanrwst.

Of this tribe came the families of Morgan, Gwibernant ; Evans, Llanrwst ; and Davies, Coedymynydd, all of which are extinct in the male line *(Pennant.)* The first of these produced that eminent and good prelate Dr. William Morgan already referred to *ante*, p. 90 ; Bishop of Llandaff in 1595, and translated in 1601 to St. Asaph, whose great work was the translation of the Bible into Welsh. He was an excellent scholar. He died on the 10th September, 1604, at St. Asaph, where he was interred the following day. See the interesting correspondence between him and Sir John Wynn of Gwydir, *ante*, pp. 134 to 142. He was also descended from two other tribes, paternally from HEDD MOLWYNOG, and maternally from MARCHUDD AB CYNAN. The first edition of Morgan's Bible is now very scarce.—*Ed.*

VII.—MAELOG CRWM.

HE was of Llechweddisaf and Creuddyn, and lived in the
time of Prince David ap Owain, about the time of our Lord
1175, as Sir Thomas William's book averreth. The most famous
men descended of him was Sir Thomas Chaloner, and others of
that name, whose ancestor Trahaiarn Chaloner was so called
because his grandfather Madoc Crwm had lived in a town in
France called Chaloner, from whence he took that name. ·He
beareth[1] *argent* on a chevron *sable* three angels *or*, by the name
of Macloc Crwm.

[1] I have seen the arms blazoned thus: *argent* on a chevron *sable* three angels
kneeling with wings displayed *or*.

· · · · —— ·

[ADDENDA.]—Llechwedd isaf and Creuddyn, of which Maelog Crwm (the hunch-
back) was lord, are both in Carnarvonshire. He was descended from Helig ab Glannawg
(Arch. Camb. 1861, p. 142), whose fine patrimony was overflowed about the commencement of the sixth century, and is now known by the name of the Lavan Sands.
Others assign to him a different pedigree to Cunedda Wledig. By "the town in
France called Chaloner" is probably meant Chalons,—either Chalons-sur-Marne, the
capital of the department of Marne ; or Chalons-sur-Saône, the capital of an
arrondissement of the department of Saône et Loire.

Trahaiarn de Chaloner was the son of Gwilym ab Madog ab Maelog Crwm, and took
the lord of Chaloner prisoner in France, took possession of his lands and assumed his
armorial bearings. He was the ancestor of the Chaloners of Lloran Ganol, Denbighshire, and of Chester, both extinct *(Hist. Powys Fadog*, iv., p. 347.) Also of the
Chaloners of Guisborough, Yorkshire, still extant and represented by Lieut-Col. and
Admiral Thomas Chaloner. C.B., and others. Sir Thomas Chaloner of this line, was
a celebrated writer and soldier, who was knighted by the Protector Somerset, at the
battle of Musselburgh in 1547 *(Burke's Landed Gentry.)* Two of his grandsons
were members of the Long Parliament, and sat as judges on the trial of Charles the
First *(Penny Cycl.)—Ed.*

VIII.—MARCHUDD AP CYNAN.

HE was Lord of Abergelcu, his house was Brynffanigl, he lived in the time of Rhodri mawr, King of the Britons, about the year of our Lord 846. Of him was Ednyfed Fychan descended, who being general of the prince's host,[1] was sent to the marches to defend the frontiers from the approach of the English army, which was ready to invade under the command of Ranulph, Earl of Chester, who met them and killed three of their chiefest captains, and a great many of the common soldiers: the rest he put to flight and triumphantly returned to Prince Llewelin ap Iorwerth his Lord, who, in recompence of his good service, gave him, among many gifts, a new coat of arms; for the coat which he and his ancestors had always given before, was the coat of Marchudd, viz. *gules* a Saracen's head erazed *proper*, wreathed *or*, whereas the new coat was *gules* between three Englishmen's heads couped a chevron *ermin.*[2] From the death of the last Prince Llewelin, this man's progeny were the greatest men of any in Wales, as by the works of

---

[1] Llewelin ap Iorwerth, commonly called Llewelin the Great, to whom Ednyfed was Privy Counsellor.

[2] After this overthrow of the English, Ednyfed Fychan is said to have sung thus :—

"Llawer bron yn llai i'r brenin ;—heddyw
　　Hawdd i galon chwerthin,
　　Llawer Sais lleibus llibin,
　　A'r gro yn do ar ei din."—*Ednyfed Fychan* ai cànt.

　　To-day the King is short of many a breast ;
　　Now to the heart 'tis easy to be gay ;
　　The length of many a Saxon licks the ground,
　　Where lies the gravel heaped upon his back.

the bards and other records is yet manifest. If I should go about to reckon all the famous men descended of him, it would far exceed the bounds of my undertaking. Let it suffice to remember Henry the Seventh, Henry the Eighth, Edward the Sixth, and Queen Elizabeth, all which are lineally and paternally descended of Ednyfed Fychan, and he of Marchudd.[1]

---

[1] After this enumeration of crowned heads it may savour a little of the *Bathos* to particularize any descendants of inferior rank, such as Sir William Griffith of Penrhyn, surnamed the liberal, Chamberlain of North Wales, and the Lord Keeper Williams, Archbishop of York, and prior to them Llewelin ab Gwilym of Cryngae, near Newcastle Emlyn, Carmarthenshire, the patron of the Muses in his time, who was murthered at St. Dogmael's, near Cardigan, and whose fate was lamented by his favourite bard, Dafydd ab Gwilym, in a poem to be found in that bard's works lately published, page 459. Of the above, Llewelin ap Gwilym is lineally descended ; a gentleman now living who does honour to his great ancestor by his taste for encouragement of learning, and who himself has not unsuccessfully paid his devotion to the Muses, Maurice Morgan, Esq., the sole surviving representative of the ancient house of Llanbylan, Pembrokeshire.

N.B.—This gentleman is author of the ingenious Essay on the character of Shakespeare's Falstaff.

[ADDENDA.]—To begin with royalty, the descent of Henry the Seventh from GRIFFITH AP CYNAN, head of the first Royal Tribe, has been already given, *ante*, p. 73, *note.* His descent from MARCHUDD, the founder of this important Tribe, was as follows :—Henry the Seventh was the son of Edmund Tudor, Earl of Richmond by his wife, Margaret Beaufort, daughter of John, Duke of Somerset, and granddaughter of John of Gaunt ; Edmund Tudor was the son of Sir Owen Tudor of Penmynydd, Anglesey, by Catherine of Valois, Queen and widow of Henry the Fifth. He was beheaded and buried at Hereford after the battle of Mortimer's Cross in 1461. Besides Edmund, who predeceased him, he had issue, Jasper Tudor, Earl of Pembroke (who died without issue) ; Owen Tudor, who became a monk ; and Tacina Tudor, wife of Reginald, Lord Grey de Wilton. Sir Owen Tudor was the son of Meredith, the son of Tudor, the son of Goronwy, the son of Tudor, the son of Goronwy, the son of Ednyfed Fychan, who was ninth in direct descent from Marchudd the head of this Tribe.

Ednyfed Fychan, the able general and minister of Prince Llewelyn, lived about 1220, chiefly at Tregarnedd, near Llangefni, Anglesey, but occasionally also at Llys Bryn Eurin, near Abergele. He was twice married ; first, to Gwenllian, daughter of the Lord Rhys, grandson of RHYS AB TEWDWR, founder of the second Royal Tribe, by whom he had Gruffudd of Henglawdd ; Goronwy, Lord of Trecastle, Anglesey (ancestor of the Tudors) ; Gwenllian and Angharad ; secondly, to Eva, daughter of LLYWARCH AB BRAN, who brought him Tudor, who had Nant and Llangynhafal ; Howell, who became Bishop of St. Asaph ; Llewelyn and Cynwrig, who had the Creuddyn ; Rees, who had Garth Garmon ; and Iorwerth, who had Abermarlais, and was the ancestor in the maternal line of the redoubtable Sir Rhys ab Thomas (*Dwnn's Vis.*, i., p. 331 ; and ii., p. 101).

From the above, it will be seen that the Tudors were descended from no less than *three* of the Royal and Noble Tribes of Wales. Sir Owen Tudor's first cousin, Morfydd, heiress of Penmynydd, married Gwilym ab Gruffydd of Cochwillan and Penrhyn, also a direct descendant from Ednyved Fychan, from whom lineally descended the Tudors, Theodors, and Owens of Penmynydd, the last of whom, Margaret, the heiress of the estate, married Coningsby Williams, Esq., M.P., who died without issue in 1707, where-upon her aunt, Mary, wife of Rowland Bulkeley, Esq. of Porthamel, inherited the property. Their daughter and heiress, Jane, wife of Richard Meyrick, Esq. of Bodorgan, also died without issue. The last descendant, male or female, of the once powerful and illustrious family of Tudor, which supplied England with a race of Kings, is supposed to have been a humble individual named Moses Tudor, who kept a little school at Gaerwen in Anglesey, and who died in 1793. Penmynydd was sold in 1722 to Viscount Bulkeley, and now forms part of the Baron Hill estate (*Arch. Camb.* 1869, p. 379, where a very full account may be found of Penmynydd and the Tudors).

Gwilym ab Gruffydd was also the direct ancestor of Sir William Griffith of Penrhyn, above-named. Sir William was twice married, and had five sons and ten daughters, who married into some of the best Welsh and Cheshire families, and whose descendants are to this day very numerous. Pyrs Gruffydd (Sir William's grandson), bought and fitted out a ship at his own expense, and was present at the defeat of the Spanish Armada. He also accompanied Drake and Raleigh in a subsequent expedition against the Spaniards, but falling into pecuniary difficulties, his estate of Penrhyn was sold in 1616, but in 1622 was purchased again by Lord Keeper Williams, who himself was a descendant through a female from its former possessors. Pyrs Gruffydd was buried in Westminster Abbey in 1628. The Penrhyn estate continued for several generations in the Williams family. Upon the death without issue of Sir Griffith Williams, Bart., it became vested in his eldest sister, Frances, wife of Lord Edward Russell. She also died without issue, and it passed to her sisters, Anne, wife of Thomas Warburton, Esq., and Gwen, wife of Sir Walter Yonge. Mrs. Warburton's moiety descended to her grand-

z

daughter, Susannah Anne Warburton, who, on 6th December, 1765, married Richard Pennant, Esq., afterwards created Lord Penrhyn, by whose father, John Pennant, Esq. (of the line of TUDOR TREVOR), the other moiety had been purchased from the Yonge family. His lordship died without issue in 1808, when the title became extinct, and by his Will, the estate passed to his cousin, George Hay Dawkins, Esq., who, on the site of the ancient castle of Penrhyn, erected one of the most magnificent modern baronial mansions in these kingdoms. It is now the property of his grandson, the second Lord Penrhyn of the second creation (*Dwnn's Vis.*, ii., p. 168.)

Of Marchudd's descendants the following families are still extant in the male line :— Wynn of Melai and Maenan Abbey, now represented by Lord Newborough (see *ante*, p. 186) ; Foulkes of Eriviatt, whose present representative is John Jocelyn Foulkes, Esq. ; Lloyd of Forest, Pontruffydd and Pengwern, now represented by Lord Mostyn (*Hist. Powys Fadog*, v., p. 300) ; Wynn of Coed Coch and Trefarth or Trofarth, represented by Henry John Lloyd Wynn, Esq. of Coed Coch (*Ib.*, p. 322) ; Griffith of Garreglwyd, represented by Miss Conway Griffith, of Garreglwyd ; Williams of Marl, a branch of the Cochwillan family, now represented by Sir Richard Williams-Bulkeley, Bart. of Baron Hill ; Williams of Ystumcolwyn, another branch of the same family now represented by Rhys Buckley Williames, Esq. of Pennant, Montgomeryshire ; and Morgan of Golden Grove, Flintshire, now represented by George Augustus Morgan, Esq. of that place (*Dwnn's Vis.*, ii., p. 297).

The following appear to be extinct or merged in other families through inter-marriage :—Wynne of Garthewin, who became extinct in the male line on the death (30th November, 1844) of Lieut. Col. R. William Wynn ; Wynn of Dyffryn Aled, whose heiress, Diana, was married to Philip Yorke, Esq. of Erthig, author of *The Royal Tribes of Wales*, and his family is now represented by Pierce Wynne Yorke, Esq. of Dyffryn Aled, and Simon Yorke, Esq. of Erthig ; Lloyd of Gydros ; Roberts of Gwysaney ; Lloyd of Dol Edeyrn (*Dwnn's Vis.*, ii., p. 253) ; Lloyd of Trebul ; Vaughan of Henblas and Bronheulog ; Llewelyn of Llanelian ; Jones of Maesygarnedd, of whom was Col. Jones "the Regicide" (*Byegones*, 1872-3) ; Jenkin of Efenechtyd ; Howel of Maelienydd ; Griffith of Festiniog ; Dr. William Hughes, bishop of St. Asaph, whose daughter and heiress married a member of the Mostyn family (*Dwnn's Vis.*, ii., p. 299) ; Smith, Chancellor of St. Asaph ; Wynn of Giler (*Hist. Powys Fadog*, v., p. 393) ; Hughes of Cefnygarlleg and Prestatyn ; Conway of Nant ; Lloyd of Kinmael, whose heiress married a Holland, and after some generations, the heiress of Kinmael (a Holland) married Sir John Carter, one of Cromwell's officer's (see *ante*, p. 113, *note*) ; Lloyd of Plymog (see *ante*, p. 109, *note*) ; Anwyl of Garth Garmon (*Hist. Powys Fadog*, v., p. 301); Williams of Cochwillan, Vaynol, and Meillionydd, one of the greatest families in Carnarvonshire in its day, who intermarried with the powerful families of Wynn of Gwydir, Salesbury of Denbigh, &c. The elder branch of

Cochwillan has been extinct for many generations. One of its most distinguished members was the redoubtable Lord Keeper Williams, already referred to, who was in great favour with James the First and Charles the First. He was promoted to the Bishopric of Lincoln in 1621, and translated to the Archbishopric of York, 4th December, 1641. He died 25th March, 1650. The extinction of the Vaenol branch has already been shewn *(ante,* p. 187); and the Meillionydd branch ended in Sir Robert Williames Vaughan, Bart., who died in 1859. The learned Dr. John Davies of Mallwyd, was also of this tribe, see *ante.* p. 93.—*Ed.*

IX.—HEDD MOLWYNOG.

HE was of Uwch Aled in Denbighshire, his lands and Lordships were Llanfair Talhaiarn, Dyffryn Elwy, and Nant Aled, the which his three sons, Menter, Gwillonon, and Gwrgi divided, whose posterity have enjoyed and still do enjoy some part of them, even to our time. Rhys ap Ievan ap Llywelin Chwith of Chwibren, was an Esquire of the body to King Edward the Fourth, who, with his cousin german David Jenkin, were both very unruly in the Lancastrian war. Meurick Llwyd of Llwynymaen, near Oswestry, a descendant of Hedd Molwynog, was a valiant captain under the Earl of Arundel, who, by his prowess, achieved a very noble coat of arms, viz. *argent* an eagle displayed with two heads *sable.* And here I think Iolo Goch, Owain Glyndwr's bard, whose mother was the Countess of Lincoln (as Griffith Hiraethog saith), may well bear a place among the worthies descended from this line, who, for his lofty strain and singular skill in the British poetry, was, and is as as famous and renowned as any that hath been these four hundred years; and also Tudur Aled, another learned bard and a doctor of the Chair in his profession. But their works which are still preserved will better speak for them. The arms given by this tribe are *sable* a hart passant *argent* attired *or.*

[ADDENDA.]—Hedd Molwynog was descended from Rhodri Mawr, King of all Wales, and flourished during the latter half of the twelfth century. He lived at Henllys, in the parish of Llanfair Talhaiarn, Denbighshire, where the site of his palace may still be seen; and in Pennant's time, a field called "Maes y Bendithion" (the field of blessings), marked the spot where the poor received his alms. He was steward to Prince David ab Owen Gwynedd (1170-1195), whom he assisted to carry fire and sword through England, even to the walls of Coventry.

The descendants of Hedd Molwynog in the male line are supposed to be all extinct at the present day. The most important, perhaps, of the families that have become extinct was that of Lloyd of Hafodunos (near Abergele). The founder of this house was Bleddyn ap Bleddyn Fychan, who, according to Pennant, first assumed the name of Llwyd, and " peopled North Wales with Llwyds." Meurig Llwyd, referred to in the text, was his son. He, resenting the injuries which he and his tenants received from the English judges and officers, slew one of the first, and hanged several of the latter, on the oaks of his woods, by which he forfeited to the Crown his lands. He secured his life by taking refuge within a sanctuary at Halston. He afterwards placed himself under the protection of the Earl of Arundel, and was made captain over a band of soldiers, with whom he joined the Crusades. He had a command at the Siege of Acre, where he distinguished himself in recovering from the enemy the standard of the Emperor, by whom he was rewarded with a new coat of arms as stated above. On his return to Wales, he married Annesta, heiress of Llwynymaen and Llanforda, and was the progenitor of the Lloyds of those places and of Drenewydd (Whittington), Blaen Iâl, and Blaen y Ddol. Edward Llwyd, the eminent Welsh antiquary (who died in 1709), was a natural son of Edward Lloyd, the last male representative of the Llanforda branch. The estate had been sold in 1675, to Sir William Williams, Bart., and it still remains the property of his descendant, Sir Herbert Lloyd Watkin Williams Wynn, Bart.

The last male representative of the Lloyds of Hafod Unos (Hedd Lloyd), died without issue in 1739. His sister, Phœbe Lloyd, heiress of Hafodunos, married Howell Lloyd, Esq. of Wigfair, descended from EDNOWAIN BENDEW (Tribe xiii). Their descendant, the Rev. Thomas Hugh Clough, in 1830-1, sold Hafodunos to Samuel Sandbach, Esq.

Geoffrey Lloyd of Dyffryn Erethlyn, was the ancestor of the Lloyds of Palau, near Corwen. Evan Lloyd of Palau, married 12th July, 1591, being then sixteen years of age, and his wife eleven, by whom he had two sons and ten daughters. The male line ended in 1863 on the death of David Maurice Lloyd, Esq. of Palau, and some years afterwards the Palau estate was sold to Henry Robertson, Esq. *(Hist. Powys Fadog,* vi., p. 105.)

The Lloyds of Bach Eurig *(Hist. Powys Fadog,* iv., p. 183); Lloyd of Erw Cynddel *(Ib.* p. 184) ; Lloyd of Rhandir *(Ib.* p. 388) ; Wynn of Bryn Cynwrig *(Ib.)* ; Wynn of Giler *(Ib.* v., p. 391); and according to Pennant, Parry of Llangernyw ; Griffiths of Bodychwyn; Griffiths of Hafodygarreg; Griffiths of Blaen Ial; and Griffiths of Plasnewydd ; to whom may be added the Lloyds of Llansannan, afterwards of Plas Power, and now represented in the female line by T. L. Fitzhugh, Esq. ; were all of this Tribe, but have long been extinct or may be traced now in the female line only.

Iolo Goch, above referred to, was one of the most eminent poets of the Principality. He was lord of Llechryd and resided at Coed Pantwn, Llanefydd, Denbighshire. His stirring Odes roused the spirit of his countrymen against the English during Owen Glyndwr's insurrection. · He obtained extreme old age, and was living in 1402. Some of his poems have lately been published by the Cymmrodorion Society.

Tudur Aled lived at Garth Geri, Llansannan, Denbighshire, and was a Dominican friar. He was a nephew and pupil of Dafydd ab Edmund, another very eminent poet, and flourished from 1480 to 1520.

Edmund Prŷs, the learned Archdeacon of Merioneth, and one of the most eminent poets of his time, is stated *(ante,* p. 93, *note)* to have belonged to the Tribe of Marchudd, but according to a pedigree in *Dwnn's Vis.,* ii., p. 285, he descended from Hedd Molwynog. He was born at Gerddi Bluog, Llandecwyn, Merionethshire, about 1541 ; but resided, in after life, at Tyddyn Du, Maentwrog. He composed the Welsh metrical version of the Psalms still in use, and assisted Bishop Morgan in translating the Bible into Welsh. He died in 1624.—*Ed.*

X.—BRAINT HIR.

He was of Is Dulas, and lived about the time of the sons of Roderick the Great. His progeny did not much increase, for there are not many at present known to be descended of him, His arms are *vert* a Cross Fleury *or.*

[ADDENDA.]—The time above ascribed to the founder of this Tribe, by Gutyn Owain and others, is the latter half of the ninth century. Rhodri Mawr (Roderick the Great) died in 877. The Welsh Bruts, however (see " Brut Tysilio," *Myv. Arch.*, Gee's Edition, p. 473), say that he lived at a much earlier date, being nephew of Cadwallon, King of North Wales, 630-632; that he first distinguished himself in his uncle's service against Edwin, King of Northumberland, but the latter being victorious, he was compelled to flee to Ireland, and thence to Brittany; that his return to Britain was prevented for some time by Edwin with the help of Pelidys, a Spanish magician; but that at length, Braint disguised as a vagabond with a staff, in the head of which was a blade of iron, went over and reached York where Edwin held his court, and when the magician came out to distribute alms, Braint slew him with the blade of his staff, and then went to Exeter, where he summoned the Britons to join him, and was thus enabled to recover the country from the Saxons and restore the sovereignty to Cadwallon, who slew Edwin in the battle cf Hatfield, 633 *(Williams's Em. Welshmen.)* There is not, it seems, a single family at the present day that can trace its descent direct through the male line to Braint Hir. Pennant and Yorke *(Tracts of Powys)* mention the family of Vaughan of Pont y Gwyddyl, now extinct, as belonging to this Tribe.—*Ed.*

XI.—MARCHWEITHIAN.

He was called Lord of Isaled, his lands were Carwed Fynydd, Dincadfael, Prees, Berain, Llyweni, Gwytherin, and many other townships within the said hundred of Isaled in Denbighshire, as appears by the Extent of the Lordship and Honour of Denbigh, made in the eighth year of Edward the Third, at what time Cynwric Fychan, being the ninth in descent from Marchweithian lived, whereby some aim may be made of the time when the head of this tribe flourished. The families descended of him are many, but the most eminent are these:—Berain, now incorporated to the house of Llyweny by the marriage of Catherine, daughter and heir of Tudur ap Robert Fychan of Berain, Esq., with John Salisbury, son and heir of Sir John Salisbury of Llyweni,

Knight, after whose death she married Richard Clough of Denbigh, Esq., a Hamburgh merchant; and for her third husband, Moris Wynn of Gwyder, Esq.; and for her fourth, Edward Thelwall of Plas-y-ward, Esq. Of Marchweithian are likewise descended Wynn of Foelas; Price of Rhiwlas, whose ancestor, Robert ap Rees, being chaplain to Cardinal Wolsey, was a very great man in the time of Henry the Eighth. Ellis Price of Plâs Iollin, doctor of laws, who was one of the scholars of Cambridge that disputed with one Throgmorton and other scholars of Oxford and Cambridge, in the year of our Lord, 1532, and got the best, as Caius in the first book of the antiquities of Cambridge affirmeth; Vaughan of Pant Glâs, and many others. Marchweithian gave for his arms, *gules* a lion rampant *argent* armed *azure*.

[ADDENDA.]—Marchweithian was lineally descended from Coel Godhebog, King of Britain, and lived about the middle of the eleventh century. His palace was at Llyweni in the Vale of Clwyd, now little better than a farmhouse.

Some particulars have already been given *(ante,* p. 82, *note)* respecting the famous Catherine of Berain, her four husbands, and her numerous descendants. Her second, and it seems her favourite husband, Sir Richard Clough, was an eminent merchant and partner of the celebrated Sir Thomas Gresham, who, at his suggestion erected the Royal Exchange.

Rhys Fawr ab Meredydd, twelfth in descent from Marchweithian, was entrusted with the Standard of England, by the Earl of Richmond, at the Battle of Bosworth, after Sir William Brandon had been prostrated by King Richard the Third, and was, as his name implies a man of great stature. He and his descendants bore *gules* a lion rampant *argent* holding in its paws a rose of the second seeded *or,* stem and leaves *proper.* He was buried at Ysbytty Ifan Church, Denbighshire, where alabaster effigies of himself and his wife may now be seen. The latter was Lowry, daughter and heiress of Howel ab Gruffydd Goch, Lord of Rhos and Rhufoniog, by whom Rhys had five sons, namely,

Howel, Maurice, Robert, David, and Cadwaladr ; and six daughters, Eva, Gwenhwyfar, Margaret, Annes, Catherine, and Elizabeth *(Dwnn's Vis.*, ii., p. 343). From Rhys Fawr descended the families of Voelas, Rhiwlas, Cerniogau, Pantglas, Giler, and several others.

Maurice ap Rhys Fawr had two sons, Cadwalader and Robert Wynn Gethin, who obtained Grants from Henry the Eighth, of Voelas, Cerniogau, and other lands. By Deed of Partition in 1546, between them, Cadwalader took Voelas, and Robert, Cerniogau, with their adjacent tenements respectively *(Camb. Journal*, 1855, p. 181). Cadwalader's son, Robert, took the name of Wynn. His lineal descendant, Jane Wynn, daughter and heiress of Watkin Wynne, Esq., was married in 1775 to the Hon. Charles Finch, second son of the Earl of Aylesford, and the estate now belongs to their great grandson, Col. Charles Arthur Wynne Finch. Robert Wynn Gethin of Cerniogau's great granddaughter and heiress of that estate, married Richard Kenrick, Esq. of Woore Manor, whose descendants are now extinct in the male line. The estate was sold to a Mr. Blair, and about 1840, purchased of him by Mr. Wynne of Voelas, whereby the two estates became re-united in the line of their ancient possessors *(Ib.)* The Prices of Gilar also descended from Cadwalader ap Maurice. To this family belonged Robert Price, Baron of the Exchequer and afterwards Chief Justice of the Common Pleas, who successfully opposed the grant by William the Third, to William Bentinck, Earl of Portland, of the Townships of Denbigh, Bromfield, and Yale. He died in 1732 *(Arch. Camb.*, 1860, p. 121).

Robert ap Rhys Fawr, Chaplain and Cross bearer to Cardinal Wolsey, obtained a grant of the lands of Cwm Tirmynach and Moch or Boch Rhaiadr, now comprised in the estate of Rhiwlas held by his descendants. He was the father of thirteen sons and four daughters, among the former being Dr. Ellis Prys of Plas Iolyn ; Cadwaladr of Rhiwlas (ancestor of R. J. Lloyd Price, Esq. of Rhiwlas, near Bala) ; Richard, Abbot of Aberconwy (from whom came the Wynns of Plas Newydd, now extinct) ; Hugh, an Abbot, &c. *(Dwnn's Vis.*, ii., pp. 229 and 344). Ellis Prys, known as "the Red Doctor," represented Merioneth in three Parliaments, and was Sheriff of that and other Counties no less than fifteen times, namely, of Merioneth eight times, Carnarvon once, Anglesey twice, and Denbigh four times. He obtained grants from the Crown, of lands of the Knights Hospitallers in Yspytty Ifan. Pennant describes him as "a creature of Dudley, Earl of Leicester, and devoted to all his bad designs." He was living in 1605. His son, Capt. Thomas Prys of Plas Iolyn, was an excellent poet. He fitted out a privateer against the Spaniards, and he and Capt. William Middleton and Capt. Huet (or Koet), are said to have been the first who smoked tobacco in the streets of London. His great granddaughter, Elizabeth Pryse, heiress of Plas Iolyn, and Lady of the Manor of Yspytty Ifan, married Robert Edwards, Esq. of Gallt y Celyn, Yspytty Ifan *(Hist. Powys Fadog*, iv., p. 107).

Dr. Humphrey Humphreys, an eminent Bishop of Bangor, and afterwards of Hereford, was of this tribe. He was born in 1648, and died in 1712, and was the author of additions to Wood's *Athenæ Oxonienses*. He inherited Cesail Gyfarch, in the County of Carnarvon, from his mother. He married Margaret, daughter of Dr. Robert Morgan, Bishop of Bangor, by whom he had two daughters.

The following families are also named by Pennant, as descended from Marchweithian, all of them, however, I believe, being now extinct or only represented in the female line, namely, Wynn of Llangynhafal; Panton of Coleshill Manor, Flintshire; Parry of Tywysog and Pistyll *(Hist. Powys Fadog*, vi., p. 437) ; Price of Tyddyn Sieffrey; Price of Cwm Mein ; Price of Fedw deg ; Price of Llanrwst; Price of Dugoed, Penmachno; Wynn of Hafod y Maidd ; Foulkes of Llys Llywarch *(Ib.*, p. 238) ; Foulkes of Carwed Fynydd, and Meiriadog *(Ib.*, p. 235) ; Vaughan of Pantglas, whose eventual heiress, Anne Vaughan, married Sir Hugh Williams, Bart. of Marl *(Hist. Powys Fadog*, v., p. 407) ; Vaughan of Blaenycwm ; Vaughan of Llysfaen ; Williams of Aberconwy ; Williams of Hafod Garregog ; Wynn and Foulkes of Plasnewydd ; and Davies of Llathwryd.—*Ed.*

XII.—EDWIN.

EDWIN, commonly called King of Tegaingl, had a son, Owen, whose daughter, Angharad, was married to Gruffudd ab Cynan, King of Gwynedd or North Wales. Many worthy and noble gentlemen in Flintshire and Denbighshire, are descended of him, as the Bishop of Bangor now living;[1] Thomas Owen, a Judge of the Common Pleas, in the reign of Queen Elizabeth, father of Sir Roger Owen, late of Condover, Knight; Howel Gwynedd, a very valiant and stout man, who, siding with Owen Glyndwr against Henry the Fourth, did much annoy the English; but

---

[1] Probably Dr. William Roberts, consecrated Bishop of Bangor, September, 1637, and who died in August, 1665, aged eighty. He was a prelate distinguished for his piety and charity. His portrait is preserved at Pontruffydd, near Denbigh.—*Ed.*

Aa

on a time being more secure than he ought to have been, he was taken by his adversaries of the town of Flint, who, upon a place called Moel-y-gaer, cut off his head. And long before that time one Owen ap Aldyd, grandchild to Edwin, by force of arms kept all Tegaingl in subjection nothwithstanding all the power of King, Lord, and Country to the contrary. He beareth *argent* between four Cornish crows armed *gules* a cross Fleury engrailed *sable*.[1]

---

[1] From Edwin was descended Sir Thomas Powell, one of the Judges of the Kings Bench in the time of William the Third, and the present family of Nanteos in Cardiganshire; as likewise the Gwyns of Mynachdy, in the same County. [Sir Thomas Powell was appointed Judge, in April, 1687, but his judicial career terminated a few months afterwards with the flight of the King, James the Second.—*Ed.*]

[ADDENDA.]—Edwin was the great great grandson of Hywel Dda, and flourished about the middle of the eleventh century. His mother was Ethelfleda, daughter and heiress of Edwin, Earl of Mercia, and relict of Edmund Ironside, King of England. His patrimony of Tegaingl is a division of Flintshire, comprising the hundreds of Rhuddlan, Coleshill, and Prestatyn; and he held his Court at a place called Llys Edwin, in the parish of Llaneurgain *(Anglicè*, Northop). He married Gwerydd or Ewerydda, sister of BLEDDYN AB CYNFYN, by whom he had three sons, Owain, Uchdryd, and Hywel. He was slain in 1073, and buried at Northop.

Owain succeeded his father as Prince of Tegaingl. He bore *gules* three men's legs conjoined at the thighs in triangle *argent*. He died of consumption in 1103. By his wife, Morfudd, daughter of Goronwy ab EDNOWAIN BENDEW (chief of the thirteenth Noble Tribe), he had, besides the daughter, Angharad above referred to as the wife of GRUFFUDD AB CYNAN, five sons, Goronwy, Meilir, Llewelyn, Aldud, and Rhirid. These were the ancestors of the Lloyds of Hersedd, Ffern, and Llwyn Yn; Pryse, Llwyn Yn; Edwards of Stansty, Rhual, Gallt Celyn, Crogen Iddon, and Glyn; Evans, Coedllai and Treuddyn; Lloyd, Pentrehobin; Wynn, Copa'r Ieni; Parry, Llaneurgain; Griffith of Garn; Wynn of Nerquis.

Uchdryd became lord of Cyfeiliog and Meirion. His first wife was Agnes, daughter of Llewelyn Aurdorchog ("of the golden torque"), lord of Iâl, who bore him Iorwerth, Idnerth Benfras, Llawdden, and Philip of Cyfeiliog, ancestor of the old families of

Abergwidol, Gelligoch, Caelan, and others in the hundred of Cyfeiliog. By his second wife, Angharad, daughter of Meredydd ab Bleddyn, he had a son, Meredydd, ancestor of the Owens of Llynlloedd, Tedsmore, Woodhouse, Condover, and Bettws Cedewain ; the Powells of Nanteos ; and the Bromfields of Bromfield.

Hywel married Janet, daughter of Ithel ab Eynydd, lord of Trefalun.

Howel Gwynedd, referred to in the text, was seventh in descent from Uchdryd ab Edwin.

Sir Thomas Owen, above referred to, was a man of great legal erudition, and was Judge of the Common Pleas, from January 21st, 1594, until his death, December 21st, 1598. His son, Sir Roger Owen, distinguished himself among the literary men of his day, and was an active Member of Parliament. Both he and several of his successors filled the office of Sheriff, and the estate of Condover still remains with the family ; though this and the other branches of the Owen family above named, have long been extinct in the direct male line.

Dr. David Powell, Vicar of Rhiwabon, a learned divine and eminent antiquary, born about 1522, died in 1598, was descended from Uchdryd ab Edwin. He was Chaplain to Sir Henry Sidney, Lord President of the Marches, published several works of great learning, and rendered essential assistance to Dr. Morgan in the translation of the Bible into Welsh.

The only families of this tribe that I can find to be still extant in the male line, are those of Griffith of Garn, now represented by William Douglas Wynne Griffith, Esq. of Garn, near Rhyl ; and Powell of Nanteos.

In addition to the other families above named, all of which are extinct, or only extant in the male line, may be added the Mostyns of Llys Pengwern, Mostyn and Talacre, who are maternally descended from Edwin *(Hist. Powys Fadog ; Arch. Camb. ; Dwnn's Vis., &c.)—Ed.*

XIII.—EDNOWAIN BENDEW.

HE was Lord of Tegaingl in the year of our Lord 1079, as the book of Ednop saith, and it is said by Peter Ellis the counsellor to be the chief of the fifteen Peers of North Wales. Of him are descended Ithel ap Rotpert, Archdeacon of Tegaingl;

all the Bithels; the Hanmers; and many other noted families. He beareth *argent* between three Boars' heads couped a chevron *sable.*

———————— - -

[ADDENDA.]—Ednowain Bendew ("the strong skulled"), is supposed to have lived at Llys y Coed, in the parish of Cilcain, in the county of Flint ; and that he had a mansion also at Tymaen, in the parish of Whiteford, in the same county *(Pennant's Tours in Wales,* iii., pp. 159 and 446). His wife was Gwerful, daughter of Lluddoca ab Tudor Trevor, Earl of Hereford, head of the Tribe of the Marches. An old MS. states of him that " he was brave, for he killed a wild boar without help" *(Dwnn's Vis.,* ii., p. 83),

Ithel ap Rotpert, above referred to, was living in 1393 *(Pennant's Hist. of Whiteford and Holywell,* p. 119).

Dr. Richard Davies, Bishop successively of St. Asaph and St. David's, one of the translators of the Old Testament into English, and of the New Testament and Liturgy into Welsh, was of this Tribe (see *ante,* p. 92, *note).*

Pennant *(Tours in Wales,* iii., p. 446) gives the following list of families in his time extant in the male line :—Lloyd of Wigfair ; Foulkes of Mertyn ; Griffith of Rhual ; Hughes of Halkin and Bagillt ; and Griffith of Plas isaf, Caerwys. The Lloyds of Wigfair, became extinct in the male line on the death of John Lloyd, Esq., F.R.S. and M.P. for Flintshire in 1815, unmarried. John Inglis Jones, Esq. of Derry Ormond, in the county of Cardigan, also claims direct descent from Ednowain Bendew *(Nicholas's County Families,* p. 197).

The following families are enumerated by Pennant; among those that are extinct or only represented in the female line belonging to this tribe, all in Flintshire :—

Wynns of Galedlom and Caerwys ; the Facknalts of Facknalt ; Pugh of Ysceifiog ; Piers of Llanasaph ; Parry of Coleshill and Basingwerk ; Griffith of Pantyllongdy, Llanasa ; Griffith of Caerwys Hall ; Evans of Llancurgain (Northop). The heiress of this family (Martha, daughter of Thomas Hughes, Esq.), about the middle of last century, married Edward Pryse Lloyd, Esq. of Glansevin, in the county of Carmarthen, whose descendant, Morgan Pryse Lloyd, Esq. of that place, is now the representative of this family *(Arch. Camb.,* 1863, p. 248), and *(Dwnn's Vis.,* ii., p. 326). Jones of Ysceifiog ; of this family was John Jones, Esq. of Gelli lyfdy, a great collector of Welsh MS., which now form part of the Hengwrt collection at Peniarth (see *ante,* p. 115)! Williams, Colomendy, Ysceifiog ; and Hughes of Coedybrain.—*Ed.*

XIV.—EFNYDD.

COMMONLY called the son of Gwenllian, the daughter of Rhys ap Marchen, who was Lord of seven townships in Dyffryn Clwyd, called Ruthin land, viz. Tref Ben-y-Coed, and Efenechdyd, y Groes-lwyd, Pant Meugen, and three more, all freehold land, and had no children only Gwenllian aforesaid, which by the means of Bleddyn ap Cynfin, King of Wales, was given in marriage to this Efnydd's father, being of a near kindred unto the said King, who gave him seven[1] other townships, viz. Almor, Tref Alen, Gresfordd in Bromfield, Lleprog-fawr, Lleprog-fechan, and Trêf y nant in Tegaingl, &c. He had a daughter called Hunydd, who was the wife of Meredydd ap Bleddyn, Prince of Powys. Of this Efnydd, was descended John Almor, one of the Marshalls of the Hall to King Henry the Seventh, father of John Almor, Serjeant at Arms to King Henry the Eighth, who bore for his arms, *azure* a lion rampant *or* armed and langued *gules*. Sir William Meredith of England, is also of this tribe. Efnydd's Coat was, *azure* a lion saliant *or*, wherewith he quartered his mother's, being *azure* between three Nag's heads erased *argent* a fess *or*.

---

[1] Only six townships are named.—*Ed.*

[ADDENDA.]—Of Efnydd or Eunydd, who flourished about the close of the eleventh century, some particulars have already been given *(ante, p. 43, note)*. His father was, it is there stated, Gwernwy, a cousin of BLEDDYN AB CYNFYN, but Dwnn *(Vis., ii., pp. 83 and 355)* states him to have been Morien ap Morgeneu ap Gwerystan ap Gwaethfoed, lord of Powys, and that Eunydd, with HEDD MOLWYNOG and MARCHWEITHIAN, had the distinction of being constituted heads of tribes conferred upon them on account of their bravery at the Battle of Coventry *(Ib.)*

Eunydd married Eva, daughter and heiress of Llywelyn ab Dolphyn ab Llywelyn Aurdorchog, lord of the townships of Aelhaiarn, Llygadog, Ucheldref, Garthaiarn, Llandderfel, Caer Gilor, and Saith Marchog. By this lady he had issue, two sons, Ithel and Heilyn, and a daughter, Hunydd above named *(Hist. Powys Fadog,* iii., p. 193).

Pennant gives the following list of Eunydd's descendants, all extinct, or in the female line only :—Simunt of Coedllai ; Prichard of Caergwrle ; Rogers of Flint ; Meredydd of Trefalun ; Meredith of Pentrebychan ; Meredith of Stansty ; Almor of Almor ; Alynton of Alynton ; and Lloyd of Gresford and Alynton.

The Almors and Alyntons took their names from the townships where they resided— the latter being simply a translation of Trefalun. The first to assume the name of Almor, was John ap Ievan ap David, ninth in descent from Eunydd, through his son Ithel. The Almors became extinct in the male line about the commencement of the seventeenth century *(Dwnn's Vis.,* ii., p. 355).

Mallt, the heiress of Trefalun, married Richard Trevor, descended from Ednyfed Gam of Llys Pengwern. By this alliance, the Trevors became possessed of Trefalun, which is still in the possession of their descendants *(Hist. Powys Fadog,* iii., p. 194). Of this family was Sir Thomas Trevor, Lord Chief Justice of England, created Baron Trevor in 1711.

The Merediths of Pentrebychan maternally descended from Eunydd, are now represented by Lieut.-Col. Henry Warter Meredydd (see *ante,* p. 106).

Sir Frederick Hughes, Bart. of East Bergholt, Suffolk (being the seventh Bart.), claims direct descent from Eunydd *(Nicholas's County Families,* p. 397).—*Ed.*

XV.—EDNOWAIN AP BRADWEN.[1]

HE is by many writers called Lord of Merionydd ; but I apprehend erroneously, for the Princes and their issue were always Lords of Merionydd. Howbeit it might be that he (as others) took the same to farm and therefore might be called lord

---

[1] William Lleyn, the bard, out of an old book written in the days of Edward the First, by one David Scrivenor, to one Iorwerth ap Llewelyn ap Tudur, a descendant of this chief, gives the Bradwen [Pedigree] thus :—Bradwen ap Mael ap Bleddyn ap

thereof. Yet, certain it is that he and his issue were possessed of all Tal-y-bont, save Nanney, and the Prince's demesnes, and for the most part of the Hundred of Estimaner in like manner. He is said to have lived in Gruffudd ap Cynan's time. The ruins of his house, Llys Bradwen,[1] are to be seen in the township of Cregenan, in the hundred of Tal-y-bont Is-cregenan in Merionethshire. Llywelin ap Tudur ap Gwyn ap Peredur ap Ednowain ap Bradwen lived in the time of Edward the First and did him homage with the lords and gentry of Wales, as by the said king's records is manifest. Aron, the grandchild of this Llywelin ab Tudur by his son Ednyfed had two sons more eminent than the rest of his children, Ednyfed and Gruffudd, of the which William David Lloyd of Peniarth, Esq., lately deceased,

Morudd ap Cynddelw ap Cyfnerth ap Cadifor ap Run ap Mergynawc ap Cynfawr ap Hefan ap Cadifor ap Maeldaf hynaf ap Unwch Unarchon ap Ysbwys ap Ysbwch, which Ysbwys and Ysbwch, father and son came into this island out of Spain with Aurelius, Ambrosius, and Uther, A.D. 466, and first inhabited Moelysbidion, viz. the Strangers Mount, and when Aurelius had recovered his crown from Vortigern the Usurper, he rewarded those men, being his retinue, with the whole hundred of Talybont, and part of Estimaner in Merionethshire, where their posterity flourish to this day.

[1] These ruins, which I have seen, consisting of large stones, as usually laid to form the foundations of buildings, mark the form as well as the simplicity of the habitations of the ancient Reguli of Wales, agreeing exactly with the account given of them by Whitaker in his *History of Manchester*, who says " they were commonly placed in the hollow of a valley ; and either upon the margin of one stream, or the confluence of two, for the conveniency of water and security from winds. And the followers lived immediately about the person of their chief, or in little bodies along the windings of the valley, to be within reach of the usual signals of the lord, the striking of the shield or the blowing of the horn." The Ichnography of Llys Bradwen presents nearly this figure ()‾] the outward circular apartment being the audience hall and Court of Judicature ; the oblong building the chief's own retirement : around this principal building there were the traces of several others of various forms and dimensions.

was descended, whose inheritance is come to Margaret, the
mother of Lewis Owen, Esq. of Peniarth, deceased.

Ednyfed ab Aaron is said to have entertained Owain Glyndwr
when he was overcome by King Henry the Fourth, the Usurper;
but secretly in a cave by the sea-side, in the parish of Celynnin,
which of him is called Ogof Owain. Of this Ednyfed was
descended Morgan ap Gruffudd ap Einion, a courageous stout
man, who as it is reported by his kinsmen, by chance in the
streets of the city of London, far in the night, met with King
Henry the Eighth with a small guard about him, coming to see
what rule was kept in the city, and when neither would yield
to the other, they drew and fought hardly, until Morgan's companion that was with him bade him take heed what he did; for
that he feared it was the king with whom he fought, whereupon
Morgan crying mercy yielded and craved pardon, and the king
did let him go saying that he was a lusty man, and ever after
he was called lusty Morgan, a tradition to which the following
couplet from a bard of those times seems to countenance :—

> " Morgan hir mawr gan Harri,
> Mae Llundain dan d'adain di."

Ednowain ap Bradwen bore for his arms *gules* three snakes
rowed in a triangular knot *argent*.[1]

---

[1] Llewelin Dalran, of this tribe, came to South Wales, and, marrying Jennet, daughter
and heiress of Gwilym ap Sitsyllt, Lord of Aberaeron, Cardiganshire, laid the
foundation of several families of note in that country, such as the Lewes's of
Abernantbychan and Coedmore, now extinct ; the Lewes's of Llysnewidd ; and the
Lewes's of Gellydowill, a family which centres in Thomas Lewes, Esq., Captain of the
Sampson Man of War, and his brother Brigadier-General Lewes, at present serving in

the West Indies, an Officer of distinguished merit, who arrived not at the rank he now possesses by forced marches, but who from long and arduous services had an irresistible claim on those rewards, which longer to have with-held would have been a reproach to the fountain of preferment, an Officer who will be spoken of with honour so long as cool intrepid bravery and discipline shall continue to be the best recommendation of a British soldier. Nor can another descendant of the above Llewelin Dalran be here overlooked ; Sir Watkin Lewes, Knight, Member of Parliament for the City of London, the first Welshman since the days of Sir Hugh Middleton who has filled the Civic Chair, and on [sic] whom no man has experienced a greater accumulation of City honours, or passed through them with more credit to himself and utility to the public, discharging the duties of a Magistrate with humanity, firmness and discretion, suited to times the most trying and critical, who may boast himself almost the only one of all the swarm of Patriots that clustered some years ago round the standard of liberty, who has never disgraced his principles by becoming either the slave of a popular faction or the tool of ministerial influence.

[ADDENDA.]—Ednowain ab Bradwen is supposed by the best authorities to have lived somewhat later than the period above ascribed to him. The most correct date would probably be the latter half of the twelfth century. His wife was Margaret, daughter of Cynan ab Owain Gwynedd *(Dwnn's Vis.*, i., p. 39) ; or as other pedigrees have it, Jane, daughter of Philip ab Uchdryd, lord of Cyfeiliog, son of EDWIN AB GORONWY *(Hist. Powys Fadog*, v., p. 100).

The mother of Lewis Owen, Esq. of Peniarth, in the text called Margaret, is elsewhere *(Dwnn's Vis.*, ii. p. 238; and *(Arch. Camb.*, 1879, p. 122) called Elizabeth. She was William David Lloyd, Esq.'s sister and heiress, and married Griffith Owen, Esq. of Talybont, fourth son of Baron Lewys Owen, who was murdered near Mallwyd, in October, 1555 (see *ante*, p. 114). Her inheritance passed by marriage to the Owen's of Morben, and from them, through the Williams's, a branch of the families of Wynnstay and Bodelwyddan, to the Wynne's of Peniarth, now represented by William Robert Maurice Wynne, Esq. One of Griffith Owen's grandsons was that eminent and learned divine, Dr. John Owen, the Puritan Dean of Christ Church, Oxford. Hugh Owen of Bronyclydwr, a Puritan preacher of some celebrity, who died 15th March, 1699, was also of the same family. Two branches of this family, those of Owen, Caerberllan and Owen of Garthangharad, were still extant in 1846 according to the learned annotator of *Dwnn's Visitations* (vol. ii., p. 237) and it is believed are so now. The Hon. Griffith Humphrey Pugh Evans of Lovesgrove, and Lewis Pugh Pugh, Esq. of Abermaide, both in Cardiganshire, claim to represent other branches of the same family *(Nicholas's County Families*, pp. 195 and 210).

Lb

The Lewes's of Llysnewydd (Carmarthenshire), above referred to are now represented by Col. William Price Lewes of that place; and Col. John Lewes of Llanllyr, Cardiganshire *(Ib.*, pp. 200 and 293).

According to Dwnn *(Vis.*, ii., p. 284), Rhys Nanmor, an eminent poet who flourished from about 1440 to 1480, and resided at Maenor Vynwy in Pembrokeshire, was paternally descended from Ednowain ab Bradwen, and maternally from Ednyfed Fychan of the tribe of MARCHUDD.

The Lloyds of Nantymynach, Mallwyd *(Dwnn's Vis.*, ii., p. 242); and according to Pennant and Yorke *(Tracts of Powys)*, the Griffiths of Garth and Cloddiau Cochion, long extinct, belonged also to this tribe; also the Morgans of Caelan, Llanbrynmair, Montgomeryshire.—*Ed.*

XVI.—TUDOR TREVOR.

TUDOR TREVOR, the Tribe of March[1] called likewise in our books Llwyth Maelor (or the Tribe of Maelor), was the son of Ynyr ap Cadfarch, descended of Cadell Deyrnllug, King of Powys. He is said to have been the founder of, and to have resided at Whittington Castle, which continued in his posterity for many generations after. His mother was Rhiengar, daughter to Lluddocca ap Caradoc Vreichfras, Earl of Hereford, who was one of the Knights of King Arthur's Round Table. Tudor had large possessions in Herefordshire, in right of his mother, as well as in that country called Ferlys, which lies between the rivers Wye and Severn. He was contemporary with Howel Dda, King of Wales, whose daughter, Angharad, he married, by whom he had three sons and one daughter. Powell of

---

[1] So called, because a great number of the gentlemen in the Marches of England and Wales are descended from him.

Edenhope, in his *Pentarchia*, describes his arms in the following
manner :—

Erminus fulgens Theodori parma Trevori,

Dat rapidum fulvumque sinistro verte leonem ;

Mostonis sunt nota satis simul arma Trevoris—

Which may be thus expressed in plain English: " Parted per
bend sinister *ermine* and *ermines*, over all a lion rampant *or ;*
the well-known arms of the Mostyns, and also of the Trevors."

[ADDENDA.]—Tudor Trevor lived during the first half of the tenth century. In
907 he married Angharad, daughter of Howel Dda, by whom he had three sons,
Goronwy, Lluddocaf, and Dingad.

Goronwy (who died in his father's lifetime), married Tangwystl, daughter of Dyfnwal
ab Alan, a direct descendant from Rhodri Mawr, and by her had an only daughter and
heiress, Rhiengar, who succeeded to her grandfather's lands in Hereford, Gloucester,
Erging, and Ewyas. Rhiengar married Cyhelin ab Ifor, by whom she was mother of
ELYSTAN GLODRUDD (Royal Tribe V.) Many of Goronwy's descendants have therefore,
been already dealt with in the account of that Tribe (*ante*, pp. 125 to 133).

Lluddocaf was lord of Chirk, Whittington, Oswestry and Maelor Saesonaeg ; and
was the ancestor of, among others, the Mostyns of Mostyn, Talacre, Bryngwyn, and
Segroid ; the Trevors of Brynkinallt, Plas-teg, and Trefalun ; the Wynns of Eyarth ;
the Lloyds of Leaton Knolls ; the Youngs of Bryn Yorkin ; the Edwards of Sansaw
Hall ; the Trevors of Trevor Hall, and Thomas of Coed-helen ; the Lloyds of
Halchdyn, Plas Madog, Berth, and Rhagatt ; the Eytons of Park Eyton ; the
Vaughans of Burlton Hall ; the Pennants of Downing and Penrhyn Castle ; and the
Dymocks of Penley Hall (*Mont. Coll.*, ii., p. 265).

Dingad was lord of Maelor Gymraeg or Bromfield, and was the ancestor of the
families of Jones Parry of Llwynon ; Lloyd of Llwynycnotiau ; Roberts of Hafodybwch ;
Jones of Croes Foel ; Edwards of Sealyham and Lord Kensington ; Erddig of Erddig ;
Trafford of Esclusham ; Davies of Hafod y wern ; Madog yr Athraw of Plas Madog
and Erbistock ; Bersham of Bersham ; Wynn of Gerwyn fawr ; Eyton of Eyton
uchaf ; Sontley of Sontley ; Bady of Rhiwabon ; Jefferies of Acton ; Broughton of

Broughton and Marchwiail ; Powell of Alrhey ; Ellis of Alrhey and Wyddial Hall, Hertfordshire ; and others *(Ib.*, p. 266).

Of the above, the following at least have become extinct, or are to be found only in the female line :—Mostyn of Bryngwyn (merged in the family of Owen of Woodhouse) ; Trevor of Brynkinallt, Plas-teg, and Trefalun (now represented by Boscawen Trevor Griffith, Esq.) ; Young of Bryn Yorkin ; Pennant of Downing and Penrhyn Castle ; Dymock of Penley Hall ; Erddig of Erddig ; Trafford of Esclusham ; Bersham of Bersham ; Sontley of Sontley ; Bady of Rhiwabon ; Jefferies of Acton ; Davies of Hafod y Wern ; Broughton of Broughton ; Powel of Alrhey ; Ellis of Alrhey ; and Lloyd of Halchdyn.

Reference has already been made *(ante,* p. 96) to Sir John Trevor of Brynkinallt, Commissioner of the Great Seal, Master of the Rolls, and Speaker of the House of Commons in the time of James the Second and William the Third. Sir Thomas Trevor of Trefalun, was a Baron of the Exchequer in the reign of Charles the First. Sir John Trevor of Trefalun, was Secretary of State to Charles the Second. He married Ruth, a daughter of the celebrated John Hampden, and one of his sons, Thomas, became Chief Justice of the Common Pleas in 1701, which office he also filled during the whole of Queen Anne's reign, and in December 31st, 1711, he was called to the peerage by the title of Baron Trevor of Bromham. In 1726 he was made Lord Privy Seal, and in 1730, Lord President of the Council. He was an able and upright, but reserved, grave and austere judge. His third son, who became fourth Lord Trevor, was a distinguished diplomatist, and having published a volume of poems is enrolled in Horace Walpole's list of *Royal and Noble Authors.* Having become possessed of the Hampden estates, he took the name and arms of Hampden, and was, in 1766, created Viscount Hampden, a title, which, as well as the Barony of Trevor, became extinct in 1824. Another of the first Lord Trevor's sons became Bishop of Durham in 1752.—*Ed.*

THE END.

INDEX.

Alleluiatic victory over the Saxons, 86
Alliteration, characteristic of Welsh poetry, 60
Almor of Aimor, 206
Alynton of Alynton, 206
Alphonsus, son of Edward I., 66
Angharad, Queen of Gruffudd ab Cynan, 26
Anwyl of Park, 18
ATHELSTAN GLODRUDD, see ELYSTAN GLODRUDD
Athelstan, King of England, God-father to Elystan Glodrudd, 125; imposes tribute on his country, 125

Bady of Rhiwabon, 211
Bagots, Lords of Stafford and Dukes of Buckingham, 70, 71
Bala, celebrated by Lord Lyttelton, 21
Bangor Monachorum, 42
Bards, their massacre by Edw. I. not authenticated, 59
Baugé, battle of, 75
Bellot, Bishop of Chester, 20
Berain, Catherine of, 82, 198, 199
Bersham, 211
Bevan of Fosbury, 123
Beveridge, Bishop, interview with Sir John Wynn, 11
Bible, its Translators into Welsh, 90, 93
Bishops, Trial of the Seven, 100, 129
Blayney of Gregynog, 158
Blayney, Arthur, his character, 155
BLEDDYN AB CYNFYN, 39—119; his arms, 40; death, 40; wives, 116; sons 116
Bodville of Bodvel, 186
Bodwrda of Bodwrda, 186
Bottwnog School, founder of, 187
Bradwen, Llys, 207
BRAINT HIR, 197, 198; his arms, 198
Bridgeman, Sir Orlando, 104
British Chronicles, The, 42
Brochwel Ysgithrog, 42
Brogyntyn, 17
Brogyntyn, Owain, 47, 54, 107, 108; his arms, 109; his cup and dagger, 109
Bromfield of Bromfield, 203
Bromley, Lord Chancellor, 120
Broughton, 211
Brynkir, 21

Cadwaladr, Queen Victoria's descent from, 73
Cadwgan ab Bleddyn, 40, 109; his arms, 40, 109; his death, 40, 109; his sons, 110
Cadwgan ab Elystan, 126; his arms, 126.
Caer Hywel, 44
Camden's partiality as a historian, 92
Caractacus, ancestor of Iestyn ab Gwrgant, 120
Caradog Vreichfras, 210
Caradog ab Iestyn, 122; his descendants, 122
Carbery, Earl of, 106, 107
Carno, Battle of, 2

Carreg Hwfa Castle taken and plundered, 62
Carter, Col., of Kinmael, 113, 194
Catherine of Berain, "Mother of Wales," 82, 198, 199
Catherine Tudor, Widow of Henry V., 15, 192
Celynin of Llwydiarth, 118; his descendants, 118
Cesail Gyfarch, 14, 201
Chaloner, Sir Thomas, 190
Chaloner of Chester, 190
Chaloner of Guisborough, 190
Chaloner of Lloran Ganol, 190
Charlton, Sir John, first English Lord of Powys, 58
Charlton, Sir John, second English Lord of Powys, 69
Charlton, Sir John, third English Lord of Powys, 70
Cheshire, first represented in the House of Commons, 68
Chirk Castle, 55, 96
CILMIN TROED-DU, 181—183; his arms, 182
Clough, Sir Richard, 82, 199
Cobhnm, Lord, 71
Coetmore Howel, 22
Coytmore of Coytmore, 186
COLLWYN AB TANGNO, 184—188; arms, 185; sons, 186; extinct families, 188
Corbet of Ynysymaengwyn, 102, 127
Corsygedol, 17
Court of Marches, its institution, 6
Criccieth Castle, 185
Crogen or Chirk, Battle of, 48
Cromwell descended from Cadwgan ab Bleddyn, 111; his protection of Protestants, 112
Crown Manors in Wales, observations on, 159
Cwmhir, Abbey of, 126
Cyfeiliog, 57
Cyfeiliog, Huw, 45
Cyfeiliog, Owain, 45; his Castle at Tafolwern, 57; death, 58; distinguished poet, 58; interview with Henry II. at Shrewsbury, 64.
Cymry, their origin, 41
Cynddelw Brydydd Mawr, 54, 117
Cynfelyn ab Dolphyn of Manafon, 118; his descendants, 118
Cynfyn, Rhiwallon ab, 39
Cynwrig Efell, 47, 54; his arms, 98
Cynwrig Hir, 3

Dafydd ab Owain's embassy to the Lord Rhys, 48
Dafydd Llwyd ab Llywelyn of Mathafarn, 56
Dafydd, lord of Denbigh, barbarously executed, 22
Daron, Dean of Bangor, 124
Dates, uncertainty of, in Welsh Chronology, 69, 125
Davies of Coedymynydd, 189
Davies of Hafodywern, 211
Davies, Dr. John of Mallwyd, Grammarian and Lexicographer, 93, 195
Davies, Dr. Richard, Bishop of St. Asaph and St. David's, 92, 204
Davies, John of Henblas, the Genealogist, 119

Davies, Robert of Llannerch, the Antiquary, 87
Davies of Trewylan, 119
Derwas of Cemmes, 118
Dighy, Sir Kenelm, dubbed Knight, 79
Dinas Bran Castle, 52
Dingad ab Ednowain ab Bradwen, 211
Dolben, Dr., Bishop of Bangor, 101
Dolforwyn Castle, 40
Done, Margaret, Anecdote of, 95
Drunkenness in the French army, 75
Dymock of Penley Hall, 211

EDNOWAIN AB BRADWEN, 207—210; extinct families,
EDNOWAIN BENDEW, 203, 204; extinct families, 204
Ednyfed ab Aaron, 208
Ednyfed Fychan, 179, 191, 193: his wife Gwenllian, 36:
    his arms, 191; his sons, 193; his illustrious descend-
    ants, 192
Edward I. nominated Prince of Wales, 51
Edwards of Nanhoron, 187
Edwards of Sansaw Hall, 211
Edwards of Sealyham, 211
EDWIN, 201—203; his arms, 202; sons, 202; extinct
    families, 203
EFNYDD or EUNYDD, 43, 205, 206; his arms, 205;
    descendants, 206
Eglwysegl, 86
Einion ab Collwyn, 28, 120
Einion ab Ithel, 13
Einion Efell, 47, 54; his arms, 98
Ellis of Alrhey and Wyddial, 212
Ellis of Bronyfoel and Ystumllyn, 186
ELYSTAN GLODRUDD, 125—133; his arms, 126; his
    sons, 126; his death, 126; his descendants, 126,
    127, 128, 132; extant families, 132; extinct fami-
    lies, 133
Erddig of Erddig, 211
Esquires, several classes of 10
Evans, Rev. Evan, collector of Welsh MSS, 115
Evans of Eleirnion, 183
Evans of Llanrwst, 189
Evans of Llaneurgain, 204
Evans of Lovesgrove, 209
Evans of Tanybwlch, 188
Evans of Trecastell, 38
Evans of Watstay, 9
Extent of North Wales, The, 173
Eyton of Leeswood, 88
Eyton of Park Eyton, 211
Eyton of Rhiwabon, 9

Facknalt of Facknalt, 204
Ferlys, the country between the Severn and Wye, 125,
    210
FIFTEEN NOBLE TRIBES, THE, 171, 172
Fitzwalter, Milo's gallant conduct, 32
Fitzwarren, Fulke's encounter with Gruff. ab Cynan, 3
Fitzpeter, Jeffrey, Justiciary of England, 63
Fitzhamon invades Glamorgan, 120
Foulkes of Eriviatt, 194
Foulkes of Carwedd Fynydd and Meiriadog, 201
Foulkes of Gwernygron, 181
Foulkes of Llys Llywarch, 201
Foulkes of Mertyn, 204

Founders of Five Royal Tribes, 1
French writers, their Latin Prosody, 55
Fychan, Sir Gruffudd of Byrgedwyn, 44, 72; behended,
    76
Fychan, Sir Gruffydd, of Caer Hywel, 84

Gavelkind, derivation of the term, 42; its effect upon
    estates, 14, 39, 40, 41, 42, 45, 47, 53, 67, 102
Gerald de Windsor, Constable of Pembroke, 29; Nest,
    wife of, 29; revenge on Owain ab Cadwgan, 30
Gethin of Fedwdeg, 22
Gethin, Rhys, 22
Giraldus Cambrensis, 38
Gloucester, Humphrey Duke of, 75
Glyndyfrdwy, 56
Glyndwr, Owain, 38; his arms, 118; his descendants,
    117
Glyn of Ewell, 183
Glyn of Gaunts, 183
Glynn of Bryngwdion, 183
Glynn of Glynllifon, 182, 183
Glynn of Hawarden, 182, 183
Glynn of Lleuar, 182, 183
Glynn of Nantlle, 182, 183
Glynne, Sir John of Hawarden, 83
Glynne, Sir Stephen Richard of Hawarden, 183
Glynne, Sir William, of Glynllifon, 179
Goch, Dafydd, killed at Pennal, 179
Godolphin, Col. Sydney, 103
Goodman, Dr. Gabriel, Dean of Westminster, 91
Goodman, Dr. Godfrey, Bishop of Gloucester, 91; Will
    of, 160
Gore, Ormsby, 17, 103
Goronwy ab Ednowain ab Bradwen, 211
Goronwy Owen on Welsh Poetry, 59
Gresford Vicarage, Inscription on, 155
Grey, Sir Edward, lord of Powys, 78
Grey, Sir Henry, lord of Powys, 76
Grey, Sir John, lord of Powys, 73, 74
Griffith ab Chwaen, 176
Griffith of Garreglwyd, 178, 194
Griffith of Garn, 203
Griffith of Garth and Cloddiau Cochion, 210
Griffith of Pantyllongdy, 204
Griffith of Plas Isaf, Caerwys, 204
Griffith of Rhual, 204
Griffith, Sir William, of Penrhyn, 16, 192, 193
GRUFFUDD AB CYNAN, 1—26; his captivity at Chester,
    3; his arms, 4; reforms of music, 5; character
    and reign, 23; life, 23; benefactions, 24; death,
    25; personal appearance, 25; Queen Angharad,
    26; sons, 26
Gruffudd ab Dafydd Goch, 22
Gruffudd ab Gwenwynwyn, 64; his wife, 65
Gruffudd ab Llywelyn, death of, 51
Gruffudd ab Llywelyn ab Seisyllt, 39
Gruffydd ab Madog, 50; alliance with Edward the
    First, 51; wife, Emma, 52; death and burial, 52
Gruffydd ab Maredudd, 57
Gruffydd ap Rhys ab Tewdwr, 29; his wife, Gwenllian,
    31; death, 32
Gruffydd ap the Lord Rhys, 37
Gruffydd Fychan ab Gruffudd ab Gwenwynwyn, 66
Gruffydd Fychan of Glyndyfrdwy, 38

Gruffydd Maelor, 10, 47 ; death and burial, 48; wife, Angharad, 48 ; children, 48 ; arms, 49
Gruffydd, Pyrs of Penrhyn, 193
Gwasannau, origin of the name, 86
GWEIRYDD AP RHYS GOCH, 180, 181 ; his arms, 180 ; sons, 180
Gwenllian, daughter of Bleddyn ab Cynfyn. 119
Gwenllian, wife of Ednyfed Fychan, 36
Gwenllian, mother of Eunydd, 43, 205
Gwenwynwyn, 57, 61 ; arms, 64 ; wife, 64 ; sons, 66.
Gwenwynwyn, Gruffudd ab, 64, 65
Gwgan of Caereinion's embassy, 48
Gwydir, 8
Gwydir family, History of the, 5
Gwyn ab Bleddyn, 118
Gwyn of Baron's Hall, 175
Gwyn, Mynachdy, 202
Gwynedd, Hywel, 201, 203
Gwynedd, Owain, 4, 33 ; arms, 4

Haer, wife of Bleddyn ab Cynfyn, 116
Hafod Lwyfog, 14
Hampden, Viscount, 212
Hanmer, Sir Thomas, Speaker of the House of Commons, 100; his Epitaph, 164; the same paraphrased, 166
Harlech, Baron, 17, 103, 175 ; Castle, 184 ; its brave defence, 89
Hawys Gadarn married to Sir John de Charleton, 66 ; buried at Shrewsbury, 69
HEDD MOLWYNOG, 195—197 ; his sons, 195 ; arms and descendants, 196
Helig ab Glanawg's patrimony overflowed, 190
Hengwrt MSS, 115
Henry II marches to Oswestry, 33 ; puts out the eyes of hostages, 33 ; makes peace with the Lord Rhys, 34 ; battle of Crogen, the king's life in danger, 48 ; reproved by Owain Cyfeiliog, 64
Henry IV.'s cruel statutes against the Welsh, 59
Henry VII.'s Welsh descent, 192
Henry VIII.'s Regulations in North Wales, 68
Herbert, Sir Edward piurchases Powys Castle and lordship, 78
Herbert, Lady Mary, Pope's lines to, 80
Herbert of Cherbury, Edward Lord, 81
Herbert, Richard, beheaded at Banbury, 81
Herbert, William Earl of Pembroke, 79
Herberts, The, of Powys Castle, 79
Hirlas, Owain, 59
Hirwaen Wrgant, battle of, 28
Holt Castle built, 55
Holland of Berw, 178
Holland of Kinmael, 113
Holland William's letter to Sir John Wynn, 144
Hope Castle, 144
Hughes of Beaumaris, 180
Hughes of Coedybrain, 204
Hughes of East Bergholt, 206
Hughes of Gwerclas, 108, 109, 170
Hughes of Halkin and Bagillt, 204
Hughes of Kinmael, 175, 176
Hughes of Plascoch, 179
Hughes, Dr. William, Bishop of St. Asaph, 19, 194
Humphreys, Dr., Bishop of Bangor, 201

Hunydd, daughter of Bleddyn ab Cynfyn, 119
HWFA AB CYNDDELW, 172—176 ; his arms, 174 ; extinct families, 176
Hywel ab Ieuaf of Talgarth, 126
Hywel ab Owain Gwynedd, 60
Hywel y Fwyall, Sir, 184, 187
Hywel y Pedolau, Sir, 65, 173

Idwal, Prince, his murder, 188
IESTYN AB GWRGANT, 27, 50, 120—122 ; his treachery, 120 ; arms, 120 ; descent from Caractacus, 120 ; descendants, 120—122 ; children, 122
Ieuan ab Maredudd, 13, 14
Iolo Goch, 195. 197
Iorwerth Drwyndwn, 46
Iorwerth Goch, 44
Irish allies of Griffith ab Cynan, 2

James I. at Chester in 1617, 80 ; his aversion to a drawn sword, 79 ; knighting Sir William Morice, 80
Jefferies of Acton, 211
Jefferies, Chancellor, Anecdotes of, 97
John ab Gruffudd ab Gwenwynwyn, 66
John ab Maredudd, 14, 16
John Dafydd Rhys the Grammarian, 94
Jones, Inigo, 8, 26
Jones, Col. " the Regicide," 194
Jones, Sir William, Chief Justice of England, 187
Jones of Castellmarch, 187
Jones of Croes Foel, 211
Jones of Derry Ormond, 204
Jones of Dol, 120, 121
Jones of Gellilyfdy, 204
Jones of Haim, 38
Jones of Llyfnant, 179
Jones Parry of Llwynon, 188, 211

Kensington, Lord, 211
Kenyon, Lord, 175
Kyffin, origin of the name, 99
Kyffin of Bodfach, 99
Kyffin of Glascoed, 99
Kyffin of Maenan, 98
Kyffin, Maurice, the translator and poet, 99
Kynaston, claim to the Barony of Powys, 75 ; family, 44, 82
Kynaston, Arthur of Pantylyrsle, 84
Kynaston, Humphrey, the Wild, 44, 85
Kynaston, Sir John Roger, 84
Kynaston, Sir Roger, 84
Kynaston of Bryngwyn, 83
Kynaston of Hordley and Hardwick, 84
Kynaston of Otley, 83
Kynaston of Stocks, 84, 85
Kynaston of Trewylan, 83

Lewes of Abernantbychan, 208
Lewes of Coedmore, 208
Lewes of Gellidywyll, 208
Lewes of Llanllyr, 210
Lewes of Llysnewydd, 208, 210
Lewes, Brigadier General, 208
Lewes, Captain Thomas, 208
Lewes, Sir Watkin, Mayor and M.P. for London, 209

Lewis of Harpton Court, 38
Lewis of Llanddyfnan, 174
Lewis of Presaddfed, 174, 175
Lewis of Trysglwyn, 175, 176
Lewys of Cemlyn, 176
Lewys, Robert, Chancellor of Bangor, 176
Lewys Glyn Cothi, and the inhabitants of Chester, 89
Linen scarce in the fifteenth century, 43
Lisburne, Earl of, 185
Lollards persecuted by Henry V., 71
Lord Rhys, his great feast at Cardigan, 35
Lumley, the Barony of, 106
Llanegwest, or Valle Crucis Abbey, 50
Llannerch Gardens and Waterworks, 87
Llanrwst burned by the Earl of Pembroke, 81
Llewelyn Aurdorchog, his arms and descendants, 119, 202, 206
Llewelyn ab Gruffydd, 51, 52
Llewelyn ab Tudor ab Gwyn, 207
Llewelyn Dalran, 208
Lloyd, Humphrey, Bishop of Bangor, 19
Lloyd, John, Bishop of St. David's, 132
Lloyd, Rev. John of Caerwys, 111
Lloyd, Sir Richard of Holt, 19
Lloyd, William, Bishop of St. Asaph, 179
Lloyd, of Aston, 104
Lloyd of Bach Eurig, 197
Lloyd of Berth, 211
Lloyd of Blaenyglyn, 111
Lloyd of Boxllith, 106
Lloyd of Cwmbychan, 111
Lloyd of Dolglessyn, 108
Lloyd of Dyffryn Erethlyn, 196
Lloyd of Erw Cynddel, 197
Lloyd of Forest, Pontruffydd and Pengwern, 194
Lloyd of Foxhall, 105
Lloyd of Glanhafon, 14
Lloyd of Glansevin, 204
Lloyd of Gwaredog, 180, 181
Lloyd of Hafodunos, 196
Lloyd of Halchdyn, 211
Lloyd of Hersedd, Ffern, and Llwyn Yn, 202
Lloyd of Kinmael, 194
Lloyd of Leaton Knolls, 211
Lloyd of Llai or Leighton, 72
Lloyd of Llugwy, 181
Lloyd of Llwynycnotiau, 211
Lloyd of Maesmawr, 72
Lloyd of Marrington, 72
Lloyd of Nantymynach, 210
Lloyd of Palau, 196
Lloyd of Peniarth, 207
Lloyd of Pentrehobin, 202
Lloyd of Plasmadog, 211
Lloyd of Plas uwch Clawdd, 38
Lloyd of Plas Power, 197
Lloyd of Rhagatt, 211
Lloyd of Rhandir, 197
Lloyd of Rhiwgoch, 180
Lloyd of Tregayan, 188
Lloyd of Wigfair, 204
Lluddocaf ab Ednowain ab Bradwen, 21'
Llwyd, Edward, the Antiquary, 145
Llwyd, Humphrey, the historian, 43, 105; his descendant's claim to the barony of Lumley, 106

Llwyd, Meurig of Llwynymaen, 195, 196
Llwyd of Esclusham and Dulasseu, 19
Llwynymaen, 102
LLYWARCH AB BRAN, 177—180; his sons, 177; arms, 178; extinct families, 180
Llywarch ab Gruffudd ab Gwenwynwyn, 66

Mac in Erse synonymous with the Welsh ap or ab, 12
Madog ab Bleddyn, 116, 119
Madog ab Gruffudd Maelor, 10, 49; his sons, 50
Madog ab Gruffudd's children murdered at Holt, 55
Madog ab Iestyn, 123
Madog ab Maredudd, 45; his death and burial, 46; his descendants, 46, 47; his Norman wife's treachery, 46
Madog grupl, 53
Madog yr Athraw, 211
Madryn of Madryn, 188
MAELOG CRWM, 190
Maelor, the lordship of Bromfield, why so called, 47
Maelor, Gruffudd, 47
Maesmor of Maesmor, 108
Malta, Knights of, 44
March, Mortimer Earl of, 67
Marches, Court of, its institution, 6
Marchers, The Lords, 67
MARCHUDD AB CYNAN, 191—195; extant and extinct families, 194
MARCHWEITHIAN, 198—201; arms, 199; extinct families, 201
Maredudd ab Bleddyn, 42; his wives, 43; descendants, 44, 117
Maredudd ab Owain of South Wales, 38
Marsh, Dr., Archbishop of Armagh, 20
Matthew of Llandaff, 123, 133
Matthews of Esgair Foel Eirin, 118
Mathrafal Castle destroyed, 50
Maurice of Lloran, 102, 127
Mealy of Perfeddgoed, 124
Meredith, Sir William, 205
Meredith of Glantanad, 104
Meredith of Pentrebychan, 106, 121, 206
Meredith of Monachdy Gwyn, 180
Meredith of Trefalun, 206
Meyrick of Bodorgan and Goodrich Court, 179
Militia for the Scotch war raised in North Wales by Edward II., 67
Mold Castle destroyed, 65
Morgan Hir ab Iestyn and his descendants, 122
Morgan of Golden Grove, 194
Morgan ap Gruffudd ap Einion, 208
Morgan, Dr. William, Bishop of St. Asaph, 90, 189; his letters to Sir John Wynn, 134, 142; his letter to Mr. Martyn, 139; Sir John Wynn's reply, 136
Morice of Clenenneu, 16, 17
Morice, Dr. Andrew, Dean of St. Asaph, 18
Morice, Dr. David of Bettws, 18
Morice, Sir William, Secretary of State to Charles II., 17; knighted by James I., 80
Mortimer, Roger, 55
Mostyn family, 12, 211; surname first assumed, 12
Mostyn, Lord, 99
Mostyn of Bryngwyn, 83, 211
Mostyn of Segrwyd, 180
Music and Bardism regulated by Gruffudd ab Cynan, 4, 5
Myddelton, Charles, 95

Myddelton, Foulk, 95, 106
Myddelton, Sir Hugh, 95
Myddelton, Pierce, 95
Myddelton, Richard, 94
Myddelton, Robert, 95
Myddelton, Sir Thomas, 95, 96
Myddelton, Captain William, 94, 95
Myddelton of Chirk Castle, 14
Myddelton of Gwaenynog, 14
Mutton, Sir Peter, 9
Mwsoglen family, 178, 179
Mytton of Garth, 72
Mytton of Halston, 67
Mytton of Halston, John, his reckless expenditure, 67

Nanmor, Rhys, the poet, 210
Nanney of Cefndeuddwr and Gwynfryn, 118, 176
Nanney of Maesyneuadd, 17
Nanney of Nannau, 109 ; their arms, 110
NEFYDD HARDD, 188, 189
Ness Cliff, Wild Kynaston's retreat, 44
Nest, mother of Robert of Gloucester, 29
Newborough, Lord, 186
Newmarch, Bernard seizes the lordship of Brecknock, 28
Newton of Haethle, 121
Norman invasion of South Wales, 28
North Wales, its Princes paramount, 2, 46

Oakeley of Tanybwlch, 188
Offa's Laws revived by Harold, 116
Officers of the Welsh Court, 1
Oldcastle, Sir John, apprehended in Powysland, 71
Orwel, Jane, mistress of Edward de Charleton, 77
Osborn, Fitzgerald, or Osbwrn Wyddel, 16, 182
Owain ap Aldyd, 202
Owain ap Cadwgan, a turbulent chieftain, 30
Owain ap Edwin of Tegaingl, 202
Owain ap Gruffudd ab Gwenwynwyn, 66
Owain Cyfeiliog, see Cyfeiliog, Owain
Owain Glyndwr, 53 ; his children and descendants, 117 ;
    arms, 118 ; wife, 181 ; hid in a cave, 208
Owain Gwynedd, see Gwynedd, Owain
Owain Tudor, 15, 192
Owen, Griffith of Talybont, 209
Owen, Hugh of Bronyclydwr, 209
Owen, Dr. John, the Puritan divine, 209
Owen, Sir John of Clenenneu, 18, 175
Owen, Lewis, Baron of the Exchequer, his murder,
    113, 114, 209
Owen, Sir Roger of Condover, 201, 203
Owen, Sir Thomas, Judge, 201, 203
Owen of Bettws Cedewain, 203
Owen of Bodeon and Orielton, 174, 179
Owen of Bodsilin, 18
Owen of Caerberllan, 209
Owen of Cefnhafodau and Glansevern, 38
Owen of Clenenneu, 174
Owen of Condover, 203
Owen of Garthangharad, 209
Owen of Hengwrt, 113
Owen of Llynlloedd, 203
Owen of Morben, 209
Owen of Peniarth, 208
Owen of Plasdu, 187

Owen of Rhiwsaeson, 127
Owen of Tedsmore, 203
Owen of Woodhouse, 203

Panton of Coleshill, 201
Parry, Dr. Richard, Bishop of St. Asaph, 28, 90 ; his
    letter to Sir John Wynn, 142
Parry of Cefn Llanfair, 186
Parry of Coleshill and Basingwerk, 204
Parry of Llwyn Yn, 90
Parry of Plasnewydd, 90
Parry of Tywysog and Pistyll, 201
Parry of Wernfawr, 176
Pelidys, a magician, 198
Pembroke, Earl, beheaded at Banbury, 81
Pennant of Downing, 211
Pennant of Penrhyn Castle, 194, 211
Penrhyn Castle, 194
Pen Rhys, Monastery of, 29
Pentarchia, a MS. History of the Royal Tribes in Latin
    verse, 40, 52, 55, 127
Philip of Cyfeiliog, 202
Piers of Llanasaph, 204
Piozzi, Mrs., 82
Plas Dinas, Manor of, 78
Porthamel, 178
Powel, Dr. David, the historian, 90, 203
Powell, Sir Thomas of Nanteos, 202
Powell of Alrhey, 212
Powell of Brandlesome Hall, 38
Powell of Ednop, 127
Powell of Nanteos, 203
Powell of Worthen, 126
Puwis Castle, 40, 62, 67 ; taken by Sir Thomas Mydde!-
    ton, 79
Powys, Barony of, conveyed from the Greys to the
    Herberts, 78 ; claims to it, 75
Powys Fadog, so called, 45, 57
Powys, Wenwynwyn   do.   45, 57
Powys, Earls of, 81, 133
Powys, William, Duke of, 80
Powys, William, Marquis of, 80
Presaddfed, meaning of name, 173
Price, Sir John, the friend of Leland, 78
Price, Sir Robert, Chief Justice of the Common
    Pleas, 200
Price of Cwm Mein, 201
Price of Dugoed, Penmachno, 201
Price of Fedw deg, 201
Price of Llanrwst, 201
Price of Rhiwlas, 199, 200
Price of Tyddyn Sieffrey, 201
Pritchard of Caergwrle, 206
Pritchard of Dincun, 176
Prophecies, pretended, instrumental in bringing in
    Henry VII., 57
Pryce, Sir Edward Manley, Newtown Hall, 128
Pryce, Sir John Powell   do.   128
Pryce, Sir John   do.   129 ;
    his letter to Bridget Bostock, 129
Pryce of Cyfronydd, 117
Pryce of Esgairweddan, 133
Pryce of Glwysegl, 122
Pryce of Llanfyllin, 122

CC

218

Pryce of Llwyn Yn, 202
Pryce of Newtown Hall, 128, 131
Pryce of Vaynor, 133
Prys, Edmund, Archdeacon of Merioneth, 90, 93, 177
Prys, Ellis, Plas Iolyn, 199
Prys, Captain Thomas, Plas Iolyn, 200
Prytherch of Myvyrian, 178
Pugh of Abermaide, 209
Pugh of Ysceifiog, 204

Ranulph de Poer put to death, 35
Reinalli ap Gruffudd of the Tower, 89
Reynolds, John of Oswestry, 119
Rhaiadr Castle built, 35
Rhiwaedog, 17
Rhydderch of Tregayan, 188
Rhys ab Gruffudd, 37
Rhys ab Llewelyn ab Hwlcyn, 175
RHYS AB TEWDWR, 27—38; his death and arms, 29; extinct families, 38; extant families, 38
Rhys Fawr ab Maredudd, Standard Bearer of England, 199
Rhys Goch o'r Eryri, 186
Rhys Nanmor, 210
Rhys, Dr. John David, 94
Rhys, The Lord, 32; invades Cardigan, 33; his successes, 34; submits to Henry II., 34; feast at Cardigan, 35; builds Rhaiadr Castle, 35; dies of the plague, 37; his children, 37
Ririd ab Bleddyn, 116, 119
Ririd Flaidd Lord of Penllyn, 14, 95, 116
Robert of Gloucester, 29
Robert ab Rhys, Chaplain to Cardinal Wolsey, 199
Robert of Lygun, 186
Robert of Rhuddlan, slain by Gruffudd ab Cynan, 3
Roberts, Dr. William, Bishop of Bangor, 201
Roberts, of Hafodybwch, 211
Roberts of Llangedwyn, 104
Robinson, Dr. Nicholas, Bishop of Bangor, 23, 173
Rogers of Flint, 206
Rowlands, Dr. Henry, Bishop of Bangor, 187

Salesbury, Col. E. W., Vaughan of Rug, 56, 57, 107
Salesbury of Lleweni, 82, 83
Salesbury, William, the translator of the New Testament, 57, 92
Salisbury, Col. William, Governor of Denbigh Castle, 170
Sanctuaries violated, 30
Scolan, alleged destruction by him of Welsh MSS., 116
Sherlock, Bishop of Bangor, 13
Shrewsbury taken by the Welsh, 46
Sidney, Sir Henry and Sir Philip, 43
Simunt of Cuedllai, 206
Smith, Chancellor of St. Asaph, 194
Smith of Vaenol, 187
Sontley of Sontley, 211
South Wales, fall of its independency, 28
Sparrow of Red Hill, 175
Stafford, Viscount, his attainder and its reversal, 71
Strata Florida Abbey or Ystrad Fflur, 35, 126
Strata Marcella Abbey or Ystrad Marchell, 58, 64
Sudeley, Lord, 158
Surnames first adopted by the Welsh, 12; variety of in one family, 108

Tafolwern Castle, 57
Taliesin's Poem on the Tombs of the Warriors, 61
Tanad of Abertanad, 72, 102
Tanad of Blodwel, 104
Tankerville, Henry Earl of, 75
Taylor, Bishop Jeremy, 107
Thelwal of Plasyward, 82
Thelwal of Ruthin, 21
Thomas of Coedhelen, 179, 211
Thomas, Sir Rhys ab, of Dinevor, 132, 179
Thomas, Sir William, of Coedhelen, 132
Tiptoft, Earl of Worcester, 77
Tower of London, repository for Welsh MSS., 116
Trafford, 211
Tracy of Gregynog, 158
Trahaiarn ab Caradog slain, 2
Trevor, Sir John, 96, 212
Trevor, Sir Thomas, 206, 212
Trevor, Lord, 212
Trevor of Brynkinallt, 178
Trevor of Trefalun, &c., 206, 211
Triads, The, 61
Tribes, Fifteen Noble, 171, 172
Tribes, Royal, 1
Tribute of Hounds, Hawks and Wolves' heads, 125, 126
Tudor, Catherine, Queen and Widow of Henry V., 15
Tudor, Owen, 15, 192
Tudor of Penmynydd, 192, 193
TUDOR TREVOR, 210—212; arms, 211; sons and descendants, 211
Tudur Aled, an eminent poet, 197
Turberville, Sir Payne of Coety, 123
Tyndale, William, translator of the Bible, 111
Tyssilio, the author of Geoffrey of Monmouth's Chronicle, 42

Uchdryd, lord of Cyfeiliog and Meirion, 202

Valle Crucis Abbey built, 50
Vanbutchell, Epitaph on Mary, 168; translation of same, 169
Vaughan, Sir John, 97, 185
Vaughan, Dr. Richard, Bishop of London, 90, 187
Vaughan, Robert, the antiquary, 115
Vaughan, Sir Robert Williames, Bart., 110, 114, 195
Vaughan, Rowland of Caergai, the translator, 170
Vaughan of Aberkin, 187
Vaughan of Blaenycwm, 201
Vaughan of Burlton, 211
Vaughan of Corsygedol, 17, 38, 187
Vaughan of Glanllyn, 14
Vaughan of Golden Grove, 106
Vaughan of Llwydiarth, Caergai and Glanllyn, 104, 118, 122, 133
Vaughan of Llysfaen, 201
Vaughan of Nannau, arms of, 110
Vaughan of Pantglas, 201
Vaughan of Plasben, 187
Vaughan of Talgarth and Tretower, 123
Vaughan of Talhenbont, 187
Vaughan of Wengraig, 113

Wales, its union with England, a blessing to both, 66
Wales, North, its boundary by the Treaty of 1264, 52

Watstay, 9
Welsh chieftains, causes of their domestic feuds, 41
Welsh metres, 59
Welsh poetry, 67
Whittington Castle, 210
Wilcock, Mowddwy, 66
William or Wilcock ab Gruffudd ab Gwenwynwyn, 66
William, Sir Thomas ab, of Trefriw, 93, 177
Williams, Archbishop, 192, 193, 195 ; his letters to Sir
    John Wynn, 143, 145, 146, 150
Williams, Lord of Thame, 124
Williams, Rev. Richard of Fron and Machynlleth, 98
Williams, Sir William of Llanforda, 83
Williams, Sir William, Speaker, 99, 104, 181, 196 ; his
    monument in Llansilin Church, 167
Williams, Sir William of Vaenol, 187
Williams of Aberarch, 188
Williams of Aberpergwm, 123
Williams of Bodelwyddan, 101
Williams of Cochwillan, 194
Williams of Colomendy, 204
Williams of Fron, 95
Williams of Hafod Garregog, 201
Williams of Marl and Pantglas, 18, 194
Williams of Meillionydd, 194
Williams of Penbedw, 101
Williams of Vaynol, 194
Williams of Ystumcolwyn, 194
Willoughby de Eresby, Lady, 8
Wynn, Henry of Gwydir, 9, 180
Wynn, John of Bodvel, 186
Wynn, Sir John of Gwydir, 5 ; his children, 7 ; corres-
    pondence with Bishop Morgan and Mr. Martyn,
    134—142 ; instructions to his Chaplain, 151 ;
    inventory of his wardrobe, 152
Wynn, John (his son) of Gwydir, 7 ; his wife, 7
Wynn, Sir John of Wynnstay, 9 ; his monument in
    Ruabon church, 11
Wynn, Maurice of Gwydir, 82
Wynn, Sir Owen of Gwydir, 8
Wynn, Sir Richard of Gwydir, 7 ; contract with
    Bernard Lyndesey, 154 ; inscription on monu-
    ment, 154

Wynn, Sir Thomas of Bodvean, 186
Wynn, Sir Watkin Williams, Bart., 11, 83, 104
Wynn of Berthddu, 12
Wynn of Bodewrid, 180
Wynn of Bodvel, 186
Wynn of Bodychen, 175
Wynn of Bodysgallen, 12
Wynn of Bryn Cynwrig, 197
Wynn of Cerniogau, 200
Wynn of Coed Coch, 194
Wynn of Coedllai, 38
Wynn of Coparleni, 202
Wynn of Dolbachog, 38
Wynn of Dyffryn Aled, 162
Wynn of Eyarth, 211
Wynn of Galedlom and Caerwys, 204
Wynn of Garth, 72
Wynn of Garthewin, 162
Wynn of Gerwyn fawr, 211
Wynn of Giler, 197, 200
Wynn of Glyn Ardudwy, 17
Wynn of Glynllifon, 186
Wynn of Gwynfryn, 187
Wynn of Hafod y Maidd, 201
Wynn of Llangynhafal, 201
Wynn of Llwyn, 11
Wynn of Melai, 162, 194
Wynn of Pantglas, 200
Wynn of Pennardd, 186
Wynn of Penyberth, 186 ·
Wynn of Plasnewydd, 201
Wynn of Tower, 88
Wynn of Wern, 21
Wynne of Peniarth, 209
Wynne of Voelas, 199, 200
Wynnstay, 9, 10 ; destroyed by fire and rebuilt, 10
Wythan of Trewythan, 110

Yale of Plas yn Yale, 17
Young of Bryn Yorkin, 211

REFERENCE TO THE PLATES.

	PAGE.
Lord Chancellor ELLESMERE ...	... 6
Sir THOMAS MYDDELTON ...	... 8
Sir JOHN WYNN	... 10
HUMPHREY Duke of Buckingham	... 70
CATHERINE of Berain	... 82
GEORGE Lord Jefferies	... 96
Chief Justice VAUGHAN ...	... 98
Sir JOHN TREVOR	... 100
Sir ORLANDO BRIDGEMAN ...	... 104
HUMPHREY LLWYD	... 106
Sir THOMAS HANMER	164
Sir WILLIAM WILLIAMS ...	... 168

I. FOULKES, 18, BRUNSWICK STREET, LIVERPOOL.

www.ingramcontent.com/pod-product-compliance
Lightning Source LLC
Chambersburg PA
CBHW020847270326
41928CB00006B/593